SOLILOQUIES IN ENGLAND

AND LATER SOLILOQUIES

BY

George Santayana

NEW INTRODUCTION BY RALPH ROSS

Ann Arbor Paperbacks

THE UNIVERSITY OF MICHIGAN PRESS

PREFACE

MANY of these Soliloquies have appeared in *The Athenaeum* and one or more in *The London Mercury, The Nation, The New Republic, The Dial,* and *The Journal of Philosophy.* The author's thanks are due to the Editors of all these reviews for permission to reprint the articles.

For convenience, three Soliloquies on Liberty, written in 1915, have been placed in the second group; and perhaps it should be added that not a few of the later pieces were written in France, Spain, or Italy, although still for the most part on English themes and under the influence of English impressions.

NEW INTRODUCTION
by Ralph Ross

I HAVE liked *Soliloquies in England and Later Soliloquies* immensely ever since I first read it. It is an ideal sample of Santayana's work: It contains philosophy, literary criticism, social characterization, personal likes and dislikes, even three sonnets. The first soliloquies were written in 1914, when Santayana was 51, and all were edited and published in 1922, when he was 59. In all, the work of vigorous maturity.

Underlying the *Soliloquies* is the philosophy of civilization that Santayana published in 1905 in five volumes as *The Life of Reason*. Although Santayana later decried *The Life of Reason* as immature and rewrote it (not alone, it seems) in one large volume not nearly so good as the original five, the basic naturalism of the earlier work stamps the pages of the *Soliloquies*. Its underlying principle, which he insisted he found in Aristotle, is still that everything ideal has a natural basis and everything natural an ideal development. Santayana's last great philosophical effort, the volumes called *Realms of Being,* had not yet appeared, but he was already working at them and one can see here intimations of that system of philosophy of which he said, "...my system is not mine, nor new."

Santayana has many admirers but no disciples. Like Spinoza, one of his masters in philosophy or, on a lesser scale, Musorgski in music and Redon in painting, Santayana's achievement is memorable and distinctive, but it has opened no doors for others to enter, or they have refused to do so. Bertrand Russell suggested that Santayana's philosophy was not original (which might be the reason he has no followers) and Santayana seemed happy to accept that judgment on the ground that he sought truth, not originality, always intimating that the two were probably incompatible in our time. "...I am an ignorant man, almost a poet," he wrote, "and I can only spread a feast of what everybody knows." And in the *Soliloquies* he says of most latter-day philosophers, "Bent on some specific reform or wrapped up in some favorite notion, they have denied the obvious because other people had pointed it out...."

Perhaps Santayana is a philosopher without a school because he wove so complete an intellectual pattern, not so much suggestive or stimulating as final, a consummation to be contemplated and enjoyed, not to be finished or even applied. Perhaps it is because of the Olympian detachment of his prose style, that brought much assent but warmed no hearts. Perhaps, above all, it is because his viewpoint was alien, partly Latin and traditional, yielding to no fashion, appreciative of much in other cultures and modern views, but dispassionate in that appreciation and coolly critical of all existence. Santayana never fully belonged to America, nor to Anglo-Saxon civilization; he was too Latin and Catholic for that. Yet he was not properly a Latin either. He wrote in English, was literally an atheist, and professed a technical philosophy that marked him an American. In the language of the schools, he was a naturalist and a critical realist.

One can be alien to his time and place, even alienated from them, and still attract an army of followers if only he places himself in the avant-garde, or preaches action, or at least sets forth a program. Santayana did none of these. He was committed to traditional wisdom, to thinking about the world, not changing it, to being a philosopher, not just doing philosophy. He had no party line to enunciate, no activity to advocate. And he rejected the common notion that his thought represented a state of society or a stage of civilization, even that it was influenced by his time, his place, and his life in any essential way. Implicitly he was claiming that *his* thought *was* philosophy, not because it was his but because it was honest, and that disagreement with him yielded only ideology. The evidence is in many places, but very explicit in *Scepticism and Animal Faith* where he wrote: "My philosophy is justified, and has been justified in all ages and countries, by the facts before every man's eyes; and no great wit is requisite to discover it, only (what is rarer than wit) candour and courage.... In the past or in the future, my language and my borrowed knowledge would have been different, but under whatever sky I had been born, since it is the same sky, I should have had the same philosophy."

In the end, if he was anything, Santayana was an American, and he knew it. His language and his education were American, and his place in intellectual history is that of an American philosopher. Yet English was not his native tongue—he only came to America at nine—and he blamed that for his being only

a minor poet. He still could be a major prose writer: rare as
that is for those not born to the language they write, Conrad
and Nabokov are proof that it is possible. As a final ambival-
ence, Santayana never relinquished his Spanish citizenship and
so was able to live in Mussolini's Italy during World War II
on a Spanish passport, even though Italy and America were at
war.

How little of World War I enters *Soliloquies in England,*
although it was written in England in 1914-18. Yet how clearly
Santayana saw the fantasy in slogans like the war to end war
and the war to save democracy. All that is apparent in the
soliloquy "Tipperary." How apt indeed is the term "soliloquy"
rather than the obvious "essay." More than other men, Santayana
addressed no one but himself. More than other men, he wrote
to clarify and order his ideas, not to persuade his readers. The
reason for this, if there is a reason beyond temperament, can
be found in the implication in "John Bull and His Philosophers"
that one who trusts his inner man has an impulse to soliloquize.
And Santayana always proclaimed his trust in his own inner
man and in his philosophy which, if not his particularly, was
true. Where he got that philosophy—and with it, perhaps, his
trust in himself—is described admirably in this book in "The
Progress of Philosophy."

I suspect that critics have been misled by the stance Santayana adopted of being the voice of inherited traditions. Insofar
as originality of mind is possible, Santayana's mind was extra-
ordinarily original. It was acute and perceptive, incredibly
sensitive to some aspects of experience and to the color of other
men's minds, able to sustain thought at great length, basically
very powerful but with some weakness I cannot define that
kept Santayana from the full measure of greatness that seems
his natural right. Just as a guess, I think his pretended un-
originality was a shield from attack, his vaunted love of life
really a love of mind, his Olympian and detached style a barrier set up against others. As compared with William James's
vigor and easy masculinity, Santayana too often sounds finicky,
afraid to soil his hands with the world's hot blood.

Still, how much has been made by today's philosophers, so
many of whom have forgotten Santayana or never read him,
of ideas offered so casually in the *Soliloquies:* grammar creates
metaphysics, which reads the structure of languages and minds

into the universe ("...nature, in the works of the metaphysicians, held the mirror up to man."); Plato's world is a mythical statement of moral states and stages; a philosopher should blush to maintain that the movement of history is dialectical, and to think of it as triadic is to reveal a superstitious reverence for the number three. And how many philosophers have yet caught up with Santayana's realization that, contrary to Locke, ideas (and words) are not the objects of knowledge, but the knowledge of objects.

The *Soliloquies* shows Santayana at his best and at his worst; and at his worst his prose is pretentious. He is at his best when he writes simply, and it is then that his poetic quality is clearest. When he is not simple, he too readily becomes turgid or purple. But when he is simple, he is a natural epigrammatist: "The love of friends is not, like the love of woman, a lyrical prologue to nest-building"; "...what can we relish if we recoil at vulgarity"; "To embroider upon experience is not to bear false witness against one's neighbor, but to bear true witness to oneself."

Santayana's literary criticism has much of the quality of his philosophical criticism: it is based on omnivorous reading and a chameleon's sensitivity. Santayana feels every writer's internal temperature, sees the world as he does, and describes it as he might if he wrote Santayana's expository prose. Then Santayana looks at that world through his own eyes and marks the disparities. It is a method that might be called impressionistic except for Santayana's thoroughness and rigor. It is not a method that can be taught, like that of the New Criticism, for it is intensely personal, although without a personal tone. Some critics have learned much from it, but as with his philosophy, it has no avowed disciples. The discipline behind it is evident when we see in this book how much of Dickens has been captured and enjoyed by the aloof Castilian don.

The *Soliloquies* has many tones and voices; it is not one book but a collection of discrete pieces, only held together by a devotion to England. What makes it a whole is the single philosophy that welds all the soliloquies; that, and the fact that all the tones and voices, like the philosophy, belonged uniquely to one man.

Claremont, California
August 1966

CONTENTS

PROLOGUE

THE outbreak of war in the year 1914 found me by chance in England, and there I remained, chiefly at Oxford, until the day of the peace. During those five years, in rambles to Iffley and Sandford, to Godstow and Wytham, to the hospitable eminence of Chilswell, to Wood Eaton or Nuneham or Abingdon or Stanton Harcourt,

Crossing the stripling Thames at Bab-lock-hithe,

these Soliloquies were composed, or the notes scribbled from which they have been expanded. Often over Port Meadow the whirr of aeroplanes sent an iron tremor through these reveries, and the daily casualty list, the constant sight of the wounded, the cadets strangely replacing the undergraduates, made the foreground to these distances. Yet nature and solitude continued to envelop me in their gentleness, and seemed to remain nearer to me than all that was so near. They muffled the importunity of the hour ; perhaps its very bitterness and incubus of horror drove my thoughts deeper than they would otherwise have ventured into the maze of reflection and of dreams. It is a single maze, though we traverse it in opposite moods, and distinct threads conduct us ; for when the most dire events have assumed their punctiform places in the history of our lives, where they will stand eternally, what are they but absurd episodes in a once tormenting dream ? And when our despised night-dreams are regarded and respected as they deserve to be (since all their troubles are actual and all their tints evident), do they prove more arbitrary or less significant than our waking thoughts, or than those more studious daylight fictions which we call history or philosophy ? The human mind at best is a sort of song ; the music of it runs away with the words, and even the words, which pass for the names of things, are but poor wild symbols for their unfathomed objects. So are these Soliloquies compared with their occasions ; and I should be the first to hate their verbiage, if a certain spiritual happiness did not seem to breathe through it, and redeem its irrelevance. Their very abstraction from the time in which they were written may commend them to a free mind. Spirit refuses to be caught in a vice ; it triumphs over the existence which begets it. The moving world which feeds it is not its adequate theme. Spirit hates its father and its mother. It spreads from its burning focus into the infinite, careless whether that focus burns to ashes or not. From its pinnacle of earthly time it pours its little life into spheres not temporal nor earthly, and half in playfulness, half in sacrifice, it finds its joy in the irony of eternal things, which know nothing of it.

Spirit, however, cannot fly from matter without material wings ; the most abstract art is compacted of images, the most mystical renunciation obeys some passion of the heart. Images and passion, even if they are not easily recognizable in these Soliloquies as now coldly written down, were not absent from them when inwardly spoken. The images were English images, the passion was the love of England and, behind England, of Greece. What I love in Greece and in England is contentment in finitude, fair outward ways, manly perfection and simplicity. Admiration for England, of a certain sort, was instilled into me in my youth. My father (who read the language with ease although he did not speak it) had a profound respect for British polity and British power. In this admiration there was no touch of sentiment nor even of sympathy ; behind it lay something like an ulterior contempt, such as we feel for the strong man exhibiting at a fair. The performance may be astonishing but the achievement is mean. So in the middle of the nineteenth century an intelligent foreigner, the native of a country materially impoverished, could look to England for a model of that irresistible energy and public discipline which afterwards were even more conspicuous in Bismarckian Germany and in the United States. It was admiration for material

progress, for wealth, for the inimitable gift of success ;
and it was not free, perhaps, from the poor man's illusion,
who jealously sets his heart on prosperity, and lets it blind
him to the subtler sources of greatness. We should none
of us admire England to-day, if we had to admire it only
for its conquering commerce, its pompous noblemen, or its
parliamentary government. I feel no great reverence
even for the British Navy, which may be in the junk-shop
to-morrow ; but I heartily like the British sailor, with his
clear - cut and dogged way of facing the world. It is
health, not policy nor wilfulness, that gives true strength
in the moral world, as in the animal kingdom ; nature and
fortune in the end are on the side of health. There is, or
was, a beautifully healthy England hidden from most
foreigners ; the England of the countryside and of the
poets, domestic, sporting, gallant, boyish, of a sure and
delicate heart, which it has been mine to feel beating,
though not so early in my life as I could have wished. In
childhood I saw only Cardiff on a Sunday, and the docks
of Liverpool ; but books and prints soon opened to me
more important vistas. I read the poets ; and although
British painting, when it tries to idealize human subjects,
has always made me laugh, I was quick to discern an
ethereal beauty in the landscapes of Turner. Furgueson's
Cathedrals of England, too, and the great mansions in the
Italian style depicted in the eighth edition of the *Encyclopaedia Britannica*, revealed to me even when a boy the
rare charm that can envelop the most conventional things
when they are associated with tender thoughts or with
noble ways of living.

It was with a premonition of things noble and tender,
and yet conventional, that after a term at the University
of Berlin I went to spend my first holidays in England.
Those were the great free days of my youth. I had lived
familiarly in Spain and in the United States : I had had
a glimpse of France and of Germany, and French literature
had been my daily bread : it had taught me how to think,
but had not given me much to think about. I was not
mistaken in surmising that in England I should find a
tertium quid, something soberer and juster than anything
I yet knew, and at the same time greener and richer.

I felt at once that here was a distinctive society, a way of living fundamentally foreign to me, but deeply attractive. At first all gates seemed shut and bristling with incommunication ; but soon in some embowered corner I found the stile I might climb over, and the ancient right of way. Those peaceful parks, and those minds no less retired, seemed positively to welcome me ; and though I was still divided from them by inevitable partitions, these were in places so thin and yielding, that the separation seemed hardly greater than is requisite for union and sympathy between autonomous minds. Indeed, I was soon satisfied that no climate, no manners, no comrades on earth (where nothing is perfect) could be more congenial to my complexion. Not that I ever had the least desire or tendency to become an Englishman. Nationality and religion are like our love and loyalty towards women : things too radically intertwined with our moral essence to be changed honourably, and too accidental to the free mind to be worth changing. My own origins were living within me ; by their light I could see clearly that this England was pre-eminently the home of decent happiness and a quiet pleasure in being oneself. I found here the same sort of manliness which I had learned to love in America, yet softer, and not at all obstreperous ; a manliness which when refined a little creates the gentleman, since its instinct is to hide its strength for an adequate occasion and for the service of others. It is self-reliant, but with a saving touch of practicality and humour ; for there is a becoming self-confidence, based on actual performance, like the confidence of the athlete, and free from any exorbitant estimate of what that performance is worth. Such modesty in strength is entirely absent from the effusive temperament of the Latin, who is cocky and punctilious so long as his conceit holds out, and then utterly humbled and easily corrupted ; entirely absent also from the doctrinaire of the German school, in his dense vanity and officiousness, that nothing can put to shame. So much had I come to count on this sort of manliness in the friends of my youth, that without it the most admirable and gifted persons seemed to me hardly *men* : they fell rather into an ambiguous retinue, the

camp followers of man, cleverer but meaner than himself—
the priests, politicians, actors, pedagogues, and shop-
keepers. The *man* is he who lives and relies directly on
nature, not on the needs or weaknesses of other people.
These self - sufficing Englishmen, in their reserve and
decision, seemed to me truly men, creatures of fixed
rational habit, people in whose somewhat inarticulate
society one might feel safe and at home. The low pressure
at which their minds seemed to work showed how little
they were alarmed about anything : things would all be
managed somehow. They were good company even when
they said nothing. Their aspect, their habits, their
invincible likes and dislikes seemed like an anchor to me
in the currents of this turbid age. They were a gift of the
gods, like the sunshine or the fresh air or the memory of
the Greeks : they were superior beings, and yet more
animal than the rest of us, calmer, with a different scale
of consciousness and a slower pace of thought. There were
glints in them sometimes of a mystical oddity ; they loved
the wilds ; and yet ordinarily they were wonderfully sane
and human, and responsive to the right touch. Moreover,
these semi-divine animals could talk like men of the world.
If some of them, and not the least charming, said little
but " Oh, really," and " How stupid of me," I soon
discovered how far others could carry scholarly distinction,
rich humour, and refinement of diction. I confess, however,
that when they were very exquisite or subtle they seemed
to me like cut flowers ; the finer they were the frailer, and
the cleverer the more wrong-headed. Delicacy did not
come to them, as to Latin minds, as an added ornament,
a finer means of being passionate, a trill in a song that
flows full-chested from the whole man ; their purity was
Puritanism, it came by exclusion of what they thought
lower. It impoverished their sympathies, it severed them
from their national roots, it turned to affectation or
fanaticism, it rendered them acrid and fussy and eccentric
and sad. It is truly English, in one sense, to fume against
England, individuality tearing its own nest ; and often
these frantic poses neutralize one another and do no harm
on the whole. Nevertheless it is the full-bodied Englishman
who has so far ballasted the ship, he who, like Shakespeare,

can wear gracefully the fashion of the hour, can play
with fancy, and remain a man. When he ceases to be
sensual and national, adventurous and steady, reticent and
religious, the Englishman is a mad ghost ; and wherever
he prevails he turns pleasant England, like Greece, into a
memory.

Those first holidays of mine, when I was twenty-three
years of age, laid the foundation of a life-long attachment—
of which these Soliloquies are a late fruit—to both Oxford
and Cambridge : not so much to the learned society of
those places as to their picturesque aspects and to the
possibility of enjoying there in seclusion the intense companionship of the past and of the beautiful ; also the
intense companionship of youth, to which more advanced
years in themselves are no obstacle, if the soul remains
free. I have never liked the taste of academic straw ; but
there are fat grains and seeds of novelty even at universities,
which the lively young wits that twitter in those shades
pick up like hungry sparrows, yet without unmitigated
seriousness ; and unmitigated seriousness is always out of
place in human affairs. Let not the unwary reader think
me flippant for saying so ; it was Plato, in his solemn old
age, who said it. He added that our ignominious condition
forces us, nevertheless, to be often terribly in earnest.
Wanton and transitory as our existence is, and comic as
it must appear in the eyes of the happy gods, it is all in
all to our mortal nature ; and whilst intellectually we may
judge ourselves somewhat as the gods might judge us, and
may commend our lives to the keeping of eternity, our
poor animal souls are caught inextricably in the toils of
time, which devours us and all our possessions. The artist
playing a farce for others suffers a tragedy in himself.
When he aspires to shed as much as possible the delusions
of earthly passion, and to look at things joyfully and
unselfishly, with the clear eyes of youth, it is not because
he feels no weight of affliction, but precisely because he
feels its weight to the full, and how final it is. Lest it
should seem inhuman of me to have been piping soliloquies
whilst Rome was burning, I will transcribe here some
desperate verses extorted from me by events during those
same years. I am hardly a poet in the magic sense of the

word, but when one's thoughts have taken instinctively a
metrical form, why should they be forbidden to wear it ?
I do not ask the reader to admire these sonnets, but to
believe them.

A PREMONITION

Cambridge, October 1913

Grey walls, broad fields, fresh voices, rippling weir,
I know you well : ten faces, for each face
That passes smiling, haunt this hallowed place,
And nothing not thrice noted greets me here.
Soft watery winds, wide twilight skies and clear,
Refresh my spirit at its founts of grace,
And a strange sorrow masters me, to pace
These willowed paths, in this autumnal year.
Soon, lovely England, soon thy secular dreams,
Thy lisping comrades, shall be thine no more.
A world's loosed troubles flood thy gated streams
And drown, methinks, thy towers ; and the tears start
As if an iron hand had clutched my heart,
And knowledge is a pang, like love of yore.

THE UNDERGRADUATE KILLED IN BATTLE

Oxford, 1915

Sweet as the lawn beneath his sandalled tread,
Or the scarce rippled stream beneath his oar,
So gently buffeted it laughed the more,
His life was, and the few blithe words he said.
One or two poets read he, and reread ;
One or two friends with boyish ardour wore
Close to his heart, incurious of the lore
Dodonian woods might murmur overhead.
Ah, demons of the whirlwind, have a care,
What, trumpeting your triumphs, ye undo !
The earth once won, begins your long despair
That never, never is his bliss for you.
He breathed betimes this clement island air
And in unwitting lordship saw the blue.

THE DARKEST HOUR

Oxford, 1917

Smother thy flickering light, the vigil's o'er.
Hope, early wounded, of his wounds is dead.
Many a night long he smiled, his drooping head
Laid on thy breast, and that brave smile he wore
Not yet from his unbreathing lips is fled.
Enough : on mortal sweetness look no more,
Pent in this charnel-house, fling wide the door
And on the stars that killed him gaze instead.
The world's too vast for hope.   The unteachable sun
Rises again and will reflood his sphere,
Blotting with light what yesterday was done ;
But the unavailing truth, though dead, lives on,
And in eternal night, unkindly clear,
A cold moon gilds the waves of Acheron.

SOLILOQUIES IN ENGLAND

1914–1918

I

ATMOSPHERE

THE stars lie above all countries alike, but the atmosphere
that intervenes is denser in one place than in another ;
and even where it is purest, if once its atoms catch the
sunlight, it cuts off the prospect beyond. In some climates
the veil of earthly weather is so thick and blotted that
even the plodder with his eyes on the ground finds its
density inconvenient, and misses his way home. The
advantage of having eyes is neutralized at such moments,
and it would be better to have retained the power of going
on all fours and being guided by scent. In fact human
beings everywhere are like marine animals and live in a
congenial watery medium, which like themselves is an
emanation of mother earth ; and they are content for the
most part to glide through it horizontally at their native
level. They ignore the third, the vertical dimension ; or
if they ever get some inkling of empty heights or rigid
depths where they could not breathe, they dismiss that
speculative thought with a shudder, and continue to dart
about in their familiar aquarium, immersed in an opaque
fluid that cools their passions, protects their intellect
from mental dispersion, keeps them from idle gazing, and
screens them from impertinent observation by those who
have no business in the premises.

The stellar universe that silently surrounds them, if
while swimming they ever think of it, seems to them
something foreign and not quite credibly reported. How
should anything exist so unlike home, so out of scale with
their affairs, so little watery, and so little human ? Their
philosophers confirm them in that incredulity ; and the
sea-caves hold conclaves of profound thinkers congregated

to prove that only fog can be real.   The dry, their council
decrees, is but a vain abstraction, a mere negative which
human imagination opposes to the moist, of which alone,
since life is moist, there can be positive experience.

As for the stars, these inspired children of the mist have
discovered that they are nothing but postulates of astro-
nomy, imagined for a moment to exist, in order that a
beautiful human science may be constructed about them.
Duller people, born in the same fog, may not understand
so transcendental a philosophy, but they spontaneously
frame others of their own, not unlike it in principle.   In
the middle of the night, when the starlight best manages
to pierce to the lowest strata of the air, these good people
are asleep ; yet occasionally when they are returning
somewhat disappointed from a party, or when illness or
anxiety or love-hunger keeps them pacing their chamber
or tossing in their beds, by chance they may catch a
glimpse of a star or two twinkling between their curtains.
Idle objects, they say to themselves, like dots upon the
wall-paper.   Why should there be stars at all, and why
so many of them ?   Certainly they shed a little light and
are pretty ; and they are a convenience sometimes in the
country when there is no moon and no lamp-posts ; and
they are said to be useful in navigation and to enable the
astronomers to calculate sidereal time in addition to solar
time, which is doubtless a great satisfaction to them.
But all this hardly seems to justify such an expense of
matter and energy as is involved in celestial mechanics.
To have so much going on so far away, and for such prodigious lengths of time, seems rather futile and terrible.
Who knows ?   Astrologers used to foretell people's character and destiny by their horoscope ; perhaps they may
turn out to have been more or less right after all, now that
science is coming round to support more and more what
our fathers called superstitions.   There may be some
meaning in the stars, a sort of code-language such as
Bacon put into Shakespeare's sonnets, which would prove
to us, if we could only read it, not how insignificant, but
how very important we are in the world, since the very
stars are talking about us.

The safest thing, however, is to agree with the great

idealists, who say there are really no stars at all. Or, if their philosophy seems insecure—and there are rumours that even the professors are hedging on the subject—we can always take refuge in faith, and think of the heavenly bodies as beautiful new homes in which we are to meet and work together again when we die ; and as in time we might grow weary even there, with being every day busier and busier, there must always be other stars at hand for us to move to, each happier and busier than the last ; and since we wish to live and to progress for ever, the number of habitable planets provided for us has to be infinite. Certainly faith is far better than science for explaining everything.

So the embryonic soul reasons in her shell of vapour ; her huddled philosophy is, as it were, pre-natal, and discredits the possibility of ever peeping into a cold outer world. Yet in time this shell may grow dangerously thin in places, and a little vague light may filter through. Strange promptings and premonitions at the same time may visit the imprisoned spirit, as if it might not be impossible nor inglorious to venture into a world that was not oneself. At last, willy-nilly, the soul may be actually hatched, and may suddenly find herself horribly exposed, cast perhaps on the Arabian desert, or on some high, scorched, open place that resembles it, like the uplands of Castile. There the rarefied atmosphere lets the stars down upon her overwhelmingly, like a veritable host of heaven. There the barren earth entwines few tentacles about the heart ; it stretches away dark and empty beneath our feet, a mere footstool for meditation. It is a thing to look away from, too indifferent and accidental even to spurn ; for after all it supports us, and though small and extinguished it is one of the stars. In these regions the shepherds first thought of God.

2

GRISAILLE

ENGLAND is pre-eminently a land of atmosphere. A luminous haze permeates everywhere, softening distances, magnifying perspectives, transfiguring familiar objects, harmonizing the accidental, making beautiful things magical and ugly things picturesque. Road and pavement become wet mirrors, in which the fragments of this gross world are shattered, inverted, and transmuted into jewels, more appealing than precious stones to the poet, because they are insubstantial and must be loved without being possessed. Mists prolong the most sentimental and soothing of hours, the twilight, through the long summer evenings and the whole winter's day. In these country-sides so full of habitations and these towns so full of verdure, lamplight and twilight cross their rays ; and the passers-by, mercifully wrapped alike in one crepuscular mantle, are reduced to unison and simplicity, as if sketched at one stroke by the hand of a master.

English landscape, if we think only of the land and the works of man upon it, is seldom on the grand scale. Charming, clement, and eminently habitable, it is almost too domestic, as if only home passions and caged souls could live there. But lift the eyes for a moment above the line of roofs or of tree-tops, and there the grandeur you miss on the earth is spread gloriously before you. The spirit of the atmosphere is not compelled, like the god of pantheism, to descend in order to exist, and wholly to diffuse itself amongst earthly objects. It exists absolutely in its own person as well, and enjoys in the sky, like a true deity, its separate life and being. There the veil of Maya, the heavenly Penelope, is being woven and rent perpetually, and the winds of destiny are always charmingly defeating their apparent intentions. Here is the playground of those early nebulous gods that had the bodies of giants and the minds of children.

In England the classic spectacle of thunderbolts and rainbows appears but seldom ; such contrasts are too violent and definite for these tender skies. Here the conflict between light and darkness, like all other conflicts, ends in a compromise ; cataclysms are rare, but revolution is perpetual. Everything lingers on and is modified ; all is luminous and all is grey.

3

PRAISES OF WATER

THE transformation of landscape by moisture is no matter of appearance only, no mere optical illusion or effect of liquid stained glass. It is a sort of echo or symbol to our senses of very serious events in prehistoric times. Water, which now seems only to lap the earth or to cloud it, was the chisel which originally carved its surface. They say that when the planet, recently thrown off from the sun, was still on fire, the lighter elements rose in the form of gases around the molten metallic core; and the outer parts of this nucleus in cooling formed a crust of igneous rock which, as the earth contracted, was crushed together and wrinkled like the skin of a raisin. These wrinkles are our mountain chains, made even more rugged and villainous by belated eruptions. On that early earth there was no water. All was sheer peaks, ledges, and chasms, red-hot or coal-black, or of such livid metallic hues, crimson, saffron, and purple, as may still be seen on the shores of the Dead Sea or in the Grand Canyon of the Colorado—rifts that allow us to peep into the infernal regions, happily in those places at least without inhabitants. This hellish sort of landscape, which we must now plunge into the depths to find, was the first general landscape of earth.

As the cooling progressed, however, the steam that was in the upper atmosphere began to condense and to fall in rain. At first the hot drops no doubt sizzled as they fell and rose again immediately in vapour, yet the meteorological cycle was established notwithstanding. The rain that evaporated descended once more, each time colder and more abundant, until it cut channels amongst the crags, ground and polished their fragments into boulders and pebbles, formed pools in the hollows, and finally covered the earth up to its chin with the oceans. Much detritus meantime was washed down from the rocks; it gathered in crevices and along the pockets and slacker reaches of rivers. This sediment was soaked

with moisture and mixed with dissolved acids , it became
the first soft layer of earth and finally a fertile soil.   Water
in this way softened the outlines of the mountains, laid the
floor of the valleys, and made a leafy and a cloudy place of
the planet.

The sages (and some of them much more recent than
Thales) tell us that water not only wears away the rocks,
but has a singular power of carrying away their subtler
elements in solution, especially carbonic acid, of which the
atmosphere also is full ; and it happens that these elements
can combine with the volatile elements of water into
innumerable highly complex substances, all of which the
atmospheric cycle carries with it wherever it goes ; and with
these complex substances, which are the requisite materials
for living bodies, it everywhere fills the sea and impregnates
the land.

Even if life, then, is not actually born of the moist
element, it is at least suckled by it ; the water-laden
atmosphere is the wet nurse, if not the mother, of the
earth-soul.   The earth has its soul outside its body, as
many a philosopher would have wished to have his.   The
winds that play about it are its breath, the water that
rains down and rises again in mist is its circulating blood ;
and the death of the earth will come when some day it
sucks in the atmosphere and the sea, gets its soul inside
its body again, turns its animating gases back into solids,
and becomes altogether a skeleton of stone.

No wonder that living creatures find things that are
fluid and immersed in moisture friendly to the watery core
of their own being.   Seeds, blood, and tears are liquid ;
nothing else is so poignant as what passes and flows, like
music and love ; and if this irreparable fluidity is sad,
anything stark and arrested is still sadder.   Life is compelled to flow, and things must either flow with it or, like
Lot's wife, in the petrified gesture of refusal, remain to
mock their own hope.

4

THE TWO PARENTS OF VISION

IT would seem that when a heavenly body ceases to shine by its own light, it becomes capable of breeding eyes with which to profit by the light other bodies are shedding ; whereas, so long as it was itself on fire, no part of it could see. Is life a gift which cooling stars receive from those still incandescent, when some ray falls upon a moist spot, making it a focus of warmth and luminous energy, and reversing at that point the general refrigeration ? It is certain, at any rate, that if light did not pour down from the sun no earthly animal would have developed an eye. Yet there was another partner in this business of seeing, who would have flatly refused to undertake it, had the sole profit been the possibility of star-gazing.

Star-gazing is an ulterior platonic homage which we pay to our celestial sources, as a sort of pious acknowledgment of their munificence in unconsciously begetting us. But this is an acknowledgment which they are far from demanding or noticing, not being vain or anxious to be admired, like popular gods ; and if we omitted it, they would continue to perform their offices towards us with the same contemptuous regularity. Star-gazing is, therefore, a pure waste of time in the estimation of the other partner in vision, besides celestial light—I mean, that clod of moist earth which the light quickens, that plastic home-keeping parent of the mind, whom we might call old mother Psyche, and whose primary care is to keep the body in order and guide it prudently over the earth's surface. For such a purpose the direct rays of the sun are blinding, and those of the moon and stars fit only to breed lunatics. To mother Psyche it seems a blessing that the view of the infinite from the earth is so often intercepted ; else it might have sunk into her heart (for she has watched through many a night in her long vegetative career), and might have stretched her comfortable industrious sanity into a sort of divine madness or reason, very disconcerting in her business. Indeed, she would never have consented to look or to see at all, except for this circumstance, that the rays coming

from heavenly bodies are reflected by earthly bodies upon
one another ; so that by becoming sensitive to light the
Psyche could receive a most useful warning of what to
seek or to avoid.   Instead of merely stretching or poking
or sniffing through the world, she could now map it at a
glance, and turn instinct into foresight.

This was a great turn in her career, wonderful in its
tragic possibilities, and something like falling in love ; for
her new art brought her a new pleasure and a new unrest,
purer and more continual than those drowsy and terrible
ones which she knew before.   Reflected light is beautiful.
The direct downpour of light through space leaves space
wonderfully dark, and it falls on the earth indiscriminately
upon the wise and the foolish, to warm or to scorch them ;
but the few rays caught by solid matter or drifting vapour
become prismatic, soft, and infinitely varied ; not only
reporting truly the position and material diversity of things,
but adding to them an orchestration in design and colour
bewitching to the senses.   It was not the stars but the
terrestrial atmosphere that the eyes of the flesh were made
to see ; even mother Psyche can love the light, when it
clothes or betrays something else that matters ; and the
fleshly-spiritual Goethe said most truly : *Am farbigen
Abglanz haben wir das Leben.*

5

AVERSION FROM PLATONISM

REPETITION is the only form of permanence that nature
can achieve, and in those Mediterranean regions that
nurtured the classic mind, by continually repeating the
same definite scenes, nature forced it to fix its ideas.
Every one learned to think that the earth and the gods
were more permanent than himself ; he perused them, he
returned to them, he studied them at arm's length, and
he recognized their external divinity.   But where the
Atlantic mists envelop everything, though we must
repeatedly use the same names for new-born things, as
we continue to christen children John and Mary, yet we
feel that the facts, like the persons, are never really alike ;

everything is so fused, merged, and continuous, that whatever element we may choose to say is repeated seems but a mental abstraction and a creature of language. The weather has got into our bones; there is a fog in the brain; the limits of our own being become uncertain to us. Yet what is the harm, if only we move and change inwardly in harmony with the ambient flux ? Why this mania for naming and measuring and mastering what is carrying us so merrily along ? Why shouldn't the intellect be vague while the heart is comfortable ?

6

CLOUD CASTLES

THE heavens are the most constant thing we know, the skies the most inconstant. Even the Olympian expanse, when blue and cloudless, is an aspect of terrestrial atmosphere in a holiday mood, a sort of gay parasol which the Earth holds up when she walks in the sun, and takes down again when she walks in the shadow; while clouds are veils wrapped more closely about her, and even more friendly to her frailty. Nor are these feminine trappings less lovely for being easily blown about, and always fresh and in the latest fashion. It is a prejudice to suppose that instability must be sad or must be trivial. A new cloud castle is probably well worth an old one ; any one of them may equal in beauty the monotonous gold and black vault which it conceals from us, and all of them together certainly surpass that tragic decoration in spiritual suggestion. Something in us no doubt regrets that these airy visions vanish so quickly and are irrecoverable; but this is a sort of fleshly sentimentality of ours and not reasonable. In nature, what disappears never narrows the range of what is yet to be. If we were immortally young, like the atmosphere, the lapse of things would not grieve us, nor would inconstancy be a vice in ourselves. Nobody's future would be blighted by his past ; and this perhaps explains the morals of the gods. Change to us is an omen of death, and only in the timeless can we feel secure ; but if we were safe in our plastic existence, like nature and the gods of nature,

fidelity to a single love might seem foolish in us ; being
and possessing any one thing would not then be incompatible
with sooner or later being and possessing everything else.
Nature and substance are like the absolute actor with an
equal affinity for every part, and changing sex, age, and
station with perfect good grace.

A great principle of charity in morals is not to blame
the fishes for their bad taste in liking to live under water.
Yet many philosophers seem to have sinned against this
reasonable law, since they have blamed life and nature for
liking to change, which is as much as to say for liking to
live. Certainly life and nature, when they produce thought,
turn from themselves towards the eternal, but it is by a
glance, itself momentary, that they turn to it ; for if they
were themselves converted into something changeless, they
could neither live, think, nor turn. In the realm of existence
it is not sinful to be fugitive nor in bad taste to be new.
Accordingly cloud castles have nothing to blush for ; if
they have a weak hold on existence, so has everything
good. We are warned that the day of judgement will be
full of surprises : perhaps one of them may be that in
heaven things are even more unstable than on earth, and
that the mansions reserved for us there are not only many
but insecure. Cloud castles are hints to us that eternity
has nothing to do with duration, nor beauty with substantial
existence, and that even in heaven our bliss would have
to be founded on a smiling renunciation. Did Mohammed,
I wonder, misunderstand the archangel Gabriel in gathering
that celestial beauties (unlike the lights and voices of
Dante's paradise) could be embraced as well as admired ?
And in promising that our heavenly brides would daily
recover their virginity, did he simply clothe in a congenial
metaphor the fact that they would be different brides every
day, and that if we wished to dwell in a true paradise, and
not in a quarrelsome and sordid harem, we must never
dream of seeing any of them a second time ?

Fidelity is a virtue akin to habit and rooted in the
inertia of animal life, which would run amok without trusty
allies and familiar signals. We have an inveterate love of
The Same, because our mortal condition obliges us to
reconsider facts and to accumulate possessions ; by instinct

both the heart and the intellect hug everything they touch, and to let anything go is a sort of death to them. This spirit of pathetic fidelity in us would certainly reproach those ethereal visions for being ephemeral, and Cupid for having wings and no heart ; but might not the visiting angels in turn reproach us for clownishness in wishing to detain them ? They are not made of flesh and blood ; they are not condemned to bear children. Their smile, their voice, and the joy they bring us are the only life they have. They are fertile only like the clouds, in that by dissolving they give place to some other form, no less lovely and elusive than themselves ; and perhaps if we took a long view we should not feel that our own passage through existence had a very different quality. We last as a strain of music lasts, and we go where it goes. Is it not enough that matter should illustrate each ideal possibility only once and for a moment, and that Caesar or Shakespeare should figure once in this world ? To repeat them would not intensify their reality, while it would impoverish and make ridiculous the pageant of time, like a stage army running round behind the scenes in order to reappear. To come to an end is a virtue when one has had one's day, seeing that in the womb of the infinite there are always other essences no less deserving of existence.

Even cloud castles, however, have a double lien on permanence. A flash of lightning is soon over, yet so long as the earth is wrapped in its present atmosphere, flashes will recur from time to time so very like this one that the mind will make the same comment upon them, and its pronouncements on its past experience will remain applicable to its experience to come. Fleeting things in this way, when they are repeated, survive and are united in the wisdom which they teach us in common. At the same time they inwardly contain something positively eternal, since the essences they manifest are immutable in character, and from their platonic heaven laugh at this inconstant world, into which they peep for a moment, when a chance collocation of atoms suggests one or another of them to our minds. To these essences mind is constitutionally addressed, and into them it likes to sink in its self-forgetfulness. It is only our poor mother Psyche, being justly afraid of growing old, who must grudge the exchange of one vision for another. Material life is sluggish and conservative ; it would gladly drag the whole weary length of its past behind it, like a worm afraid of being cut in two in its crawling. It is haunted by a ghostly memory, a wonderful but not successful expedient for calling the dead to life, in order, somewhat inconsistently, to mourn over them and be comforted. Why not kiss our successive pleasures good-bye, simply and without marking our preferences, as we do our children when they file to bed ? A free mind does not measure the worth of anything by the worth of anything else. It is itself at least as plastic as nature and has nothing to fear from revolutions. To live in the moment would indeed be brutish and dangerous if we narrowed to a moment the time embraced in our field of view, since with the wider scope of thought come serenity and dominion ; but to live in the moment is the only possible life if we consider the spiritual activity itself. The most protracted life, in the actual living, can be nothing but a chain of moments, each the seat of its irrecoverable vision, each a dramatic perspective of the world, seen in the light of a particular passion at a particular juncture. But at each moment the wholeness of mind is spiritual and aesthetic, the wholeness of a meaning or a picture, and no knife can divide it. Its immortality, too, is timeless, like that of the truths and forms in which it is absorbed. Therefore apprehension can afford to hasten all the more trippingly in its career, touching the facts here and there for a moment, and building its cloud castles out of light and air, movement and irony, to let them lapse again without a pang. Contemplation, when it frees itself from animal anxiety about existence, ceases to question and castigate its visions, as if they were mere signals of alarm or hints of hidden treasures ; and then it cannot help seeing what treasures these visions hold within themselves, each framing some luminous and divine essence, as a telescope frames a star ; and something of their inalienable distinction and firmness seems to linger in our minds, though in the exigencies of our hurried life we must turn away from each of them and forget them.

7

CROSS-LIGHTS

THEY say the sun is a very small star, and the thing is plausible enough in itself, without the proofs which presumably the astronomers can give of it. That which nature produces she is apt to produce in crowds; what she does once, if she has her way, she will do often, with a persistency and monotony which would be intolerable to her if she were endowed with memory; but hers is a life of habit and automatic repetition, varied only when there is some hitch in the clockwork, and she begins hurriedly beating a new tune. Accordingly, what any creature calls the present time, the living interest, the ruling power, or the true religion is almost always but as one leaf in a tree. The same plastic stress which created it creates a million comparable things around it. Yet it is easy for each to ignore its neighbours, and to be shocked at the notion of loving them as itself; for they all have their separate places or seasons, and bloom on their several stems, so that an accident that overwhelms one of them may easily leave the others unscathed. But for all that, they are as multitudinous and similar as the waves of the sea. Take any star at random, like our sun, or any poet, or any idea, and whilst certainly it will be the nearest and warmest to somebody, it is not at all likely to be the greatest of its kind, or even very remarkable.

Nevertheless, in a moral perspective, nearness makes all the difference; and for us the sun is a veritable ruling deity and parent of light; he is the centre and monarch of our home system. Similarly each living being is a sort of sun to itself; this spark within me, by whose light I see at all, is a great sun to me; and considering how wide a berth other spiritual luminaries seem to give me, I must warm myself chiefly by my own combustion, and remain singularly important to myself. This importance belongs to the humour of material existence, visible when I look at my seamy side; it vanishes in so far as my little light actually burns clear, and my intent flies with it to whatever objects its rays can reach, no matter how distant or alien.

Yet this very intelligence and scope in me are functions of my inward fire : seeing, too, is burning. An atomic and spark-like form of existence, prevalent in nature, is absolutely essential to spirit ; and I find it very acceptable. It is a free, happy, and humble condition. I welcome the minute bulk, the negligible power, the chance quality and oddity of my being, combined as it is with vital independence and adequate fuel in my small bunkers for my brief voyage. On a vaster scale, I think the sun, for all his littleness, has a splendid prerogative, and I honour Phoebus as a happy god. The happiest part of his condition and his best claim to deity lie in this : that he can irradiate and kindle the frozen or vaporous bodies that swim about him ; he can create the moonlight and the earthlight, much more powerful than the moonlight. This earthlight, if we could only get far enough from the earth to see it, would seem strangely brilliant and beautiful ; it would show sea-tints and snow-tints and sand-tints ; there would be greens and purples in it reflected from summer and winter zones, dotted with cinder scars and smoke-wreaths of cities. Yet all these lights are only sunlight, received and returned with thanks.

Nor is this surface shimmer, visible to telescopic observers, the only benefit gained : something is kept back and absorbed ; some warmth sinks into the substance of the earth and permeates its watery soil, initiating currents in the sea and air, and quickening many a nest of particles into magnetic and explosive and contagious motions. This life which arises in the earth is an obeisance to the sun. The flowers turn to the light and the eye follows it, animal bodies imbibe it, and send it forth again in glad looks and keen attention ; and when dreams and thoughts, even with the eyes shut, play within us like flamelets amongst the coals, it is still the light of the sun, strangely stored and transmuted, that shines in those visions. Certainly intelligence in its cognitive intent is radically immaterial, and nothing could be more heterogeneous from vibrations, attractions, or ethereal currents than the power to make assertions that shall be true or false, relevant or irrelevant to outlying things ; but this so spiritual power is profoundly natural ; it

plainly exhibits an animal awaking to the presence of
other bodies that actually surround him, resenting their
cruelty or warming to their conquest and absorption.
Apart from its roots in animal predicaments, spirit would
be wholly inexplicable in its moods and arbitrary in its
deliverance. The more ecstatic or the more tragic
experience is, the more unmistakably it is the voice of
matter. It then obviously retraces and makes incandescent the silent relations of things with things, by which
its weal or woe is decided. Sometimes it simply burns in
their midst and moves in their company like the sun
amongst the stars he ignores ; sometimes it gilds in its
highly coloured lights the surface of things turned in its
direction. Were not the distances between bodies spanned
by some universal gravitation (which we are now told
may be a sort of light), we may be sure that sense and
fancy, which are profoundly vegetative things, would
never leap from their source and discount their images
in the heroic effort to understand the world. But the
fire of life casts its passionate illumination on the dead
things that control it, and raises to aesthetic actuality
various poetic symbols of their power. Dead things possess,
of course, in their own right, their material and logical
being, but they borrow from the adventitious interest
which a living creature must needs take in them their
various moral dignities and all their part in the conscious
world. It is intelligible that moralists and psychologists
should be absorbed in those reflections of their attention
which reach them from things distant or near, and that
they should pronounce the whole universe to be nothing
but their experience of it, a sort of rainbow or crescent
kindly decorating their personal sky. On the same
principle the sun (who, being a material creature, would
also be subject to egotism) might say that the only substance
in the universe was light, and that the earth and moon
were nothing but ethereal mirrors palely reflecting his own
fire. It would seem absurd to him that the earth or its
inhabitants should profess to have any bowels. Inextin-
guishable laughter and self-assurance would seize him at
the report that any dark places existed, or any invisible
thoughts. He would never admit that, in all this, he was

himself thinking; what we should call his thoughts he would maintain (without thinking!) were evident meteors moving and shining on their own account.

Such are the cross-lights of animal persuasion. Things, when seen, seem to come and go with our visions; and visions, when we do not know why they visit us, seem to be things. But this is not the end of the story. Opacity is a great discoverer. It teaches the souls of animals the existence of what is not themselves. Their souls in fact live and spread their roots in the darkness, which embosoms and creates the light, though the light does not comprehend it. If sensuous evidence flooded the whole sphere with which souls are conversant, they would have no reason for suspecting that there was anything they did not see, and they would live in a fool's paradise of lucidity. Fortunately for their wisdom, if not for their comfort, they come upon mysteries and surprises, earthquakes and rumblings in their hidden selves and in their undeciphered environment; they live in time, which is a double abyss of darkness; and the primary and urgent object of their curiosity is that unfathomable engine of nature which from its ambush governs their fortunes. The proud, who shine by their own light, do not perceive matter, the fuel that feeds and will some day fail them; but the knowledge of it comes to extinct stars in their borrowed light and almost mortal coldness, because they need to warm themselves at a distant fire and to adapt their seasons to its favourable shining. When we are on the shady side of the earth we can, as a compensation, range in knowledge far beyond our painted atmosphere, and far beyond that little sun who, so long as he shone upon us, seemed to ride at the top of heaven; we can perceive a galaxy of other lights, no less original than he, to which his glory blinded us; we can even discover how he himself, if his hot head of burning hair would only suffer him to notice it, lives subject to their perpetual influence. Beautiful and happy god as Phoebus may be, he is not a just god nor an everlasting one. He is a lyric singer; he is not responsible save to his own heart, and not obliged to know other things. He lives in the eternal, and does not need to be perpetual. And he is often beneficent in his spontaneity, and many of us have cause to thank and to love him. There is an uncovenanted society of spirits, like that of the morning stars singing together, or of all the larks at once in the sky; it is a happy accident of freedom and a conspiracy of solitudes. When people *talk together*, they are at once entangled in a mesh of instrumentalities, irrelevance, misunderstanding, vanity, and propaganda; and all to no purpose, for why should creatures become alike who are different? But when minds, being naturally akin and each alone in its own heaven, *soliloquize in harmony*, saying compatible things only because their hearts are similar, then society is friendship in the spirit; and the unison of many thoughts twinkles happily in the night across the void of separation.

8

HAMLET'S QUESTION

To be born is painful, and the profit of it so uncertain that we need not wonder if sometimes the mind as well as the body seems to hold back. The winds of February are not colder to a featherless chick than are the surprises which nature and truth bring to our dreaming egotism. It was warm and safe in the egg; exciting enough, too, to feel a new organ throbbing here or a fresh limb growing out there. No suspicion visited the happy creature that these budding domestic functions were but preparations for foreign wars and omens of a disastrous death, to overtake it sooner or later in a barbarous, militant, incomprehensible world. Of death, and even of birth (its ominous counterpart) the embryo had no idea. It believed simply in the tight spherical universe which it knew, and was confident of living in it for ever. It would have thought heaven had fallen if its shell had cracked. How should life be possible in a world of uncertain dimensions, where incalculable blows might fall upon us at any time from any quarter? What a wild philosophy, to invent objects and dangers of which there was absolutely no experience! And yet for us now, accustomed to the buffets and ambitions of life in the open, that pre-natal vegetative dream seems worthless and contemptible, and hardly deserving the name of existence.

Could we have debated Hamlet's question before we were conceived, the answer might well have been doubtful ; or rather reason, not serving any prior instinct, could have expressed no preference and must have left the decision to chance. Birth and death are the right moments for absolute courage. But when once the die is cast and we exist, so that Hamlet's question can be put to us, the answer is already given ; nature in forming us has compelled us to prejudge the case. She has decreed that all the beasts and many a man should propagate without knowing what they are about ; and the infant soul for its part, when once begotten, is constitutionally bent on working out its powers and daring the adventure of life. To have made the great refusal at the beginning, for fear of what shocks and hardships might come, seems to us, now that we are launched, morose and cowardly. Our soul, with its fluttering hopes and alarmed curiosity, is made to flee from death, and seems to think, if we judge by its action, that to miss experience altogether is worse and sadder than any life, however troubled or short. If nature has fooled us in this, she doubtless saw no harm in doing so, and thought it quite compatible with heartily loving us in her rough way. She merely yielded to a tendency to tease which is strangely prevalent among nurses. With a sort of tyrannical fondness, to make us show our paces, she dangled this exciting and unsatisfactory bauble of life before us for a moment, only to laugh at us, and kiss us, and presently lay our head again on her appeasing breast.

The fear which children feel at being left in the dark or alone or among strangers goes somewhat beyond what a useful instinct would require ; for they are likely to be still pretty well embosomed and protected, not to say smothered. It is as if the happy inmate of some model gaol took alarm at the opening of his cell door, thinking he was to be driven out and forced to take his chances again in this rough wide world, when, in fact, all was well and he was only being invited to walk in the prison garden. Just so when the young mind hears the perilous summons to think, it is usually a false alarm. In its philosophical excursions it is likely to remain well blanketed from the truth and comfortably muffled in its own atmosphere. Groping and empirical in its habits, it will continue in the path it happens to have turned into ; for in a fog how should it otherwise choose its direction ? Its natural preference is to be guided by touch and smell, but it sometimes finds it convenient to use its eyes and ears as a substitute. So long as the reference to the vegetative soul and its comforts remains dominant, this substitution is harmless. Sights and sounds will then be but flowers in the prisoner's garden, and intelligence a maze through which at best he will find his way home again. Some danger there always is, even in such an outing ; for this walled garden has gates into the fields, which by chance may be left open. Sight and sound, in their useful ministrations, may create a new interest, and run into sheer music and star-gazing. The life the senses were meant to serve will then be forgotten ; the psychic atmosphere—which of course is indispensable— will be pierced, discounted, and used as a pleasant vehicle to things and to truths ; and the motherly soul, having unintentionally given birth to the intellect, will grumble at her runaway and thankless child. As for the truant himself, Hamlet's question will lapse from his view altogether, not because nature has answered it for him beforehand, but because his own disinterestedness and rapture have robbed it of all urgency. Intellect is passionate, and natural, and human enough, as singing is ; it is all the purer and keener for having emancipated itself, like singing, from its uses, if it ever had any, and having become a delight in itself. But it is not concerned with its own organs or their longevity ; it cannot understand why its mother, the earthly soul, thinks all the good and evil things that happen in this world are of no consequence, if they do not happen to her.

9

THE BRITISH CHARACTER

WHAT is it that governs the Englishman ? Certainly not intelligence ; seldom passion ; hardly self-interest, since what we call self-interest is nothing but some dull passion served by a brisk intelligence. The Englishman's heart is perhaps capricious or silent ; it is seldom designing or mean. There are nations where people are always innocently explaining how they have been lying and cheating in small matters, to get out of some predicament, or secure some advantage ; that seems to them a part of the art of living. Such is not the Englishman's way : it is easier for him to face or to break opposition than to circumvent it. If we tried to say that what governs him is convention, we should have to ask ourselves how it comes about that England is the paradise of individuality, eccentricity, heresy, anomalies, hobbies, and humours. Nowhere do we come oftener upon those two social abortions—the affected and the disaffected. Where else would a man inform you, with a sort of proud challenge, that he lived on nuts, or was in correspondence through a medium with Sir Joshua Reynolds, or had been disgustingly housed when last in prison ? Where else would a young woman, in dress and manners the close copy of a man, tell you that her parents were odious, and that she desired a husband but no children, or children without a husband ? It is true that these novelties soon become the conventions of some narrower circle, or may even have been adopted *en bloc* in emotional desperation, as when people are converted ; and the oddest sects demand the strictest self-surrender. Nevertheless, when people are dissident and supercilious by temperament, they manage to wear their uniforms with a difference, turning them by some lordly adaptation into a part of their own person.

Let me come to the point boldly ; what governs the Englishman is his inner atmosphere, the weather in his soul. It is nothing particularly spiritual or mysterious. When he has taken his exercise and is drinking his tea or his beer and lighting his pipe ; when, in his garden or by his fire, he sprawls in an aggressively comfortable chair ; when, well-washed and well-brushed, he resolutely turns in church to the east and recites the Creed (with genuflexions, if he likes genuflexions) without in the least implying that he believes one word of it ; when he hears or sings the most crudely sentimental and thinnest of

popular songs, unmoved but not disgusted ; when he makes
up his mind who is his best friend or his favourite poet ;
when he adopts a party or a sweetheart ; when he is
hunting or shooting or boating, or striding through the
fields ; when he is choosing his clothes or his profession—
never is it a precise reason, or purpose, or outer fact that
determines him ; it is always the atmosphere of his inner
man.

To say that this atmosphere was simply a sense of
physical well-being, of coursing blood and a prosperous
digestion, would be far too gross ; for while psychic
weather is all that, it is also a witness to some settled
disposition, some ripening inclination for this or that,
deeply rooted in the soul. It gives a sense of direction
in life which is virtually a code of ethics, and a religion
behind religion. On the other hand, to say it was the
vision of any ideal or allegiance to any principle would
be making it far too articulate and abstract. The inner
atmosphere, when compelled to condense into words,
may precipitate some curt maxim or over-simple theory
as a sort of war-cry ; but its puerile language does it injustice, because it broods at a much deeper level than
language or even thought. It is a mass of dumb instincts
and allegiances, the love of a certain quality of life, to
be maintained manfully. It is pregnant with many a
stubborn assertion and rejection. It fights under its
trivial fluttering opinions like a smoking battleship under
its flags and signals ; you must consider, not what they
are, but why they have been hoisted and will not be
lowered. One is tempted at times to turn away in despair
from the most delightful acquaintance—the picture of
manliness, grace, simplicity, and honour, apparently rich
in knowledge and humour—because of some enormous
platitude he reverts to, some hopelessly stupid little dogma
from which one knows that nothing can ever liberate
him. The reformer must give him up ; but why
should one wish to reform a person so much better than
oneself ? He is like a thoroughbred horse, satisfying to
the trained eye, docile to the light touch, and coursing in
most wonderful unison with you through the open world.
What do you care what words he uses ? Are you impatient

with the lark because he sings rather than talks ? and if he
could talk, would you be irritated by his curious opinions ?
Of course, if any one positively asserts what is contrary
to fact, there is an error, though the error may be harmless ; and most divergencies between men should interest
us rather than offend us, because they are effects of perspective, or of legitimate diversity in experience and
interests. Trust the man who hesitates in his speech and
is quick and steady in action, but beware of long arguments
and long beards. Jupiter decided the most intricate
questions with a nod, and a very few words and no gestures
suffice for the Englishman to make his inner mind felt
most unequivocally when occasion requires.

Instinctively the Englishman is no missionary, no
conqueror. He prefers the country to the town, and
home to foreign parts. He is rather glad and relieved if
only natives will remain natives and strangers strangers,
and at a comfortable distance from himself. Yet outwardly
he is most hospitable and accepts almost anybody for the
time being ; he travels and conquers without a settled
design, because he has the instinct of exploration. His
adventures are all external ; they change him so little
that he is not afraid of them. He carries his English
weather in his heart wherever he goes, and it becomes a
cool spot in the desert, and a steady and sane oracle
amongst all the deliriums of mankind. Never since the
heroic days of Greece has the world had such a sweet,
just, boyish master. It will be a black day for the human
race when scientific blackguards, conspirators, churls, and
fanatics manage to supplant him.

10

SEAFARING

ALL peoples that dwell by the sea sometimes venture out
upon it. The boys are eager to swim and sail, and the
men may be turned into habitual navigators by the spirit
of enterprise or by necessity. But some races take to the
water more kindly than others, either because they love

the waves more or the furrow less. We may imagine that sheer distress drove the Norse fishermen and pirates into their open boats. The ocean they explored was rough and desolate ; the fish and the pillaged foreigner had to compensate them for their privations. They quitted their fiords and brackish islands dreaming of happier lands. But with the Greeks and the English the case was somewhat different. There are no happier lands than theirs ; and they set forth for the most part on summer seas, towards wilder and less populous regions. They went armed, of course, and ready to give battle : they had no scruples about carrying home anything they might purloin or obtain by enormously advantageous barter, but they were not in quest of softer climes or foreign models ; their home remained their ideal. They were scarcely willing to settle in foreign parts unless they could live their home life there.

This love of home merged in their minds with the love of liberty ; it was a loyalty inwardly grounded and not a mere tribute to habit or external influences. They could consequently retain their manners wherever they went, and could found free colonies, almost as Greek or as English as the mother country ; for it was not Greece that originally formed the Greeks nor England the English, but the other way round ; the Greeks and the English, wherever they might be, spun their institutions about them like a cocoon. Certainly the geographical environment was favourable ; the skies and waters that embosomed them—when in their migrations they had reached those climes—simply met their native genius half-way and allowed it to bloom as it had not elsewhere. But the winds could carry that same seed to fructify in other soils ; and as there were many Greek cities sprung from one, so there are several local Englands in Great Britain, and others all over the world. Even people who are not heirs of these nations according to the flesh may assimilate their spirit in some measure. All men are Greek in the best sense in so far as they are rational, and live and think on the human scale ; and all are English in so far as their souls are individual, each the imperturbably dominant cell in its own organism, each faithful to its inner oracle.

Life at sea is very favourable to this empire of personal liberty. The inner man, the hereditary Psyche that breeds the body and its discursive thoughts, craves to exercise ascendancy ; it is essentially a formative principle, an organ of government. Mere solitude and monastic reverie, such as a hermit or satirist may enjoy even in great cities, weary and oppress the Englishman. He wants to do something or else to play at something. His thoughts are not vivid and substantial enough for company ; his passions are too nebulous to define their innate objects, until accident offers something that perhaps may serve. At sea there is always something doing : you must mind the helm, the sails, or the engines ; you must keep things ship-shape ; brasses must be always bright and eyes sharp ; decorum is essential, since discipline is so ; you may even dress for dinner and read prayers on Sunday. This routine does not trespass on the liberty and reserve of your inner man. You can exchange a few hearty commonplaces with the other officers and sailors, or even with a casual passenger ; now and then you may indulge in a long talk, pacing the deck beneath the stars. There is space, there is the constant shadow of danger, the chance of some adventure at sea or on a strange shore. There is a continual test and tension of character. There are degrees of authority and of competence, but the sailor's art is finite ; his ship, however complicated and delicate a creature, has a known structure and known organs ; she will not do anything without a reason ; she is not too wayward (as is the course of things on terra firma) for a clear-headed man to understand nor for a firm hand to steer. Maritime fortune in its uncertainty has after all not many forms of caprice ; its worst tricks are familiar ; your life-belt is hanging over your bunk, and you are ready.

Every one grumbles at his lot and at his profession ; but what is man that he should ask for more ? These buffeting winds, these long hours of deep breathing, these habits of quick decision and sharp movement whet your appetite ; you relish your solid plain food, whilst your accustomed drink smooths over the petty worries of the day, and liberates your private musings ; and what a companionable thing your pipe is ! The women—dear, dogmatic, fussy

angels—are not here ; that is a relief ; and yet you are
counting the weeks before you can return to them at home.
And all those tender episodes of a more fugitive sort, how
merrily you think them over now ! more merrily perhaps
than you enacted them, since you need not call to mind
the little shabby accompaniments and false notes that may
have marred them in reality. Your remoter future, too,
is smiling enough for an honest man who believes in God
and is not a snob in the things of the spirit. You see in
your mind's eye a cottage on some sunny hillside over-
looking the sea ; near it, from a signal-post that is a ship's
mast, the flags are flapping in the breeze ; your children
are playing on the beach — except the eldest, perhaps,
already a sailor. There is a blessed simplicity about the
sea, with its vast inhumanity islanding and freeing the
humanity of man.

II

PRIVACY

THE secret of English mastery is self-mastery. The Englishman establishes a sort of satisfaction and equilibrium in his
inner man, and from that citadel of rightness he easily
measures the value of everything that comes within his
moral horizon. In what may lie beyond he takes but a
feeble interest. Enterprising enough when in a roving
mood, and fond of collecting outlandish objects and ideas,
he seldom allows his wanderings and discoveries to unhinge
his home loyalties or ruffle his self - possession ; and he
remains, after all his adventures, intellectually as indolent
and secure as in the beginning. As to speculative truth,
he instinctively halts short of it, as it looms in the distance
and threatens to cast a contemptuous and chilling shadow
across his life. He would be very severe to a boy who
dreaded cold water and wouldn't learn to swim ; yet in
the moral world he is himself subject to illusions of timidity.
He does not believe, there, in the overwhelming rewards of
courage. His chosen life is indeed beautiful—as the shy
boy's might be—in its finitude ; all the more beautiful and
worth preserving because, like his country, it is an island

in the sea. His domestic thermometer and barometer have sufficed to guide him to the right hygiene.

Hygiene does not require telescopes nor microscopes. It is not concerned, like medicine or psychology, with the profound hidden workings of our bodies or minds, complexities hardly less foreign to our discoursing selves than are the mysteries of the great outer world. Hygiene regards only the right regimen of man in his obvious environment, judged by his conscious well-being. If it goes afield at all, it does so in the interests of privacy. All it asks of life is that it should be comely, spontaneous, and unimpeded : all it asks of the earth is that it should be fit for sport and for habitation. Men, to be of the right hygienic sort, must love the earth, and must know how to range in it. This the Englishman knows ; and just as, in spite of his insularity, he loves this whole terraqueous globe simply and genuinely, so the earth, turned into mud by the vain stampings of so many garrulous and sickly nations, would doubtless say : Let the Englishman inhabit me, and I shall be green again.

In matters of hygiene the Englishman's maxims are definite and his practice refined. He has discovered what he calls good form, and is obstinately conservative about it, not from inertia, but in the interests of pure vitality. Experience has taught him the uses to which vitality can be put, so as to preserve and refresh it. He knows the right degree of exertion normally required to do things well—to walk or to talk, for instance ; he does not saunter nor scramble, he does not gesticulate nor scream. In consequence, perhaps, on extraordinary occasions he fails at first to exert himself enough ; and his eloquence is not torrential nor inspired, even at those rare moments when it ought to be so. But when nothing presses, he shows abundant energy, without flurry or excess. In manners and morals, too, he has found the right mean between anarchy and servitude, and the wholesome measure of comfort. What those who dislike him call his hypocrisy is but timeliness in his instincts, and a certain modesty on their part in not intruding upon one another. Your prayers are not necessarily insincere because you pray only in church ; you are not concealing a passion if for a time

you forget it and slough it off. These alternations are
phases of the inner man, not masks put on in turn by
some insidious and calculating knave. All the Englishman's attitudes and habits—his out-of-door life, his clubs,
his conventicles, his business—when they are spontaneous
and truly British, are for the sake of his inner man in its
privacy. Other people, unless the game calls for them,
are in the way, and uninteresting. His spirit is like Wordsworth's skylark, true to the kindred points of heaven and
home ; and perhaps these points seem to him kindred only
because they are both functions of himself. Home is the
centre of his physical and moral comfort, his headquarters
in the war of life, where lie his spiritual stores. Heaven
is a realm of friendly inspiring breezes and setting suns,
enveloping his rambles and his perplexities. The world
to him is a theatre for the soliloquy of action. There is a
comfortable luxuriousness in all his attitudes. He thinks
the prize of life worth winning, but not worth snatching.
If you snatch it, as Germans, Jews, and Americans seem
inclined to do, you abdicate the sovereignty of your inner
man, you miss delight, dignity, and peace ; and in that
case the prize of life has escaped you.

As the Englishman disdains to peer and is slow to
speculate, so he resents any meddling or intrusion into his
own preserves. How sedulously he plants out his garden,
however tiny, from his neighbours and from the public
road ! If his windows look unmistakably on the street,
at least he fills his window-boxes with the semblance of a
hedge or a garden, and scarcely allows the dubious light to
filter through his blinds and lace curtains ; and the space
between them, in the most dingy tenement, is blocked by
an artificial plant. He is quite willing not to be able to
look out, if only he can prevent other people from looking
in. If they did, what would they see ? Nothing shocking,
surely ; his attitude by his fireside is perfectly seemly.
He is not throwing anything at the family ; very likely
they are not at home. Nor has he introduced any low-class
person by the tradesman's entrance, in whose company he
might blush to be spied. He is not in deshabille ; if he has
changed any part of his street clothes it has not been from
any inclination to be slovenly in private, but on the contrary

to vindicate his self-respect and domestic decorum. He does not dress to be seen of men, but of God. His elegance is an expression of comfort, and his comfort a consciousness of elegance. The eyes of men disquiet him, eminently presentable though he be, and he thinks it rude of them to stare, even in simple admiration. It takes tact and patience in strangers—perhaps at first an ostentatious indifference —to reassure him and persuade him that he would be safe in liking them. His frigid exterior is often a cuticle to protect his natural tenderness, which he forces himself not to express, lest it should seem misplaced or clumsy. There is a masculine sort of tenderness which is not fondness, but craving and premonition of things untried ; and the young Englishman is full of it. His heart is quiet and full ; he has not pumped it dry, like ill-bred children, in tantrums and effusive fancies. On the other hand, passions are atrophied if their expression is long suppressed, and we soon have nothing to say if we never say anything. As he grows old the Englishman may come to suspect, not without reason, that he might not reward too close a perusal. His social bristles will then protect his intellectual weakness, and he will puff himself out to disguise his vacuity.

It is intelligible that a man of deep but inarticulate character should feel more at ease in the fields and woods, at sea or in remote enterprises, than in the press of men. In the world he is obliged to maintain stiffly principles which he would prefer should be taken for granted. Therefore when he sits in silence behind his window curtains, with his newspaper, his wife, or his dog, his monumental passivity is not a real indolence. He is busily reinforcing his character, ruffled by the day's contact with hostile or indifferent things, and he is gathering new strength for the fray. After the concessions imposed upon him by necessity or courtesy, he is recovering his natural tone. To-morrow he will issue forth fresh and confident, and exactly the same as he was yesterday. His character is like his climate, gentle and passing readily from dull to glorious, and back again ; variable on the surface, yet perpetually self-restored and invincibly the same.

12

THE LION AND THE UNICORN

EVERY one can see why the Lion should be a symbol for the British nation. This noble animal loves dignified repose. He haunts by preference solitary glades and pastoral landscapes. His movements are slow, he yawns a good deal ; he has small squinting eyes high up in his head, a long displeased nose, and a prodigious maw. He apparently has some difficulty in making things out at a distance, as if he had forgotten his spectacles (for he is getting to be an elderly lion now), but he snaps at the flies when they bother him too much. On the whole, he is a tame lion ; he has a cage called the Constitution, and a whole parliament of keepers with high wages and a cockney accent ; and he submits to all the rules they make for him, growling only when he is short of raw beef. The younger members of the nobility and gentry may ride on his back, and he obligingly lets his tail hang out of the bars, so that the little Americans and the little Irishmen and the little Bolshevists, when they come to jeer at him, may twist it. Yet when the old fellow goes for a walk, how all the domestic and foreign poultry scamper ! They know he can spring ; his strength when aroused proves altogether surprising and unaccountable, he never seems to mind a blow, and his courage is terrible. The cattle, seeing there is no safety in flight, herd together when he appears on the horizon, and try to look unconscious ; the hyenas go to snarl at a distance ; the eagles and the serpents aver afterwards that they were asleep. Even the insects that buzz about his ears, and the very vermin in his skin, know him for the king of beasts.

But why should the other supporter of the British arms be the Unicorn ? What are the mystic implications of having a single horn ? This can hardly be the monster spoken of in Scripture, into the reason for whose existence, whether he be the rhinoceros of natural history or a slip of an inspired pen, it would be blasphemy to inquire. This Unicorn is a creature of mediaeval fancy, a horse rampant argent, only with something queer about

his head, as if a croquet-stake had been driven into it, or
he wore a very high and attenuated fool's cap. It would
be far-fetched to see in this ornament any allusion to
deceived husbands, as if in England the alleged injury
never seemed worth two horns, or divorce and damages
soon removed one of them. More plausible is the view
that, as the Lion obviously expresses the British character, so the Unicorn somewhat more subtly expresses the
British intellect. Whereas most truths have two faces,
and at least half of any solid fact escapes any single view
of it, the English mind is monocular ; the odd and the
singular have a special charm for it. This love of the
particular and the original leads the Englishman far
afield in the search for it ; he collects curios, and taking
all the nation together, there is perhaps nothing that
some Englishman has not seen, thought, or known ; but
who sees things as a whole, or anything in its right place ?
He inevitably rides some hobby. He travels through the
wide world with one eye shut, hops all over it on one leg,
and plays all his scales with one finger. There is fervour,
there is accuracy, there is kindness in his gaze, but there
is no comprehension. He will defend the silliest opinion
with a mint of learning, and espouse the worst of causes
on the highest principles. It is notorious elsewhere that
the world is round, that nature has bulk, and three if not
four dimensions ; it is a truism that things cannot be
seen as a whole except in imagination. But imagination,
if he has it, the Englishman is too scrupulous to trust ;
he observes the shapes and the colours of things intently,
and behold, they are quite flat, and he challenges you to
show why, when every visible part of everything is flat,
anything should be supposed to be round. He is a keen reformer, and certainly the world would be much simpler, right
opinion would be much righter and wrong opinion much
wronger, if things had no third and no fourth dimension.

Ah, why did those early phrenologists, true and typical
Englishmen as they were, denounce the innocent midwife
who by a little timely pressure on the infant skull com-
pressed, as they said, " the oval of genius into the flatness
of boobyism " ? Let us not be cowed by a malicious
epithet. What some people choose to call boobyism and

flatness may be the simplest, the most British, the most
scientific philosophy. Your true booby may be only he
who, having perforce but a flat view of a flat world, prates
of genius and rotundity. Blessed are they whose eye is
single. Only when very drunk do we acknowledge our
double optics ; when sober we endeavour to correct and
ignore this visual duplicity and to see as respectably as if
we had only one eye. The Unicorn might well say the
same thing of two-horned beasts. Such double and
crooked weapons are wasteful and absurd. You can use
only one horn effectively even if you have two, but in a
sidelong and cross-eyed fashion ; else your prey simply
nestles between, where eye cannot see it nor horn probe it.
A single straight horn, on the contrary, is like a lancet ;
it pierces to the heart of the enemy by a sure frontal
attack : nothing like it for pricking a bubble, or pointing
to a fact and scathingly asking the Government if they are
aware of it. In music likewise every pure melody passes
from single note to note, as do the sweet songs of nature.
Away with your demoniac orchestras, and your mad
pianist, tossing his mane, and banging with his ten fingers
and his two feet at once ! As to walking on two feet,
that also is mere wobbling and, as Schopenhauer observed,
a fall perpetually arrested. It is an unstable compromise
between going on all fours, if you want to be safe, and
standing on one leg, like the exquisite flamingo, if you
aspire to be graceful and spiritually sensitive. There is
really no biped in nature except ridiculous man, as if the
prancing Unicorn had succeeded in always being rampant ;
your feathered creatures are bipeds only on occasion
and in their off moments ; essentially they are winged
beings, and their legs serve only to prop them when at
rest, like the foot-piece of a motor-cycle which you let
down when it stops.

The Lion is an actual beast, the Unicorn a chimera ;
and is not England in fact always buoyed up on one
side by some chimera, as on the other by a sense for fact ?
Illusions are mighty, and must be reckoned with in this
world ; but it is not necessary to share them or even
to understand them from within, because being illusions
they do not prophesy the probable consequences of their

existence ; they are irrelevant in aspect to what they involve in effect. The dove of peace brings new wars, the religion of love instigates crusades and lights faggots, metaphysical idealism in practice is the worship of Mammon, government by the people establishes the boss, free trade creates monopolies, fondness smothers its pet, assurance precipitates disaster, fury ends in smoke and in shaking hands. The shaggy Lion is dimly aware of all this ; he is ponderous and taciturn by an instinctive philosophy. Why should he be troubled about the dreams of the Unicorn, more than about those of the nightingale or the spider ? He can roughly discount these creatures' habits, in so far as they touch him at all, without deciphering their fantastic minds. That makes the strength of England in the world, the leonine fortitude that helps her, through a thousand stupidities and blunders, always to pull through. But England is also, more than any other country, the land of poetry and of the inner man. Her sunlight and mists, her fields, cliffs, and moors are full of aerial enchantment ; it is a land of tenderness and dreams. The whole nation hugs its hallowed shams ; there is a real happiness, a sense of safety, in agreeing not to acknowledge the obvious ; there is a universal conspiracy of respect for the non-existent. English religion, English philosophy, English law, English domesticity could not get on without this " tendency to feign." And see how admissible, how almost natural this chimera is. A milk - white pony, elegantly Arabian, with a mane like sea-foam, and a tail like a little silvery comet, sensitive nostrils, eyes alight with recognition, a steed such as Phoebus might well water at those springs that lie in the chalices of flowers, a symbol at once of impetuosity and obedience, a heraldic image for the daintiness of Ariel and the purity of Galahad. If somehow we suspect that the poetical creature is light-witted, the stern Lion opposite finds him nevertheless a sprightly and tender companion, as King Lear did his exquisite Fool. Such a Pegasus cannot be a normal horse ; he was hatched in a cloud, and at his birth some inexorable ironic deity drove a croquet - stake into his pate, and set an attenuated crown, very like a fool's cap, between his startled ears.

13

DONS

Dons are picturesque figures. Their fussy ways and their oddities, personal and intellectual, are as becoming to them as black feathers to the blackbird. Their minds are all gaunt pinnacles, closed gates, and little hidden gardens. A mediaeval tradition survives in their notion of learning and in their manner of life ; they are monks flown from the dovecot, scholastics carrying their punctilious habits into the family circle. In the grander ones there may be some assimilation to a prelate, a country gentleman, or a party leader ; but the rank and file are modest, industrious pedagogues, sticklers for routine, with a squinting knowledge of old books and of young men. Their politics are narrow and their religion dubious. There was always something slippery in the orthodoxy of scholastics, even in the Middle Ages ; they are so eager to define, to correct, and to trace back everything, that they tend to cut the cloth on their own bias, and to make some crotchet of theirs the fulcrum of the universe. The thoughts of these men are like the Sibylline leaves, profound but lost. I should not call them pedants, because what they pursue and insist on in little things is the shadow of something great ; trifles, as Michael Angelo said, make perfection, and perfection is no trifle. Yet dry learning and much chewing of the cud take the place amongst them of the two ways men have of really understanding the world—science, which explores it, and sound wit, which estimates humanly the value of science and of everything else.

The function of dons is to expound a few classic documents, and to hand down as large and as pleasant a store as possible of academic habits, maxims, and anecdotes. They peruse with distrust the new books published on the subject of their teaching ; they refer to them sometimes sarcastically, but their teaching remains the same. Their conversation with outsiders is painfully amiable for a while ; lassitude soon puts the damper on it, unless they can lapse into the academic question of the day, or take up the circle of their good old stories. Their originality runs to interpreting some old text afresh, wearing some odd garment, or frequenting in the holidays some unfrequented spot. When they are bachelors, as properly they should be, their pupils are their chief link with the world of affection, with mischievous and merry things ; and in exchange for this whiff of life, which they receive with each yearly invasion of flowering youth, like the fresh scent of hay every summer from the meadows, they furnish those empty minds with some humorous memories, and some shreds of knowledge. It does not matter very much whether what a don says is right or wrong, provided it is quotable ; nobody considers his opinions for the matter they convey ; the point is that by hearing them the pupils and the public may discover what opinions, and on what subjects, it is possible for mortals to devise. Their maxims are like those of the early Greek philosophers, a proper introduction to the good society of the intellectual world. So are the general systems to which the dons may be addicted, probably some revision of Christian theology, of Platonic mysticism, or of German philosophy. Such foreign doctrines do very well for the dons of successive epochs, native British philosophy not being fitted to edify the minds of the young : those vaster constructions appeal more to the imagination, and their very artificiality and ticklish architecture, like that of a house of cards, are part of their function, calling for paradoxical faith and—what youth loves quite as much—for captious and sophistical argument. They lie in the fourth dimension of human belief, amongst the epicycles which ingenious error describes about the unknown orbit of truth ; for the truth is not itself luminous, as wit is ; the truth travels silently in the night and requires to be caught by the searchlight of wit to become visible. Meantime the mind plays innocently with its own phosphorescence, which is what we call culture and what dons are created to keep alive. Wit the dons often have, of an oblique kind, in the midst of their much-indulged prejudices and foibles ; and what with glints of wit and scraps of learning, the soul is not sent away empty from their door : better fed and healthier, indeed, for these rich crumbs from the banquet of antiquity, when thought was fresh, than if

it had been reared on a stuffy diet of useful knowledge,
or on some single dogmatic system, to which life-slavery
is attached. Poor, brusque, comic, venerable dons ! You
watched over us tenderly once, whilst you blew your long
noses at us and scolded ; then we thought only of the
roses in your garden, of your succulent dinners, or perhaps
of your daughters ; but now we understand that you had
hearts yourselves, that you were song-birds grown old in
your cages, having preferred fidelity to adventure. We
catch again the sweet inflection of your cracked notes, and
we bless you. You have washed your hands among the
innocent ; you have loved the beauty of the Lord's house.

14

APOLOGY FOR SNOBS

BRITISH satirists are very scornful of snobbery ; they seem
oppressed by the thought that wealth, rank, and finery
are hideously inane and that they are hideously powerful.
Are these moralists really overcome by a sense of the
vanity of human wishes ? It would hardly seem so ; for
they often breathe a sentimental adoration for romantic
love or philanthropy or adventure or mystic piety or good
cheer or ruthless will—all of them passions as little likely
as any snobbish impulse to arise without some illusion or
to end without some disappointment. Why this exclusive
hostility to the vanities dear to the snob ? Have birth,
money, and fashion no value whatever ? Do they not
dazzle the innocent and unsophisticated with a distant
image of happiness ? Are they not actually, when enjoyed,
very comforting and delightful things in their way ?
What else than this sensitiveness to better social example
—which we may call snobbery if we please—lends English
life in particular its most characteristic excellences—order
without constraint, leisure without apathy, seclusion without solitude, good manners without punctilio, emulation
without intrigue, splendour without hollowness ? Why
such bitterness about the harmless absurdities that may
fringe this national discipline ? Are these moralists in

fact only envious and sulky? Is it sour grapes? It
would sometimes seem as if, in England, the less representative a man was the more eagerly he took to literature, and
thought that by hating his fellow-men and despising their
prevalent feelings he rendered himself eminently fit to be
their guide and redeemer.

In fact, there is a philosophical principle implied in
snobbery, a principle which is certainly false if made
absolute, but which fairly expresses the moral relations
of things in a certain perspective. If we all really stood
on different steps in a single ladder of progress, then to
admire and imitate those above us and to identify ourselves with them by hook or by crook would be simply to
accelerate our natural development, to expand into our
higher self, and to avoid fatal abysses to the right and to
the left of the path marked out for us by our innate voca-
tion. Life would then be like the simple game which
children call Follow the Leader; and this scrupulous
discipleship would be perfect freedom, since the soul of
our leader and our own soul that chooses him would be
the same. This principle is precisely that of the transcendental philosophy where it maintains that there is but
one spirit in all men, and one logical moral evolution for
the world. In fact, it is the Germans rather than the
English that are solemn, convinced, and universal snobs.
If they do not seem so much snobs in particular, it is because
they are snobs *überhaupt*. It is not only from the nobility
that grateful dews descend on their sensitive hearts, as
upon open flowers; they yearn also after the professors
and the artists, and assiduously dress their domestic mind,
so far as the cloth will go, in the latest intellectual fashion.
Their respect for what holds the official stage, and holds
it for the moment, is beautiful in its completeness. They
can change their front without changing their formation.
And the occasional pricks and heartburnings of snobbery
are entirely drowned, in their case, in its voluminous
vicarious joys.

On the whole, however, snobbish sentiment and transcendental philosophy do not express the facts of nature.
Men and nations do not really march in single file, as if
they were being shepherded into some Noah's Ark. They

have perhaps a common root and similar beginnings, but they branch out at every step into forms of life between which there is no further interchange of sap, and no common destiny. Their several fruits become incommensurable in beauty and in value, like the poetry of different languages, and more disparate the more each is perfected after its kind. The whale is not a first sketch for the butterfly, nor its culmination ; the mind of an ox is not a fuller expression of that of a rabbit. The poet does not evolve into the general, nor *vice versa* ; nor does a man, in growing further, become a woman, superior as she may be in her own way. That is why snobbery is really a vice : it tempts us to neglect and despise our proper virtues in aping those of other people. If an angel appeared to me displaying his iridescent wings and treble voice and heart fluttering with eternal love, I should say, " Certainly, I congratulate you, but I do not wish to resemble you." Snobbery haunts those who are not reconciled with themselves ; evolution is the hope of the immature. You cannot be everything. Why not be what you are ?

This contentment with oneself, in its rational mixture of pride with humility, and its infinite indifference to possibilities which to us are impossible, is well understood in the great East—which is a moral as well as a geographical climate. There every one feels that circumstances have not made and cannot unmake the soul. Variations of fortune do not move a man from his inborn centre of gravity. Whatever happens and whatever people say he puts up with as he would with bad weather. He lets them thunder and rage, and continues to sit on his heels in his corner, in the shade or in the sun according to the season, munching his crust of bread, meditating on heaven and earth, and publishing on occasion to the passers-by, or to the wilderness, the revelations he receives from the spirit ; and if these are particularly vivid, he will not hesitate to cry, " So saith the Lord," with an equal dignity or assurance whether he be sage, king, or beggar. Such firmness and independence of character are admirable, so long as the expression of them remains merely poetical or moral. It is enough if confessions are sincere, and aspirations true to the heart that utters them. In the heights and the depths we are all solitary, and we are deceived if we think otherwise, even when people say they agree with us, or form a sect under our name. As our radical bodily functions are incorrigibly selfish and persistent, so our ultimate ideals, if they are sincere, must for ever deviate from those of others and find their zenith in a different star. The moral world is round like the heavens, and the directions which life can take are infinitely divergent and unreturning.

But in the world of circumstances, in matters of politics and business, information, and thrift, civilized men move together: their interests, if not identical, are parallel, and their very conflicts and rivalries arise out of this contact and relevance in their aims. Eminence in this worldly sphere is unmistakable. One fortune in money can be measured against another and may be increased to equal it; and in government, fashion, and notoriety some people are unmistakably at the top of the tree, and doubtless deserve to be there, having found the right method of climbing. It is only natural that those who wish to climb too should study and imitate them. Awe and respect for such persons is an honest expression of social idealism: it is an admiration mixed with curiosity and with the desire for propinquity, because their achievements are in our own line of business and a prospective partnership is not out of the question. Their life is the ideal of ours. Yet all such conventional values and instrumentalities, in which we are perhaps absorbed, in the end say nothing to the heart. If by chance, in the shifts of this world, we pop up near the people whom we distantly admired, and reach the crest of the wave in their company, we discover how great an illusion it was that it would be good or possible for us to resemble them; conventional friends, we have no instincts, joys, or memories in common. It is, perhaps, from quite another age or race, from an utterly different setting of worldly tasks and ambitions, that some hint of true friendship and understanding reaches us in our hermitage; and even this hint is probably a hollow reverberation of our own soliloquy. In this slippery competitive earth snobbery is not unreasonable; but in heaven and hell there are no snobs.

There every despised demon hugs his favourite vice for ever, and even the smallest of the stars shines with a singular glory.

15

THE HIGHER SNOBBERY

To call an attitude snobbish, when the great and good recommend it as the only right attitude, would be to condemn it without trial ; yet I do not know how else to name the sentiment that happiness of one sort is better than happiness of another sort, and that perfection in one animal is more admirable than perfection in another. I wish there was a word for this arrangement of excellences in higher and lower classes which did not imply approval or disapproval of such an arrangement. But language is terribly moralistic, and I do not blame the logicians for wishing to invent another which shall convey nothing to the mind with which it has any previous acquaintance. The Psyche, who is the mother of language as well as of intellect, feels things to be good or evil before she notices what other qualities they may have : and she never gets much beyond the first dichotomy of her feminine logic : wretch and darling, nasty and nice. This is perhaps the true reason why Plato, who in some respects had a feminine mind and whose metaphysics follows the lines of language, tells us in one place that the good is the highest of the Ideas, and the source of both essence and existence. Good and bad are certainly the first qualities fixed by words : so that to call a man a snob, for instance, is a very vague description but a very clear insult. Suppose we found on examination that the person in question had a retiring and discriminating disposition, that he shunned the un-washed, that he resembled persons of distinction, and recognized the superiority of those who were really his superiors ; we should conclude without hesitation that he was no snob at all, but a respectable, right-minded person. If he had been really a snob, he would have looked up stupidly to what has no true sublimity, like birth without money, would have imitated what was not becoming to his station, and would have shunned company, such as our own, which though perhaps not the most fashionable is undoubtedly the best. As I can see no scientific difference between this snob and that no-snob, I am constrained in my own thoughts to class them together ; but in order to remind myself that the same principle may be approved in one case and condemned in the other, I call snobbery, when people approve of it, the higher snobbery.

An interesting advocate of the higher snobbery is Nietzsche. Although his admiring eye is fixed on the superman, who is to supersede our common or garden humanity, the unique excellence of that future being does not seem to lie merely in that he is future, or is destined to be dominant in his day : after all, everything was once future, everything was once the coming thing, and destined to prevail in its day. It is only human to admire and copy the fashion of to-day, whether in clothes, or politics, or literature, or speculation ; but I have not yet heard of any snob so far ahead of his times as to love the fashions of doomsday. The worship of evolution, which counts for so much with many higher snobs, does not seem essential in Nietzsche. The superman no doubt is coming, but he is not coming to stay, since the world repeats its evolution in perpetual cycles ; and whilst he will give its highest expression to the love of power, it does not appear that he will care very much about controlling external things, or will be able to control them. His superiority is to be intrinsic, and chiefly composed of freedom. It was freedom, I think, that Nietzsche sighed for in his heart, whilst in his cavalierly speculations he talked of power. At least, unless by power he meant power to be oneself, the notion that all nature was animated by the lust of power would lose its plausibility ; the ambition which we may poetically attribute to all animals is rather to appropriate such things as serve their use, perfection, or fancy, and to leave all else alone. There are indications that the superman was to be a mystic and a wanderer, like a god visiting the earth, and that what spell he exercised was to flow from him almost unawares, whilst he mused about himself and about higher things. So little was his power to involve subjection to what he worked upon (which is the counterpart of all material power) that he was to disregard the interests of others in a Spartan mood ; he was to ride ruthlessly through this nether world, half a poet, half a scourge, with his breast uncovered to every treacherous shaft, and his head high in the air.

Now I will not say whether such a romantic and Byronic life is worth living in itself ; there may be creatures whose only happiness is to be like that, although I suspect that Byron and Nietzsche, Lohengrin and Zarathustra, had not mastered the art of Socrates, and did not know what they wanted. In any case, such a Dionysiac career would be good only as the humblest human existence may be so ; its excellence would lie in its harmony with the nature of him who follows it, not in its bombast, inflation, or superhumanity. Nietzsche was far from ungenerous or unsympathetic towards the people. He wished them (somewhat contemptuously) to be happy, whilst he and his superman remained poetically wretched ; he even said sometimes that in their own sphere they might be perfect, and added—with that sincerity which, in him, redeems so many follies—that nothing could be better than such perfection. But if this admission is to be taken seriously, the superman would be no better than the good slave. The whole principle of the higher snobbery would be abandoned, and Nietzsche in the end would only lead us back to Epictetus.

No, the higher snob will reply, the perfect superman may be no better than the perfect slave, but he is *higher*. What does this word mean ? For the zealous evolutionist it seems to mean later, more complicated, requiring a longer incubation and a more special environment. Therefore what is higher is more expensive, and has a more precarious existence than what is lower ; so the lady is higher than the woman, fine art is higher than useful art, and the height of the fashion in fine art is the highest point in it. The higher is the more inclusive, requiring everything else to produce it, and itself producing nothing, or something higher still. Of course the higher is not merely the better ; because the standard of excellence itself changes as we proceed, and according to the standard of the lower morality the higher state which abolishes it

will be worse.   An orchid may not be more beautiful than
a lily, but it is higher ; philosophy may not be truer than
science, nor true at all, but it is higher, because so much
more comprehensive ; faith may not be more trustworthy
than reason, but it is higher ; insatiable will may not be
more beneficent than contentment in oneself and respect
for others, but it is higher ; war is higher, though more
painful, than peace ; perpetual motion is not more reasonable than movement towards an end, and stilts are not
more convenient than shoes, but they are higher.   In
everything the higher, when not the better, means what
folly or vanity cannot bear to abandon.   Higher is a word
by which we defend the indefensible ; it is a declaration
of impenitence on the part of unreason, a cry to create
prejudice in favour of all that tyrannizes over mankind.
It is the watchword of the higher snob.   The first to use
it was Satan, when he declared that he was not satisfied
to be anything but the highest ; whereas the highest thinks
it no derogation to take the form of the lowest since the
lowest, too, has its proper perfection, and there is nothing
better than that.

16

DISTINCTION IN ENGLISHMEN

ENGLAND has been rich in poets, in novelists, in inventors,
in philosophers making new beginnings, in intrepid
travellers, in learned men whose researches are a hobby
and almost a secret.   The land was once rich in saints,
and is still rich in enthusiasts.   But the official leaders of
the English people, the kings, prelates, professors, and
politicians, have usually been secondary men ; and even
they have been far more distinguished in their private
capacity than in their official action and mind.   English
genius is anti-professional ; its affinities are with amateurs,
and there is something of the amateur in the best English
artists, actors, and generals.   Delicacy of conscience,
mental haze, care not to outrun the impulse of the soul,
hold the Englishman back midway in his achievements ;
there is in him a vague respect for the unknown, a tacit

diffidence in his own powers, which dissuade him from
venturing on the greatest things or from carrying them
out in a comprehensive manner. The truth is the British
do not wish to be well led. They are all individualistic
and aristocratic at heart, and want no leaders in ultimate
things ; the inner man must be his own guide. If they
had to live under the shadow of a splendid monarch, or a
masterful statesman, or an authoritative religion, or a
deified state they would not feel free. They wish to peck
at their institutions, and tolerate only such institutions as
they can peck at. A certain ineptitude thus comes to be
amongst them an aptitude for office : it keeps the official
from acquiring too great an ascendancy. There is a sort
of ostracism by anticipation, to prevent men who are too
good from coming forward and upsetting the balance of
British liberties ; very like the vacuum which is created in
America around distinction, and which keeps the national
character there so true to type, so much on one lively level.
But in England distinction exists, because it escapes into
privacy. It is reserved for his Grace in his library and her
Ladyship at her tea-table ; it fills the nursery with lisping
sweetness and intrepid singleness of will ; it dwells with
the poets in their solitary rambles and midnight question-
ings ; it bends with the scholar over immortal texts ; it
is shut off from the profane by the high barriers of school
and college and hunting-field, by the sanctity and silence
of clubs, by the unspoken secrets of church and home.

The greatest distinction of English people, however, is
one which, whilst quite personal and private in its scope,
is widely diffused and strikingly characteristic of the better
part of the nation ; I mean, distinction in the way of
living. The Englishman does in a distinguished way the
simple things that other men might slur over as un-
important or essentially gross or irremediable ; he is
distinguished — he is disciplined, skilful, and calm — in
eating, in sport, in public gatherings, in hardship, in
danger, in extremities. It is in physical and rudimentary
behaviour that the Englishman is an artist ; he is the ideal
sailor, the ideal explorer, the ideal comrade in a tight
place ; he knows how to be clean without fussiness, well-
dressed without show, and pleasure-loving without loud-

ness. This is why, although he is the most disliked of
men the world over (except where people need some one
they can trust) he is also the most imitated. What
ferocious Anglophobe, whether a white man or a black
man, is not immensely flattered if you pretend to have
mistaken him for an Englishman ? After all, this imitation
of the physical distinction of Englishmen is not absurd ;
here is something that *can* be imitated : it is really the
easiest way of doing easy things, which only bad education
and bad habits have made difficult for most people. There
is nothing impossible in adopting afternoon tea, football,
and boy scouts ; what is impossible, and if possible very
foolish, is to adopt English religion, philosophy, or political
institutions. But why should any one wish to adopt
them ? They have their merits, of course, and their
propriety at home ; but they are blind compromises, and it
is not in their principles that the English are distinguished,
but only in their practice. Their accents are more choice
than their words, and their words more choice than their
ideas. This, which might sound like a gibe, is to my mind
a ground for great hope and for some envy. Refinement,
like charity, should begin at home. First the body ought
to be made fit and decent, then speech and manners, and
habits justly combining personal initiative with the power
of co-operating with others ; and then, as this healthy life
extends, the world will begin to open out to the mind in
the right perspectives : not at first, perhaps never, in its
total truth and its real proportions, but with an ever-
enlarging appreciation of what, for us, it can contain.
The mind of the Englishman, starting in this proud and
humble and profound way from the inner man, pierces very
often, in single directions, to the limit of human faculty ;
and it seems to me to add to his humanity, without injury
to his speculation, that he instinctively withdraws again
into himself, as he might return home to marry and settle
after tempting fortune at the antipodes. His curious
knowledge and his personal opinions then become, as it
were, mementos of his distant adventures ; but his sterling
worth lies in himself. He is at his best when free impulse
or familiar habit takes an unquestioned lead, and when
the mind, not being expected to intervene, beats in easy

unison with the scene and the occasion, like a rider at
home in the saddle and one with his galloping horse.
Then grace returns to him, so angular often in his forced
acts and his express tenets ; the smile comes unaffectedly,
and the blithe quick words flow as they should ; arm is
linked spontaneously in arm, laughter points the bull's-
eye of truth, the whole world and its mysteries, not being
pressed, become amiable, and the soul shines happy, and
beautiful, and absolute mistress in her comely house.
Nothing in him then is gross ; all is harmonized, all is
touched with natural life. His simplicity becomes wholeness, and he no longer seems dull in any direction, but in
all things sound, sensitive, tender, watchful, and brave.

17

FRIENDSHIPS

FRIENDSHIP is almost always the union of a part of one
mind with a part of another ; people are friends in spots.
Friendship sometimes rests on sharing early memories,
as do brothers and schoolfellows, who often, but for that
now affectionate familiarity with the same old days, would
dislike and irritate one another extremely. Sometimes it
hangs on passing pleasures and amusements, or on special
pursuits ; sometimes on mere convenience and comparative
lack of friction in living together. One's friends are that
part of the human race with which one can be human.
But there are youthful friendships of quite another quality,
which I seem to have discovered flourishing more often
and more frankly in England than in other countries ;
brief echoes, as it were, of that love of comrades so much
celebrated in antiquity. I do not refer to the " friendship
of virtue " mentioned by Aristotle, which means, I suppose,
community in allegiance or in ideals. It may come to
that in the end, considered externally ; but community
in allegiance or in ideals, if genuine, expresses a common
disposition, and its roots are deeper and more physical
than itself. The friendship I have in mind is a sense of
this initial harmony between two natures, a union of one

whole man with another whole man, a sympathy between the centres of their being, radiating from those centres on occasion in unanimous thoughts, but not essentially needing to radiate. Trust here is inwardly grounded ; likes and dislikes run together without harness, like the steeds of Aurora ; you may take agreement for granted without words ; affection is generously independent of all tests or external bonds ; it can even bear not to be mutual, not to be recognized ; and in any case it shrinks from the blatancy of open vows. In such friendships there is a touch of passion and of shyness ; an understanding which does not need to become explicit or complete. There is wine in the cup ; it is not to be spilled nor gulped down unrelished, but to be sipped slowly, soberly, in the long summer evening, with the window open to the college garden, and the mind full of all that is sweetest to the mind.

Now there is a mystery here—though it need be no mystery—which some people find strange and distressing and would like to hush up. This profound physical sympathy may sometimes, for a moment, spread to the senses ; that is one of its possible radiations, though fugitive ; and there is a fashionable psychology at hand to explain all friendship, for that reason, as an aberration of sex. Of course it is such in some people, and in many people it may seem to be such at rare moments ; but it would be a plain abuse of language to call a mother's love for her children sexual, even when they are boys, although certainly she could not have that love, nor those children, if she had no sex. Perhaps if we had no sex we should be incapable of tenderness of any sort ; but this fact does not make all forms of affection similar in quality nor in tendency. The love of friends is not, like the love of woman, a lyrical prologue to nest - building. Engaging, no doubt, the same radical instincts, in a different environment and at another phase of their development, it turns them, whilst still plastic, in other directions. Human nature is still plastic, especially in the region of emotion, as is proved by the ever-changing forms of religion and art ; and it is not a question of right and wrong, nor even, except in extreme cases, of health and disease, but only a question of alternative development, whether the human capacity to love is absorbed in the family cycle, or extends to individual friendships, or to communion with nature or with God. The love of friends in youth, in the cases where it is love rather than friendship, has a mystical tendency. In character, though seldom in intensity, it resembles the dart which, in an ecstatic vision, pierced the heart of Saint Theresa, bursting the normal integument by which the blood is kept coursing through generation after generation, in the closed channel of human existence and human slavery. Love then escapes from that round; it is, in one sense, wasted and sterilized; but in being diverted from its earthly labours it suffuses the whole universe with light; it casts its glowing colours on the sunset, upon the altar, upon the past, upon the truth. The anguished futility of love corrects its own selfishness, its own illusion; gradually the whole world becomes beautiful in its inhuman immensity; our very defeats are transfigured, and we see that it was good for us to have gone up into that mountain.

That such mystic emotions, whether in religion or in friendship, are erotic was well known before the days of Freud. They have always expressed themselves in erotic language. And why should they not be erotic? Sexual passion is itself an incident in the life of the Psyche, a transitive phase in the great cycle by which life on earth is kept going. It grows insensibly out of bodily self-love, childish play, and love of sensation; it merges in the end, after its midsummer night's dream, into parental and kingly purposes. How casual, how comic, the purely erotic impulse is, and how lightly nature plays with it, may be seen in the passion of jealousy. Jealousy is in-separable from sexual love, and yet jealousy is not itself erotic either in quality or in effect, since it poisons pleasure, turns sympathy into suspicion, love into hate, all in the interests of proprietorship. Why should we be jealous, if we were simply merry? Nature weaves with a wide loom, and crosses the threads; and erotic passion may be as easily provoked peripherally by deeper impulses as be itself the root of other propensities. Lovers sometimes pretend at first to be only friends, and friends have some-

times fancied, at first blush, that they were lovers ; it is
as easy for one habit or sentiment as for the other to prove
the radical one, and to prevail in the end.   As for Englishmen, the last thing they would do would be to disguise
some base prompting in high-flown language ; they would
call a spade a spade, if there were occasion.   They are
shy of words, as of all manifestations ;   and this very
shyness, if it proves that there is at bottom a vital instinct
concerned, also proves that it is not intrinsically more
erotic than social, nor more social than intellectual.   It
is each of these things potentially, for such faculties are
not divided in nature as they are in language ; it may turn
into any one of them if accident leads it that way ; but it
reverts from every casual expression to its central seat,
which is the felt harmony of life with life, and of life with
nature, with everything that in the pulses of this world
beats our own measure, and swells the music of our
thoughts.

18

DICKENS

IF Christendom should lose everything that is now in the
melting-pot, human life would still remain amiable and
quite adequately human.   I draw this comforting assurance
from the pages of Dickens.   Who could not be happy in
his world ?   Yet there is nothing essential to it which
the most destructive revolution would be able to destroy.
People would still be as different, as absurd, and as charming as are his characters ;   the springs of kindness and folly
in their lives would not be dried up.   Indeed, there is
much in Dickens which communism, if it came, would
only emphasize and render universal.   Those schools,
those poorhouses, those prisons, with those surviving
shreds of family life in them, show us what in the coming
age (with some sanitary improvements) would be the
nursery and home of everybody.   Everybody would be a
waif, like Oliver Twist, like Smike, like Pip, and like David
Copperfield ;   and amongst the agents and underlings of
social government, to whom all these waifs would be

entrusted, there would surely be a goodly sprinkling of
Pecksniffs, Squeers's, and Fangs; whilst the Fagins
would be everywhere commissioners of the people. Nor
would there fail to be, in high places and in low, the
occasional sparkle of some Pickwick or Cheeryble Brothers
or Sam Weller or Mark Tapley; and the voluble Flora
Finchings would be everywhere in evidence, and the
strong-minded Betsey Trotwoods in office. There would
also be, among the inefficient, many a Dora and Agnes and
Little Emily—with her charm but without her tragedy,
since this is one of the things which the promised social
reform would happily render impossible; I mean, by
removing all the disgrace of it. The only element in the
world of Dickens which would become obsolete would be
the setting, the atmosphere of material instrumentalities
and arrangements, as travelling by coach is obsolete;
but travelling by rail, by motor, or by airship will emotion-
ally be much the same thing. It is worth noting how such
instrumentalities, which absorb modern life, are admired
and enjoyed by Dickens, as they were by Homer. The
poets ought not to be afraid of them; they exercise the
mind congenially, and can be played with joyfully. Consider the black ships and the chariots of Homer, the coaches
and river-boats of Dickens, and the aeroplanes of to-day;
to what would an unspoiled young mind turn with more
interest? Dickens tells us little of English sports, but he
shares the sporting nature of the Englishman, to whom
the whole material world is a playing-field, the scene
giving ample scope to his love of action, legality, and
pleasant achievement. His art is to sport according to the
rules of the game, and to do things for the sake of doing
them, rather than for any ulterior motive.

It is remarkable, in spite of his ardent simplicity
and openness of heart, how insensible Dickens was to
the greater themes of the human imagination—religion,
science, politics, art. He was a waif himself, and utterly
disinherited. For example, the terrible heritage of conten-
tious religions which fills the world seems not to exist for
him. In this matter he was like a sensitive child, with a
most religious disposition, but no religious ideas. Perhaps,
properly speaking, he had no *ideas* on any subject; what

he had was a vast sympathetic participation in the daily life of mankind ; and what he saw of ancient institutions made him hate them, as needless sources of oppression, misery, selfishness, and rancour.   His one political passion was philanthropy, genuine but felt only on its negative, reforming side ; of positive utopias or enthusiasms we hear nothing.   The political background of Christendom is only, so to speak, an old faded back-drop for his stage ; a castle, a frigate, a gallows, and a large female angel with white wings standing above an orphan by an open grave —a decoration which has to serve for all the melodramas in his theatre, intellectually so provincial and poor. Common life as it is lived was varied and lovable enough for Dickens, if only the pests and cruelties could be removed from it.   Suffering wounded him, but not vulgarity ; whatever pleased his senses and whatever shocked them filled his mind alike with romantic wonder, with the endless delight of observation.   Vulgarity—and what can we relish, if we recoil at vulgarity ?—was innocent and amusing ; in fact, for the humorist, it was the spice of life.   There was more piety in being human than in being pious.   In reviving Christmas, Dickens transformed it from the celebration of a metaphysical mystery into a feast of overflowing simple kindness and good cheer ; the church bells were still there—in the orchestra ; and the angels of Bethlehem were still there—painted on the back-curtain.   Churches, in his novels, are vague, desolate places where one has ghastly experiences, and where only the pew-opener is human ; and such religious and political conflicts as he depicts in *Barnaby Rudge* and in *A Tale of Two Cities* are street brawls and prison scenes and conspiracies in taverns, without any indication of the contrasts in mind or interests between the opposed parties.   Nor had Dickens any lively sense for fine art, classical tradition, science, or even the manners and feelings of the upper classes in his own time and country : in his novels we may almost say there is no army, no navy, no church, no sport, no distant travel, no daring adventure, no feeling for the watery wastes and the motley nations of the planet, and —luckily, with his notion of them—no lords and ladies. Even love of the traditional sort is hardly in Dickens's

sphere—I mean the soldierly passion in which a rather
rakish gallantry was sobered by devotion, and loyalty
rested on pride.   In Dickens love is sentimental or
benevolent or merry or sneaking or canine ; in his last
book he was going to describe a love that was passionate
and criminal ; but love for him was never chivalrous,
never poetical. What he paints most tragically is a
quasi-paternal devotion in the old to the young, the love
of Mr. Peggotty for Little Emily, or of Solomon Gills for
Walter Gay. A series of shabby little adventures, such as
might absorb the interest of an average youth, were
romantic enough for Dickens.

I say he was disinherited, but he inherited the most
terrible negations. Religion lay on him like the weight
of the atmosphere, sixteen pounds to the square inch, yet
never noticed nor mentioned. He lived and wrote in
the shadow of the most awful prohibitions. Hearts petrified by legality and falsified by worldliness offered, indeed,
a good subject for a novelist, and Dickens availed himself
of it to the extent of always contrasting natural goodness
and happiness with whatever is morose ; but his morose
people were wicked, not virtuous in their own way ; so
that the protest of his temperament against his environment never took a radical form nor went back to first
principles. He needed to feel, in his writing, that he
was carrying the sympathies of every man with him.
In him conscience was single, and he could not conceive
how it could ever be divided in other men. He denounced
scandals without exposing shams, and conformed willingly
and scrupulously to the proprieties. Lady Dedlock's
secret, for instance, he treats as if it were the sin of Adam,
remote, mysterious, inexpiable. Mrs. Dombey is not
allowed to deceive her husband except by pretending to
deceive him. The seduction of Little Emily is left out
altogether, with the whole character of Steerforth, the
development of which would have been so important in
the moral experience of David Copperfield himself. But it
is not public prejudice alone that plays the censor over
Dickens's art ; his own kindness and even weakness of
heart act sometimes as marplots. The character of Miss
Mowcher, for example, so brilliantly introduced, was

evidently intended to be shady, and to play a very important part in the story; but its original in real life, which was recognized, had to be conciliated, and the sequel was omitted and patched up with an apology—itself admirable—for the poor dwarf. Such a sacrifice does honour to Dickens's heart; but artists should meditate on their works in time, and it is easy to remove any too great likeness in a portrait by a few touches making it more consistent than real people are apt to be ; and in this case, if the little creature had been really guilty, how much more subtle and tragic her apology for herself might have been, like that of the bastard Edmund in *King Lear*! So, too, in *Dombey and Son*, Dickens could not bear to let Walter Gay turn out badly, as he had been meant to do, and to break his uncle's heart as well as the heroine's ; he was accordingly transformed into a stage hero miraculously saved from shipwreck, and Florence was not allowed to reward the admirable Toots, as she should have done, with her trembling hand. But Dickens was no free artist ; he had more genius than taste, a warm fancy not aided by a thorough understanding of complex characters. He worked under pressure, for money and applause, and often had to cheapen in execution what his inspiration had so vividly conceived.

What, then, is there left, if Dickens has all these limitations ? In our romantic disgust we might be tempted to say, Nothing. But in fact almost everything is left, almost everything that counts in the daily life of mankind, or that by its presence or absence can determine whether life shall be worth living or not ; because a simple good life is worth living, and an elaborate bad life is not. There remains in the first place eating and drinking ; relished not bestially, but humanly, jovially, as the sane and exhilarating basis for everything else. This is a sound English beginning ; but the immediate sequel, as the England of that day presented it to Dickens, is no less delightful. There is the ruddy glow of the hearth ; the sparkle of glasses and brasses and well-scrubbed pewter ; the savoury fumes of the hot punch, after the tingle of the wintry air ; the coaching-scenes, the motley figures and absurd incidents of travel ; the changing sights and joys of the road. And then, to balance this, the traffic of ports and cities, the hubbub of crowded streets, the luxury of shop-windows and of palaces not to be entered ; the procession of the passers-by, shabby or ludicrously genteel ; the dingy look and musty smell of their lodgings ; the labyrinth of back-alleys, courts, and mews, with their crying children, and scolding old women, and listless, half-drunken loiterers. These sights, like fables, have a sort of moral in them to which Dickens was very sensitive ; the important airs of nobodies on great occasions, the sadness and preoccupation of the great as they hasten by in their mourning or on their pressing affairs ; the sadly comic characters of the tavern ; the diligence of shop-keepers, like squirrels turning in their cages ; the children peeping out everywhere like grass in an untrodden street ; the charm of humble things, the nobleness of humble people, the horror of crime, the ghastliness of vice, the deft hand and shining face of virtue passing through the midst of it all ; and finally a fresh wind of indifference and change blowing across our troubles and clearing the most lurid sky.

I do not know whether it was Christian charity or naturalistic insight, or a mixture of both (for they are closely akin) that attracted Dickens particularly to the deformed, the half-witted, the abandoned, or those impeded or misunderstood by virtue of some singular inner consecration. The visible moral of these things, when brutal prejudice does not blind us to it, comes very near to true philosophy ; one turn of the screw, one flash of reflection, and we have understood nature and human morality and the relation between them.

In his love of roads and wayfarers, of river-ports and wharves and the idle or sinister figures that lounge about them, Dickens was like Walt Whitman ; and I think a second Dickens may any day appear in America, when it is possible in that land of hurry to reach the same degree of saturation, the same unquestioning pleasure in the familiar facts. The spirit of Dickens would be better able to do justice to America than was that of Walt Whitman ; because America, although it may seem nothing but a noisy nebula to the impressionist, is not a nebula but a concourse of very distinct individual bodies, natural and social, each with its definite interests and story. Walt Whitman had a sort of transcendental philosophy which swallowed the universe whole, supposing there was a universal spirit in things identical with the absolute spirit that observed them ; but Dickens was innocent of any such clap‑trap, and remained a true spirit in his own person. Kindly and clear-sighted, but self-identical and unequivocally human, he glided through the slums like one of his own little heroes, uncontaminated by their squalor and confusion, courageous and firm in his clear allegiances amid the flux of things, a pale angel at the Carnival, his heart aflame, his voice always flute-like in its tenderness and warning. This is the true relation of spirit to existence, not the other which confuses them ; for this earth (I cannot speak for the universe at large) has no spirit of its own, but brings forth spirits only at certain points, in the hearts and brains of frail living creatures, who like insects flit through it, buzzing and gathering what sweets they can ; and it is the spaces they traverse in this career, charged with their own moral burden, that they can report on or describe, not things rolling on to infinity in their vain tides. To be hypnotized by that flood would be a heathen idolatry. Accordingly Walt Whitman, in his comprehensive democratic vistas, could never see the trees for the wood, and remained incapable, for all his diffuse love of the human herd, of ever painting a character or telling a story ; the very things in which Dickens was a master. It is this life of the individual, as it may be lived in a given nation, that determines the whole value of that nation to the poet, to the moralist, and to the judicious historian. But for the excellence of the typical single life, no nation deserves to be remembered more than the sands of the sea ; and America will not be a success, if every American is a failure.

Dickens entered the theatre of this world by the stage door ; the shabby little adventures of the actors in their private capacity replace for him the mock tragedies which they enact before a dreaming public. Mediocrity of circumstances and mediocrity of soul for ever return to the centre

of his stage ; a more wretched or a grander existence is
sometimes broached, but the pendulum soon swings back,
and we return, with the relief with which we put on our
slippers after the most romantic excursion, to a golden
mediocrity—to mutton and beer, and to love and babies
in a suburban villa with one frowsy maid. Dickens is the
poet of those acres of yellow brick streets which the traveller
sees from the railway viaducts as he approaches London ;
they need a poet, and they deserve one, since a complete
human life may very well be lived there. Their little
excitements and sorrows, their hopes and humours are
like those of the Wooden Midshipman in *Dombey and
Son*; but the sea is not far off, and the sky—Dickens
never forgets it—is above all those brief troubles. He
had a sentiment in the presence of this vast flatness of
human fates, in spite of their individual pungency, which
I think might well be the dominant sentiment of mankind
in the future ; a sense of happy freedom in littleness, an
open - eyed reverence and religion without words. This
universal human anonymity is like a sea, an infinitive
democratic desert, chock-full and yet the very image of
emptiness, with nothing in it for the mind, except, as the
Moslems say, the presence of Allah. Awe is the counterpart
of humility—and this is perhaps religion enough. The atom
in the universal vortex ought to be humble ; he ought to
see that, materially, he doesn't much matter, and that
morally his loves are merely his own, without authority
over the universe. He can admit without obloquy that
he is what he is ; and he can rejoice in his own being,
and in that of all other things in so far as he can share it
sympathetically. The apportionment of existence and of
fortune is in Other Hands ; his own portion is contentment,
vision, love, and laughter.

Having humility, that most liberating of sentiments,
having a true vision of human existence and joy in that
vision, Dickens had in a superlative degree the gift of
humour, of mimicry, of unrestrained farce. He was the
perfect comedian. When people say Dickens exaggerates,
it seems to me they can have no eyes and no ears. They
probably have only *notions* of what things and people are ;
they accept them conventionally, at their diplomatic value.

Their minds run on in the region of discourse, where there
are masks only and no faces, ideas and no facts ; they have
little sense for those living grimaces that play from moment
to moment upon the countenance of the world. The world
is a perpetual caricature of itself ; at every moment it is
the mockery and the contradiction of what it is pretending
to be. But as it nevertheless intends all the time to be
something different and highly dignified, at the next
moment it corrects and checks and tries to cover up the
absurd thing it was ; so that a conventional world, a world
of masks, is superimposed on the reality, and passes in
every sphere of human interest for the reality itself.
Humour is the perception of this illusion, the fact allowed
to pierce here and there through the convention, whilst
the convention continues to be maintained, as if we had
not observed its absurdity. Pure comedy is more radical,
cruder, in a certain sense less human ; because comedy
throws the convention over altogether, revels for a moment
in the fact, and brutally says to the notions of mankind,
as if it slapped them in the face, There, take that !   That's
what you really are ! At this the polite world pretends to
laugh, not tolerantly as it does at humour, but a little
angrily. It does not like to see itself by chance in the
glass, without having had time to compose its features
for demure self-contemplation. " What a bad mirror," it
exclaims ; " it must be concave or convex ; for surely I
never looked like that. Mere caricature, farce, and horse
play. Dickens exaggerates ; *I* never was so sentimental as
that ; *I* never saw anything so dreadful ; *I* don't believe
there were ever any people like Quilp, or Squeers, or
Serjeant Buzfuz." But the polite world is lying ; there
are such people ; we are such people ourselves in our true
moments, in our veritable impulses ; but we are careful to
stifle and to hide those moments from ourselves and from
the world ; to purse and pucker ourselves into the mask
of our conventional personality ; and so simpering, we
profess that it is very coarse and inartistic of Dickens to
undo our life's work for us in an instant, and remind us
of what we are. And as to other people, though we may
allow that considered superficially they are often absurd,
we do not wish to dwell on their eccentricities, nor to mimic

them. On the contrary, it is good manners to look away quickly, to suppress a smile, and to say to ourselves that the ludicrous figure in the street is not at all comic, but a dull ordinary Christian, and that it is foolish to give any importance to the fact that its hat has blown off, that it has slipped on an orange-peel and unintentionally sat on the pavement, that it has a pimple on its nose, that its one tooth projects over its lower lip, that it is angry with things in general, and that it is looking everywhere for the penny which it holds tightly in its hand. That may fairly represent the moral condition of most of us at most times ; but we do not want to think of it ; we do not want to see ; we gloss the fact over ; we console ourselves before we are grieved, and reassert our composure before we have laughed. We are afraid, ashamed, anxious to be spared. What displeases us in Dickens is that he does not spare us ; he mimics things to the full ; he dilates and exhausts and repeats ; he wallows. He is too intent on the passing experience to look over his shoulder, and consider whether we have not already understood, and had enough. He is not thinking of us ; he is obeying the impulse of the passion, the person, or the story he is enacting. This faculty, which renders him a consummate comedian, is just what alienated from him a later generation in which people of taste were æsthetes and virtuous people were higher snobs ; they wanted a mincing art, and he gave them copious improviza-tion, they wanted analysis and development, and he gave them absolute comedy. I must confess, though the fault is mine and not his, that sometimes his absoluteness is too much for me. When I come to the death of Little Nell, or to What the Waves were always Saying, or even to the incorrigible perversities of the pretty Dora, I skip. I can't take my liquor neat in such draughts, and my inner man says to Dickens, Please don't. But then I am a coward in so many ways ! There are so many things in this world that I skip, as I skip the undiluted Dickens ! When I reach Dover on a rough day, I wait there until the Channel is smoother ; am I not travelling for pleasure ? But my prudence does not blind me to the admirable virtue of the sailors that cross in all weathers, nor even to the automatic determination of the sea-sick ladies, who might so easily

have followed my example, if they were not the slaves of
their railway tickets and of their labelled luggage.   They
are loyal to their tour, and I to my philosophy.   Yet as
wrapped in my great-coat and sure of a good dinner, I
pace the windy pier and soliloquize, I feel the superiority
of the bluff tar, glad of breeze, stretching a firm arm to the
unsteady passenger, and watching with a masterful thrill
of emotion the home cliffs receding and the foreign coasts
ahead.   It is only courage (which Dickens had without
knowing it) and universal kindness (which he knew he had)
that are requisite to nerve us for a true vision of this world.
And as some of us are cowards about crossing the Channel,
and others about " crossing the bar," so almost everybody
is a coward about his own humanity.   We do not consent
to be absurd, though absurd we are.   We have no fundamental humility.   We do not wish the moments of our
lives to be caught by a quick eye in their grotesque initiative, and to be pilloried in this way before our own eyes.
For that reason we don't like Dickens, and don't like comedy,
and don't like the truth.   Dickens could don the comic
mask with innocent courage ; he could wear it with a
grace, ease, and irresistible vivacity seldom given to men.
We must go back for anything like it to the very greatest
comic poets, to Shakespeare or to Aristophanes.   Who else,
for instance, could have penned this :

" It was all Mrs. Bumble.   She *would* do it," urged Mr.
Bumble ; first looking round to ascertain that his partner
had left the room.
" That is no excuse," replied Mr. Brownlow.   " You were
present on the occasion of the destruction of these trinkets,
and indeed are the more guilty of the two, in the eye of the
law ; for the law supposes that your wife acts under your
direction."
" If the law supposes that," said Mr. Bumble, squeezing
his hat emphatically in both hands, " the law is a ass, a idiot.
If that's the eye of the law, the law is a bachelor ; and the
worst I wish the law is, that his eye may be opened by
experience—by experience."
Laying great stress on the repetition of these two words,
Mr. Bumble fixed his hat on very tight, and putting his hands
in his pockets, followed his helpmate downstairs.

This is high comedy; the irresistible, absurd, intense dream of the old fool, personifying the law in order to convince and to punish it. I can understand that this sort of thing should not be common in English literature, nor much relished; because pure comedy is scornful, merciless, devastating, holding no door open to anything beyond. Cultivated English feeling winces at this brutality, although the common people love it in clowns and in puppet shows; and I think they are right. Dickens, who surely was tender enough, had so irresistible a comic genius that it carried him beyond the gentle humour which most Englishmen possess to the absolute grotesque reality. Squeers, for instance, when he sips the wretched dilution which he has prepared for his starved and shivering little pupils, smacks his lips and cries: " Here's richness ! " It is savage comedy; humour would come in if we understood (what Dickens does not tell us) that the little creatures were duly impressed and thought the thin liquid truly delicious. I suspect that English sensibility prefers the humour and wit of Hamlet to the pure comedy of Falstaff; and that even in Aristophanes it seeks consolation in the lyrical poetry for the flaying of human life in the comedy itself. Tastes are free; but we should not deny that in merciless and rollicking comedy life is caught in the act. The most grotesque creatures of Dickens are not exaggerations or mockeries of something other than themselves; they arise because nature generates them, like toadstools; they exist because they can't help it, as we all do. The fact that these perfectly self-justified beings are absurd appears only by comparison, and from outside; circumstances, or the expectations of other people, make them ridiculous and force them to contradict themselves; but in nature it is no crime to be exceptional. Often, but for the savagery of the average man, it would not even be a misfortune. The sleepy fat boy in *Pickwick* looks foolish; but in himself he is no more foolish, nor less solidly self-justified, than a pumpkin lying on the ground. Toots seems ridiculous; and we laugh heartily at his incoherence, his beautiful waistcoats, and his extreme modesty; but when did anybody more obviously grow into what he is because he couldn't grow otherwise ? So with Mr. Pickwick,

and Sam Weller, and Mrs. Gamp, and Micawber, and all
the rest of this wonderful gallery ; they are ridiculous only
by accident, and in a context in which they never intended
to appear. If Oedipus and Lear and Cleopatra do not seem
ridiculous, it is only because tragic reflection has taken
them out of the context in which, in real life, they would
have figured. If we saw them as facts, and not as
emanations of a poet's dream, we should laugh at them
till doomsday ; what grotesque presumption, what silly
whims, what mad contradiction of the simplest realities !
Yet we should not laugh at them without feeling how real
their griefs were ; as real and terrible as the griefs of
children and of dreams. But facts, however serious
inwardly, are always absurd outwardly ; and the just
critic of life sees both truths at once, as Cervantes did in
Don Quixote. A pompous idealist who does not see the
ridiculous in *all* things is the dupe of his sympathy and
abstraction ; and a clown, who does not see that these
ridiculous creatures are living quite in earnest, is the dupe
of his egotism. Dickens saw the absurdity, and understood
the life ; I think he was a good philosopher.

It is usual to compare Dickens with Thackeray, which
is like comparing the grape with the gooseberry ; there are
obvious points of resemblance, and the gooseberry has
some superior qualities of its own ; but you can't make
red wine of it. The wine of Dickens is of the richest, the
purest, the sweetest, the most fortifying to the blood ;
there is distilled in it, with the perfection of comedy, the
perfection of morals. I do not mean, of course, that Dickens
appreciated all the values that human life has or might
have ; that is beyond any man. Even the greatest philosophers, such as Aristotle, have not always much imagination to conceive forms of happiness or folly other than
those which their age or their temperament reveals to them ;
their insight runs only to discovering the *principle* of
happiness, that it is spontaneous life of any sort harmonized
with circumstances. The sympathies and imagination of
Dickens, vivid in their sphere, were no less limited in range ;
and of course it was not his business to find philosophic
formulas ; nevertheless I call his the perfection of morals
for two reasons : that he put the distinction between good

and evil in the right place, and that he felt this distinction intensely. A moralist might have excellent judgement, he might see what sort of life is spontaneous in a given being and how far it may be harmonized with circumstances, yet his heart might remain cold, he might not suffer nor rejoice with the suffering or joy he foresaw. Humanitarians like Bentham and Mill, who talked about the greatest happiness of the greatest number, might conceivably be moral prigs in their own persons, and they might have been chilled to the bone in their theoretic love of mankind, if they had had the wit to imagine in what, as a matter of fact, the majority would place their happiness. Even if their theory had been correct (which I think it was in intention, though not in statement) they would then not have been perfect moralists, because their maxims would not have expressed their hearts. In expressing their hearts, they ought to have embraced one of those forms of " idealism " by which men fortify themselves in their bitter passions or in their helpless commitments ; for they do not wish mankind to be happy in its own way, but in theirs. Dickens was not one of those moralists who summon every man to do himself the greatest violence so that he may not offend them, nor defeat their ideals. Love of the good of others is something that shines in every page of Dickens with a truly celestial splendour. How entirely limpid is his sympathy with life—a sympathy uncontaminated by dogma or pedantry or snobbery or bias of any kind ! How generous is this keen, light spirit, how pure this open heart ! And yet, in spite of this extreme sensibility, not the least wobbling ; no deviation from a just severity of judgement, from an uncompromising distinction between white and black. And this happens as it ought to happen ; sympathy is not checked by a flatly contrary prejudice or commandment, by some categorical imperative irrelevant to human nature ; the check, like the cheer, comes by tracing the course of spontaneous impulse amid circumstances that inexorably lead it to success or to failure. There is a bed to this stream, freely as the water may flow ; when it comes to this precipice it must leap, when it runs over these pebbles it must sing, and when it spreads into that marsh it must become livid and malarial. The very

sympathy with human impulse quickens in Dickens the
sense of danger ; his very joy in joy makes him stern to
what kills it. How admirably drawn are his surly villains !
No rhetorical vilification of them, as in a sermon ; no
exaggeration of their qualms or fears ; rather a sense of
how obvious and human all their courses seem from their
own point of view ; and yet no sentimental apology for
them, no romantic worship of rebels in their madness or
crime. The pity of it, the waste of it all, are seen not by
a second vision but by the same original vision which
revealed the lure and the drift of the passion. Vice is a
monster here of such sorry mien, that the longer we see
it the more we deplore it ; that other sort of vice which
Pope found so seductive was perhaps only some innocent
impulse artificially suppressed, and called a vice because
it broke out inconveniently and displeased the company.
True vice is human nature strangled by the suicide of
attempting the impossible. Those so self-justified villains
of Dickens never elude their fates. Bill Sikes is not let
off, neither is Nancy ; the oddly benevolent Magwitch does
not escape from the net, nor does the unfortunate young
Richard Carstone, victim of the Circumlocution Office.
The horror and ugliness of their fall are rendered with the
hand of a master ; we see here, as in the world, that in
spite of the romanticists it is not virtue to rush enthusiasti-
cally along any road. I think Dickens is one of the best
friends mankind has ever had. He has held the mirror up
to nature, and of its reflected fragments has composed a
fresh world, where the men and women differ from real
people only in that they live in a literary medium, so that
all ages and places may know them. And they are worth
knowing, just as one's neighbours are, for their picturesque
characters and their pathetic fates. Their names should
be in every child's mouth ; they ought to be adopted
members of every household. Their stories cause the
merriest and the sweetest chimes to ring in the fancy,
without confusing our moral judgement or alienating our
interest from the motley commonplaces of daily life. In
every English-speaking home, in the four quarters of the
globe, parents and children will do well to read Dickens
aloud of a winter's evening ; they will love winter, and

one another, and God the better for it. What a wreath
that will be of ever-fresh holly, thick with bright berries, to
hang to this poet's memory—the very crown he would
have chosen !

19

THE HUMAN SCALE

GREAT buildings often have great doors ; but great doors
are heavy to swing, and if left open they may let in too
much cold or glare ; so that we sometimes observe a small
postern cut into one leaf of the large door for more convenient entrance and exit, and it is seldom or never that
the monumental gates yawn in their somnolence. Here
is the modest human scale reasserting itself in the midst
of a titanic structure, but it reasserts itself with an ill
grace and in the interests of frailty ; the patch it makes
seems unintended and ignominious.

Yet the human scale is not essentially petty ; when
it does not slip in as a sort of interloper it has nothing to
apologize for. Between the infinite and the infinitesimal
all sizes are equally central. The Greeks, the Saracens,
the English, the Chinese, and Japanese instinctively retain
the human scale in all that part of their work which is
most characteristic of them and nearest to their affections.
A Greek temple or the hall of an English mansion can be
spacious and dignified enough, but they do not outrun
familiar uses, and they lend their spaciousness and dignity
to the mind, instead of crushing it. Everything about them
has an air of friendliness and sufficiency ; their elegance
is not pompous, and if they are noble they are certainly
not vast, cold, nor gilded.

The Saracens, Chinese, and Japanese in their various
ways use the human scale with even greater refinement,
for they apply it also in a sensuous and psychological
direction. Not only is the size of their works moderate by
preference, like their brief lyrics, but they exactly meet
human sensibility by a great delicacy and concentration
in design and a fragrant simplicity in workmanship.
Everything they make is economical in its beauty and

seems to say to us : " I exist only to be enjoyed ; there is nothing in me not merely delightful." Here the human scale is not drawn from the human body so much as from the human soul ; its faculties are treated with deference— I mean the faculties it really has, not those, like reason, which a flattering philosophy may impute to it.

An English country house which is a cottage in appearance may turn out on examination to be almost a palace in extent and appointments ; there is no parade, yet there is great profusion—too much furniture, too many ornaments, too much food, too many flowers, too many people. Everything there is on the human scale except the quantity of things, which is oppressive. The Orientals are poorer, more voluptuous, and more sensitive to calligraphy ; they leave empty spaces about them and enjoy one thing at a time and enjoy it longer.

One reason for this greater subtlety and mercifulness in the art of Orientals is perhaps the fiercer assault made on their senses by nature. The Englishman lives in a country which is itself on the human scale, clement at all seasons, charming with a gently inconstant atmospheric charm. The rare humanity of nature in his island permeates his being from boyhood up with a delight that is half sentimental, half physical and sporting. In his fields and moors he grows keen and fond of exertion ; there too his friendships and his estimates of men are shaped unawares, as if under some silent superior influence. There he imbibes the impressions that make him tender to poetry. He may not require great subtlety in his poets, but he insists that their sentiment shall have been felt and their images seen, and while the obvious, even the shamelessly obvious, does not irritate him, he hates cheap sublimity and false notes. He respects experience and is master of it in his own field.

Thus the empty spaces with which a delicate art likes to surround itself are supplied for the Englishman by his comradeship with nature, his ranging habits, and the reticence of his imagination. There the unexpressed dimension, the background of pregnant silence, exists for him in all its power. For the Saracen, on the contrary, nature is an abyss : parched deserts, hard mountains,

night with its overwhelming moon. Here the human scale
is altogether transgressed ; nature is cruel, alien, excessive,
to be fled from with a veiled face. For a relief and solace
he builds his house without windows ; he makes his life
simple, his religion a single phrase, his art exquisite and
slight, like the jet of his fountain. It is sweet and necessary
that the works of man should respect the human scale
when everything in nature so infinitely transcends it.

Why the Egyptians loved things colossal I do not
know, but the taste of the Romans for the grandiose is
easier to understand. It seems to have been part and
parcel of that yearning for the super-human which filled
late antiquity. This yearning took two distinct directions.
Among the worldly it fostered imperialism, organization,
rhetoric, portentous works, belief in the universality and
eternity of Rome, and actual deification of emperors.
Among the spiritually-minded it led to a violent abstraction
from the world, so that the soul in its inward solitude
might feel itself inviolate and divine. The Christians at
first belonged of course to the latter party ; they detested
the inflation of the empire, with its cold veneer of marble
and of optimism ; they were nothing if not humble and
dead to the world. Their catacombs were perforce on the
human scale, as a coffin is ; but even when they emerged
to the surface, they reduced rather than enlarged the
temples and basilicas bequeathed to them by the pagans.
Apart from a few imperial structures at Constantinople
or Ravenna their churches for a thousand years kept to
the human scale ; often they were diminutive ; when
necessary they were spread out to hold multitudes, but
remained low and in the nature of avenues to a tomb or a
shrine. The centre was some sombre precinct, often
subterranean, where the inward man might commune with
the other world. The sacraments were received with a
bowed head ; they did not call for architectural vistas.
The sumptuousness that in time encrusted these sanctuaries
was that of a jewel—the Oriental, interior, concentrated
sumptuousness of the cloistered arts. Yet the open-air
pagan tradition was not dead. Roman works were everywhere, and not all in ruins, and love of display and of
plastic grandiloquence lay hardly dormant in the breast

of many.   It required only a little prosperity to dispel the
mystical humility and detachment which Christianity
had brought with it at first ; and the human scale of the
Christian Greeks yielded at the first opportunity to the
gigantic scale of the Romans.   Spaces were cleared, vaults
were raised, arches were made pointed in order that they
might be wider and be poised higher, towers and spires
were aimed at the clouds, usually getting only half way,
porches became immense caverns.   Brunelleschi accomplished a *tour de force* in his dome and Michelangelo another
in his, even more stupendous.   These various strained
models, straining in divergent directions, have kept artists
uneasy and impotent ever since, except when under some
benign influence they have recovered the human scale,
and in domestic architecture or portrait painting have
forgotten to be grand and have become felicitous.

The same movement is perhaps easier to survey in
philosophy than in architecture.   Scarcely had Socrates
brought investigation down from the heavens and limited
it to morals—a realm essentially on the human scale—
when his pupils hastened to undo his work by projecting
their moral system again into the sky, denaturalizing both
morals and nature.   They imagined a universe circling
about man, tempering the light for his eyes and making
absolute his childlike wishes and judgements.   This was
humanism out of scale and out of place, an attempt to
cut not the works of man but the universe to human
measure.   It was the nemesis that overtook the Greeks
for having become too complacently human.   Earlier the
monstrous had played a great part in their religion ; henceforth that surrounding immensity having been falsely
humanized, their modest humanity itself had to be made
monstrous to fill its place.

Hence we see the temples growing larger and larger,
the dome introduced, things on the human scale piled on
one another to make a sublime fabric, like Saint Sophia,
triumphal arches on pedestals not to be passed through,
vain columns like towers, with a statue poised on the
summit like a weathercock, and finally doors so large that
they could not be opened and little doors had to be cut in
them for men to use.   So the human scale turned up

again irrepressibly, but for the moment without its native
dignity, because it had been stretched to compass a lifeless
dignity quite other than its own.

20

ENGLISH ARCHITECTURE

NESTS were the first buildings ; I suppose the birds built
them long before man ceased to be four-footed or four-
handed, and to swing by his tail from trees.   The nests
of man were coverts, something between a hole in the
ground and an arbour ; a retreat easily turned into a wig-
wam, a hut, or a tent, when once man had begun to flay
animals and to weave mats.   From the tent we can imagine
the cart developing—one of the earliest of human habitations—and from the cart the boat : tents, boats, and carts
(as the Englishman knows so well) are in a manner more
human than houses ; they are the shelters of freemen.
Some men, those destined to higher things, are migratory ;
they have imagination, being haunted by absent things,
and distance of itself allures them, even if dearth or danger
does not drive them on ; indeed, dearth and danger would
not of themselves act as incentives to migration, if some
safer and greener paradise were not present to the fancy.
Ranging into varied climates, these men feel the need of
that portable shelter which we call clothes ; and at a
slightly greater distance from their skins, they surround
themselves with a second integument, also portable, the
tent, cart, or boat.   The first home of man is appropriately
without foundations, except in the instincts of his soul ;
and it is only by a slight anchorage to the earth, in some
tempting glen or by some flowing river, that the cart,
boat, or tent becomes a dwelling-house.   Here I see the
secret of that paradox, that the English people who have
invented the word home, should be such travellers and
colonists, and should live so largely and so contentedly
abroad.   Home is essentially portable ; it has no terrene
foundation, like a tomb, a well, or an altar ; it is an
integument of the living man, as the body itself is ; and as

the body is more than the raiment, and determines its form, so the inner man is more than his dwelling, and causes it to mould and to harden itself round him like a shell, wherever he may be. Home is built round his bed, his cupboard, and his chimney-corner ; and such a nest, if it fits his habits, is home all the world over, from Hudson's Bay to Malacca ; at least, it becomes home when the inner man, as he is prompted inwardly to do, surrounds himself there with a family ; for a home is a nest, and somehow incomplete without an egg to sit on.

This seems to me to be the true genealogy of English architecture, in so far as it is English. Strictly speaking, there is no English architecture at all, only foreign architecture adapted and domesticated in England. But how thoroughly and admirably domesticated ! How entirely transmuted inwardly from the classic tragic monumental thing it was, into something which, even if in abstract design it seems unchanged, has a new expression, a new scale, a new subordination of part to part, and as it were a new circulation of the blood within it ! It has all been made to bend and to cling like ivy round the inner man ; it has all been rendered domestic and converted into a home. Far other was the character proper to nobler architecture in its foreign seats. There it had been essentially military, religious, or civic : it had begun perhaps with a slight modification or rearrangement of great stones lying on the ground, perhaps infinitely rooted in its depths. Its centre was no living person, but some spot with a magic and compulsive influence, or with a communal function ; it came to glorify three slabs—the tomb, the hearth, and the altar—and to render them monumental. The tribe or the king had a treasure to be roofed over and walled in ; the mound where the dead lay buried was marked with a heap of stones ; pillars were set up to the right and to the left of the presiding deity, to dignify the place where he delivered true oracles, and dispensed magic powers. This deity himself was a pillar, scarcely humanized in form, or fantastically named after some animal ; and as he grew colossal, and his features took form and colour, his sacred head had to be arched over with more labour and art ; and the approach to him was impressively delayed through

pylons, courts, narthex, or nave, into the sepulchral darkness
of the holy of holies. Similarly defences grew into citadels,
and judgement-seats into palaces ; and as for individual
men, if they did not sleep in the embrasure of some temple
gate, or under some public stair, they found cubicles in the
galleries of the king's court, or built themselves huts to
breed in under the lee of the fortifications.

This sort of architecture has a tragic character ; it
dominates the soul rather than expresses it, and embodies
stabilities and powers far older than any one man, and far
more lasting. It confronts each generation like an inexorable deity, like death and war and labour ; life is passed,
thoughtlessly but not happily, under that awful shadow.
Of course, there are acolytes in the temple and pages in the
palace that scamper all over the most hallowed precincts,
tittering and larking ; and the same retreats may seem
luminous and friendly afterwards to the poet, the lover,
or the mind bereaved ; yet in their essential function these
monuments are arresting, serious, silent, overwhelming ;
they are a source of terror and compunction, like tragedy ;
they are favourable to prayer, ecstasy, and meditation.
At other times they become the scene of enormous gatherings, of parades and thrilling celebrations ; but always it is
a vast affair, like a court ball, in which one insinuates
one's littleness into what corner one can, to see and feel
the movement of the whole, without playing any great
part in it. Even the most amiable forms of classic architecture have this public character. There is the theatre
and the circus, into which one must squeeze one's person
uncomfortably, in order to subject one's mind to contagious
emotions, and the judgements of the crowd ; and even
the public fountain, at which the housemaids and water-
boys wait for their turn, plays for ever far above the heads
of the people ; as if that Neptune and those dolphins
were spouting for their own pleasure, cooling the sunshine for their own bronze limbs, and never caring whether
they soused the passing mortal, or quenched his thirst.

All these forms and habits are intensely un-English, and
yet England is full of vestiges of them, not only because
its fine arts are derived from abroad, but because, however
disguised, the same tragic themes must appear everywhere.

The tomb, the temple, the fortress are obligatory things;
but they become properly English in character only when
their public function recedes into the background, and they
become interesting to the inner man by virtue of associations
or accidents which harmonize them with his sentimental
experience. They grow English in growing picturesque.
These castles and abbeys were Norman when they were
built, they were expressions of domination and fear, hard,
crude, practical, and foreign. But now the moat is grass-
grown, the cloister in ruins, the headless saints are posts
for the roses to creep over, the frowning keep has lost its
battlements and become a comfortable mansion mantled
with ivy; before it the well-dressed young people play
croquet on the lawn; and the chapel, whitewashed within,
politely furnished with pews, and politely frequented on
Sundays, is embowered in a pretty garden of a graveyard,
which the yew seems to sanctify more than the cross,
and the flowers to suit better than the inscriptions; there
is a bench there round the great tree, where the old villagers
sit of an evening, and its branches, far overtopping the
church spire with its restored sun-dial, seem to dispense
a surer grace and protection than the church itself: they
seem more unequivocally the symbol and the work of
God. So everything, in its ruin, seems in England to live
a new life; and it is only this second life, this cottage
built in the fallen stronghold, that is English.

If great architecture has a tragic character, it does not
exclude, in the execution, a certain play of fancy, a sportive
use of the forms which the needful structure imposes; and
these decorative frills or arbitrary variations of theme
might be called comic architecture. This is the side of the
art which is subject to fashion, and changes under the
same influences, with the same swiftness and the same
unanimity. But as fashions among peasants sometimes
last for ages, so certain decorative themes, although quite
arbitrary, sometimes linger on because of the inertia of
the eye, which demands what it is used to, or the poverty
of invention in the designer. The worst taste and the best
taste revel in decoration; but the motive here is play
and there display. The Englishman deprecates both; he
abominates the tawdry, the theatrical, the unnecessarily

elaborate ; and at the same time he is shy of novelty and playfulness ; give him comfortable old grey clothes, good for all weathers, and comfortable, pleasing, inconspicuous houses, where he can live without feeling a fool or being the victim of his possessions. The comic poses of architecture, which come to him from abroad, together with its tragic structure, he accordingly tones down and neutralizes as far as possible. How gently, for instance, how pleasantly the wave of Italian architecture broke on these grassy shores ! The classic line, which is tragic in its simple veracity and fixity, had already been submerged in attempts to vary it ; in England, as in France, the Gothic habit of letting each part of a building have its own roof and its own symmetry, at once introduced the picturesque into the most " classic " designs. The Italian scale, too, was at once reduced, and the Italian rhetoric in stone, the baroque and the spectacular, was obliterated. How pleasantly the Palladian forms were fitted to their English setting ; how the windows were widened and subdivided, the show pediments forgotten, the wreathed urns shaved into modest globes, the pilasters sensibly broadened into panels, and the classical detail applied to the native Gothic framework, with its gables, chimneys, and high roofs ; whence the delightful brood of Jacobean and Queen Anne houses ; and in the next generation the so genteel, so judicious Georgian mansion, with its ruddy brick, its broad windows, and its delicate mouldings and accessories of stone. The tragic and the comic were spirited away together, and only the domestic remained.

Nevertheless, at one of the greatest moments in its history, England had seemed to revel in comic art, and to have made it thoroughly its own. Domestic taste had reduced Gothic too, in England, to the human scale ; prodigies of height and width in vaulting were not attempted, doors remained modest, hooded, perhaps, with an almost rustic porch ; the vast spaces were subdivided, they were encrusted with ornament ; the lines became playful, fan-tracery was invented, and floral pendants of stone ; the walls became all glass, the ceilings carved bowers, and Gothic seemed on the point of smothering its rational skeleton altogether in luxurious trappings and the millinery

of fashion. All England seemed to become one field of the
cloth of gold ; rooms looked like gilded palanquins or
silken tents, roofs were forests of bannerets, pinnacles, and
weathercocks ; heraldry (a comic art) overspread every
garment and utensil. Poetry, too, became euphuistic and
labyrinthine and nevertheless friendly and familiar and
full of a luscious humour, like the wit of the people. Even
prose was a maze of metaphors and conceits, every phrase
was embroidered, and no self-respecting person could say
yea or nay without some artful circumlocution. It was
this outburst of universal comedy that made Shakespeare
possible—an exuberant genius in some respects not like
a modern Englishman ; he rose on the crest of a somewhat
exotic wave of passion and vivacity, which at once subsided.
Some vestiges of that spirit seem to linger in American
manners ; but for the most part puritanism killed it ; and
I do not think we need regret its loss. What could England
have been but for the triumph of Protestantism there ?
Only a coarser France, or a cockney Ireland. The puritan
stiffening was essential to raise England to its external
dignity and greatness ; and it was needed to fortify the
inner man, to sober him, and persuade him to be worthy of
himself. As for comic art, there is enough of it elsewhere,
in the oriental and the French schools, and in painting and
drawing, if not in architecture, all the younger artists are
experimenting with it. The sort of aestheticism which was
the fashion in London at the end of the nineteenth century
tried to be playful, and to dote on art for its own sake ;
but in reality it was full of a perverted moralism ; the
aesthetes were simply Ruskin's pupils running away from
school ; they thought it immensely important to be choice,
and quite disgraceful to think of morals. The architecture
of that time was certainly not comic in my sense of the
word, it did not give a free rein to exuberant fancy : it
was only railway Gothic. But in England the mists and
the ivy and the green sward and the dark screening trees
can make endurable even that abortion of the ethics of
Ruskin : and with better models, and less wilfulness, I see
the fresh building of to-day recovering a national charm :
the scale small, the detail polyglot, the arrangement
gracious and convenient, the marriage with the green earth

and the luminous air, foreseen and prepared for. Domestic
architecture in England follows to the letter the advice
of Polonius :

> Costly thy garment as thy purse can buy,
> But not expressed in fancy : rich, not gaudy.

21

THE ENGLISH CHURCH

COMPROMISE is odious to passionate natures because it
seems a surrender, and to intellectual natures because it
seems a confusion ; but to the inner man, to the profound
Psyche within us, whose life is warm, nebulous, and plastic,
compromise seems the path of profit and justice. Health
has many conditions ; life is a resultant of many forces.
Are there not several impulses in us at every moment ?
Are there not several sides to every question ? Has not
every party caught sight of something veritably right and
good ? Is not the greatest practicable harmony, or the
least dissension, the highest good ? And if by the word
" truth " we designate not the actual order of the facts,
nor the exact description of them, but some inner symbol
of reconciliation with reality on our own part, bringing
comfort, safety, and assurance, then truth also will lie in
compromise : truth will be partly truth to oneself, partly
workable convention and plausibility. A man's life as it
flows is not a theorem to which there is any one rigid
solution. It is composed of many strands and looks to
divers issues. There is the love of home and the lure of
adventure ; there is chastity which is a good, and there is
love which is a good also ; work must leave room for sport,
science for poetry, and reason for prejudice. Can it be a
man's duty to annul any of the elements that make up
his moral being and, because he possesses a religious
tradition, shall he refuse the gifts of his senses, of his
affections, of his country and its history, of the ruling
science, morality, and taste of his day ? Far from it :
religion, says the inner man, ought rather to be the highest
synthesis of our nature, and make room for all these things.

It should not succumb to any dead or foreign authority
that ignores or dishonours them. The Englishman finds
that he was born a Christian, and therefore wishes to
remain a Christian ; but his Christianity must be his own,
no less plastic and adaptable than his inner man ; and it
is an axiom with him that nothing can be obligatory for
a Christian which is unpalatable to an Englishman.

Only a few years ago, if a traveller landing in England
on a Sunday and entering an Anglican church, had been
told that the country was Catholic and its church a branch
of the Catholic church, his astonishment would have been
extreme. " Catholic " is opposed in the first place to
national and in the second place to Protestant ; how then,
he would have asked himself, can a church be Catholic
that is so obviously and dismally Protestant, and so
narrowly and primly national ? Why then this abuse of
language ? And why this silly provincialism of insisting
on always calling Catholics Roman Catholics, as if there
were any others, and they were not known by that name
all the world over ? Nevertheless, the restoration of an
elder Anglicanism in our day has somewhat softened these
paradoxes ; and when we remember how fondly the English
screen their instincts in legal fictions and in genteel shams,
the paradoxes vanish altogether.

What is Protestantism ? It is all things to all men, if
they are Protestants : but I see in it three leading *motifs* :
to revert to primitive Christianity, to inspire moral and
political reform, and to accept the religious witness of the
inner man. Now the Church of England, intensely Protestant as it seemed until the other day, is not Protestant
in any of these respects. No established national church
could possibly be so. The subjection to Parliament which
renders the English church not Catholic, renders it also
not Protestant. To a primitive Christian, to a puritan
reformer or to a transcendental mystic, a religion established by lay authority is a contradiction in terms ; a lay
government may be more or less inspired by righteousness, but it cannot mediate salvation. A Protestant is
essentially a nonconformist. Moreover, if we examine the
theology of the English church, we see that whilst inci-
dentally very heretical, it is still fundamentally Catholic ;

it admits only a single deposit of faith and one apostolic fountain of grace for all mankind. But in its view heresy in any branch of the church does not cut it off from the tree. Heresy is something to which all churches are liable ; the pope of Rome and the patriarch of Constantinople fall into it hardly less often or less desperately than the archbishop of Canterbury himself. Heresy is to be conceived as eccentricity within the fold, not as separation from it ; it is the tacking of the ship on its voyage. Saint Peter or Saint Paul or both of them must have been heretical in their little controversies ; and Christ himself must have had at times, if not always, but a partial view of the truth ; for instance, in respect to the date and the material nature of his second coming. Accordingly, although it may be a little trying to the nerves, it is no essential scandal that a curate should be addicted to Mariolatry, or that a dean should be unfortunately ambiguous on the subject of the Incarnation : such rapids and backwaters in the stream of Christian thought only prove how broad and full it is capable of being.

That many Catholic bodies, if not all, should be constantly schismatic or heretical, is therefore no paradox with this conception of the church ; and it is obvious that Rome itself is heretical and schismatic on this theory, since it has laid an exaggerated weight on the text about Peter and the keys, and has claimed a jurisdiction over the eastern patriarchates which was certainly not primitive, and which these patriarchates have never honestly acknowledged. On the other hand, the Church of England belonged to the Western Empire and its Christianity has always been Latin. It broke away from the patriarchate of Rome not at all in sympathy with the claims of Antioch or Constantinople, but notoriously in sympathy with German Protestantism. This revolt was based on the same anti-Catholic and inconsistent motives as the German Reformation—namely, greed and desire for absolute power in princes, zeal in puritan reformers, and impatience of moral and intellectual constraint in the body of the clergy and laity. Nationalism, faith, learning, and licence were curiously mingled in those turbid minds, and the Church of England inherits all that indescribable spiritual confusion.

It is national in its morals and manners, mincing in its scholarship, snobbish in its sympathies, sentimental in its emotions. Spiritual minds in the church—of which there are many—suffer under this heredity incubus of worldliness ; but what can they avail ? Some join the socialists ; a few escape to Rome ; there at least the worldliness, however conspicuous, is regarded as a vice and not as a virtue. The convert will find no dearth of petty passions, machinations, vanities, tricks, and shameless disbelief ; but all this will be, like debauchery, a crust of corruption, avowedly corrupt. It is dirt on the skin, not cancer at the heart. But then the true Catholic has made the great surrender ; he has renounced, or never thought of maintaining, the authority of his inner man. He is a catechumen ; his teachers will read for him the symptoms of health or disease visible in his thoughts and dispositions ; by their discipline—which is an ancient science—they will help him to save his soul ; a totally different thing from obeying the impulses or extending the adventures of the transcendental self. The inner man, for the Catholic as for the materialist, is only a pathological phenomenon. Therefore the Englishman, as I conceive him, living in and by his inner man, can never be really a Catholic, either Anglican or Roman ; if he likes to call himself by either name, it is equally a masquerade, a fad like a thousand others to which the inner man, so seriously playful, is prone to lend itself. He may go over to Rome on a spiritual tour, as he might abscond for a year and live in Japan with a Japanese wife ; but if he is converted really, and becomes a Catholic at heart, for good, and in all simplicity, then he is no longer the man he was. Words cannot measure the chasm that must henceforth separate him from everything at home. I am not surprised that he recoils from so desperate a step. It is not only the outward coarseness and laxity of Catholic manners that offend him ; these vices are not universal, and he would not need to share them. But for him, a modern Englishman, with freedom and experiment and reserve in his blood, always nursing within himself the silent love of nature and of rebellion, to go over to Rome is an essential suicide : the inner man must succumb first.

Such an Englishman might become a saint, but only by becoming a foreigner.

There is another sense altogether in which the English church might be catholic if it chose. Suppose we lay it down as an axiom that whatever is acceptable to the inner man is good and true, and that whatever is good and true is Christian—Christianity would then be open to every influence which, whilst apparently denaturalizing it, might help to manifest its fulness. It would cast off husk after husk of doctrine, developing the living spirit and feeding it with every substance which it was fitted to absorb. There is nothing new in this process. Christianity was born of such a marriage between the Jewish soul and the Greek. Greek philosophy was absorbed with magnificent results; the restoration of Pauline theology, and the other insights of Protestantism, led to German philosophy, which has been absorbed too; the sloughing off of monasticism and ecclesiasticism have put Christianity in a position to understand and express the modern world; the reduction of revelation, by the higher criticism of the Bible, to its true place in human history, will involve a new change of front; and the absorption of modern science and of democracy would complete the transformation.

To justify this method the church might appeal to an archbishop of Canterbury who—this was in the old days— was also a saint and a great philosopher. Saint Anselm has a famous proof of the existence of God which runs as follows : God exists, because God is, by definition, the most real of beings. According to this argument, if it should turn out that the most real of beings was matter, it would follow that matter was God. This might be thought a consequence drawn in mockery ; but I do not mean to deride Saint Anselm, whom I revere, but on the contrary to lay bare the nerve of his argument which if the age had given him scope, and he had not been Arch- bishop of Canterbury, he might have followed to its sublime conclusion, as Spinoza did after him. There is a dignity in existence, in fact, in truth which to some speculative and rapt natures absorbs and cancels every other dignity : and on this principle the English church might, without any sudden or distressing negation, gradually turn its worship to the most real of beings, wheresoever it may be found ; and I presume the most real of beings will be the whole of what is found everywhere. A narrower conception of God might at each step give place to a wider one ; and the church, instead of embodying one particular revelation and striving to impose it universally through propaganda, might become hospitable to all revelations, and find a place for the inspirations of all ages and countries under the aegis of its own progressive traditions. So the religion of ancient Rome domesticated all the gods ; and so the English language, if it should become the medium of international intercourse, might by translation or imitation of other literatures or by the infiltration into it of foreign words and styles, really become a vehicle for all human ideas.

I am not sure whether one party in the English church might not welcome such a destiny ; but at present, so far as I can see, the tenderer and more poetical spirits in it take quite another direction. They are trying to recover the insights and practices of mediaeval piety ; they are archaistic in devotion. There is a certain romance in their decision to believe greatly, to feel mystically, to pray perpetually. They study their attitudes, as they kneel in some correctly restored church, hearing or intoning some revived early chant, and wondering why they should not choose a divine lady in heaven to be their love and their advocate, as did the troubadours, or why they should not have recumbent effigies of themselves carved on their tombs, with their legs crossed, like the crusaders. " *Things*," cried the rapturous young priest who showed me the beautiful chapel of Pusey House, " what we need is *Things* ! "

22

LEAVING CHURCH

PROTESTANT faith does not vanish into the sunlight as Catholic faith does, but leaves a shadowy ghost haunting the night of the soul. Faith, in the two cases, was not faith in the same sense ; for the Catholic it was belief in a report or an argument ; for the Protestant it was confidence in an allegiance. When Catholics leave the church they do so by the south door, into the glare of the market-place, where their eye is at once attracted by the wares displayed in the booths, by the flower-stalls with their bright awnings, by the fountain with its baroque Tritons blowing the spray into the air, and the children laughing and playing round it, by the concourse of townspeople and strangers, and by the soldiers, perhaps, marching past ; and if they cast a look back at the church at all, it is only to admire its antique architecture, that crumbling filigree of stone so poetically surviving in its incongruous setting. It is astonishing sometimes with what contempt, with what a complete absence of understanding, unbelievers in Catholic countries look back on their religion. For one cultivated mind that sees in that religion a monument to his racial genius, a heritage of poetry and art almost as precious as the classical heritage, which indeed it incorporated in a hybrid form, there are twenty ignorant radicals who pass it by apologetically, as they might the broken toys or dusty schoolbooks of childhood. Their political animosity, legitimate in itself, blinds their imagination, and renders them even politically foolish ; because in their injustice to human nature and to their national history they discredit their own cause, and provoke reaction.

Protestants, on the contrary, leave the church by the north door, into the damp solitude of a green churchyard, amid yews and weeping willows and overgrown mounds and fallen illegible gravestones. They feel a terrible chill ; the few weedy flowers that may struggle through that long grass do not console them ; it was far brighter and warmer and more decent inside. The church— boring as the platitudes and insincerities were which you listened to there for hours—was an edifice, something protective, social, and human ; whereas here, in this vague unhomely wilderness, nothing seems to await you but discouragement and melancholy. Better the church than the madhouse. And yet the Protestant can hardly go back, as the Catholic does easily on occasion, out of habit, or fatigue, or disappointment in life, or metaphysical delusion, or the emotional weakness of the death-bed. No,

the Protestant is more in earnest, he carries his problem
and his religion within him. In his very desolation he
will find God. This has often been a cause of wonder to
me : the Protestant pious economy is so repressive and
morose and the Catholic so charitable and pagan, that I
should have expected the Catholic sometimes to sigh a
little for his Virgin and his saints, and the Protestant
to shout for joy at having got rid of his God. But the
trouble is that the poor Protestant can't get rid of his God ;
for his idea of God is a vague symbol that stands not
essentially, as with the Catholic, for a particular legendary
or theological personage, but rather for that unfathomable
influence which, if it does not make for righteousness, at
least has so far made for existence and has imposed it upon
us ; so that go through what doors you will and discard
what dogmas you choose, God will confront you still
whichever way you may turn. In this sense the enlightened Catholic, too, in leaving the church, has merely
rediscovered God, finding him now not in the church alone,
but in the church only as an expression of human fancy,
and in human life itself only as in one out of a myriad
forms of natural existence. But the Protestant is less
clear in his gropings, the atmosphere of his inner man
is more charged with vapours, and it takes longer for the
light dubiously to break through ; and often in his wintry
day the sun sets without shining.

23

DEATH-BED MANNERS

In all Protestant countries I have noticed a certain hush
about death, an uncomfortable secrecy, and a fear as if of
blasphemy whenever the subject threatens to come up.
Is it that hell is still felt to lie, for the vast majority,
immediately behind the curtain ? Or is it that people
have encouraged themselves to live and love as if they
were immortal, and to this lifelong bluff of theirs death
brings a contradiction which they have not the courage
to face ? Or is it simply that death is too painful, too

sacred, or too unseemly for polite ears ? That a desire to ignore everything unpleasant is at the bottom of this convention seems to be confirmed by an opposite attitude towards death which I have observed among English people during this war. Some of them speak of death quite glibly, quite cheerfully, as if it were a sort of trip to Brighton. " Oh yes, our two sons went down in the *Black Prince*. They were such nice boys. Never heard a word about them, of course ; but probably the magazine blew up and they were all killed quite *instantly*, so that we don't mind half so much as if they had had any of those bad lingering wounds. They wouldn't have liked it at all being crippled, you know ; and we all think it is probably much better as it is. Just *blown to atoms* ! It is *such* a blessing ! "

Of course, the poor parents feel their hearts sink within them in private ; but their affectation of cheerfulness has its logic. Death is a fact ; and we had better accept it as such as we do the weather ; perhaps, if we pretend not to care, we really shan't care so much. The men in the trenches and hospitals have often been bitterly unreconciled and rebellious, and haunted by the cruel futility of their sufferings : but the nursing everywhere has been devoted and heroic : and my impression of the mourning at home is, that it has been philosophical.

English manners are sensible and conducive to comfort even at a death-bed. No summoning of priests, no great concourse of friends and relations, no loud grief, no passionate embraces and poignant farewells ; no endless confabulations in the antechamber, no gossip about the symptoms, the remedies, or the doctors' quarrels and blunders ; no breathless enumeration of distinguished visitors, letters, and telegrams ; no tearful reconciliation of old family feuds nor whisperings about the division of the property. Instead, either silence and closed doors, if there is real sorrow, or more commonly only a little physical weariness in the mourners, a little sigh or glance at one another, as if to say : We are simply waiting for events ; the doctors and nurses are attending to everything, and no doubt, when the end comes, it will be for the best. In the departing soul, too, probably dulness and indifference. No

repentance, no anxiety, no definite hopes or desires either
for this life or for the next. Perhaps old memories returning,
old loves automatically reviving ; possibly a vision, by
anticipation, of some reunion in the other world : but how
pale, how ghostly, how impotent this death-dream is ! I
seem to overhear the last words, the last thoughts of a
mother : " Dear children, you know I love you. Provision
has been made. I should be of little use to you any longer.
How pleasant to look out of that window into the park !
Be sure they don't forget to give Pup some meat with his
dog-biscuit." It is all very simple, very much repressed,
the pattering echo of daily words. Death, it is felt, is not
important. What matters is the part we have played in
the world, or may still play there by our influence. We are
not going to a melodramatic Last Judgement. We are
shrinking into ourselves, into the seed we came from, into a
long winter's sleep. Perhaps in another springtime we may
revive and come again to the light somewhere, among those
sweet flowers, those dear ones we have lost. That is God's
secret. We have tried to do right here. If there is any
Beyond, we shall try to do right there also.

<h1 style="text-align:center">24</h1>

<h2 style="text-align:center">WAR SHRINES</h2>

In many an English village there is nowadays a calvary.
The novel object merges with wonderful ease into the
landscape, and one would almost think it had always been
there. The protecting wooden eaves have already lost
their rigidity and their varnish ; the crucifix no longer
reminds one of the shop-window from which it came ; it
does not suggest popish aggression nor the affectations of
ritualism. Flecks of sunlight play upon it familiarly, as
upon the wayside stones, and it casts its shadow across the
common like any natural tree. The flowers in the pots
before it have withered, they droop half hidden in the
ivy that has overgrown them. Even the scroll of names
has modified its official ghastliness—all those newly dead
obscure souls starkly ticketed and numbered ; the tragic

page has got somewhat weather-stained and illegible, and is curling up at the edges; it has become a dead leaf. Decidedly the war-shrine is at home in the scene. It is a portion of that unspoken truth which every one carries about with him, and the people seem again to breathe freely under the shadow of the cross.

What does the cross signify? We are told that Christ died to save us, and various analogies, legal, sentimental, or chivalrous, are put forward to make that notion acceptable. I respect the sentiments of duty and devotion which this doctrine of legal redemption can inspire; they express readiness to do well, and in a certain moral sense, as Hamlet says, the readiness is all; yet it is a conception of religion borrowed from ancient lawyers and rhetoricians, a sort of celestial diplomacy. The cross can mean something else; it can symbolize poetically a general truth about existence and experience. This truth is the same which the Indians express more philosophically by saying that life is an illusion—an expression which is itself figurative and poetical. It is certainly not an illusion that I have now the experience of being alive and of finding myself surrounded, at least in appearance, by a tolerably tractable world, material and social. It is not an illusion that this experience is now filling me with mixed and trooping feelings. In calling existence an illusion, the Indian sages meant that it is fugitive and treacherous : the images and persons that diversify it are unsubstantial, and myself the most shifting and unsubstantial of all. The substance and fine mechanism which I do not doubt underlie this changing apparition are out of scale with my imagined units, and (beyond a certain point) out of sympathy with my interests. Life is an illusion if we trust it, but it is a truth if we do not trust it; and this discovery is perhaps better symbolized by the cross than by the Indian doctrine of illusion. I will not say that not to exist would not be better ; existence may be condemned by the very respectable criterion of excellence or " reality " which demands in all things permanence and safety ; but so long as we exist, however precariously or " unreally," I think it the part of wisdom to find a way of living well, rather than merely to deprecate living. The cross is certainly a most violent image, putting suffering and death before us with a rude emphasis ; and I can understand the preference of many for the serene Buddha, lifting the finger of meditation and profound counsel, and freeing the soul by the sheer force of knowledge and of sweet reason. Nevertheless, I am not sorry to have been born a Christian : for the soul cannot be really freed except by ceasing to live ; and it is whilst we still exist, not after we are dead to existence, that we need counsel. It is therefore the crucified spirit, not the liberated spirit, that is our true master.

Certainly the spirit is crucified, first by being incarcerated in the flesh at all, and then again, after it has identified itself with the will of the flesh, by being compelled to renounce it. Yet both this painful incarnation and this painful redemption have something marvellously sweet about them. The world which torments us is truly beautiful ; indeed, that is one of its ways of tormenting us ; and we are not wrong in loving, but only in appropriating it. The surrender of this untenable claim to exist and to possess the beautiful, is in its turn beautiful and good. Christ loved the world, in an erotic sense in which Buddha did not love it : and the world has loved the cross as it can never love the Bo-tree. So that out of the very entanglements of the spirit come marvellous compensations to the spirit, which in its liberation leave it still human and friendly to all that it gives up. I do not at all accept the morality of the Indians in so far as it denies the values of illusion ; the only evil in illusion is that it deceives ; there is beauty in its being. True insight, true mercy, is tender and sensitive to the infinite pulsations of ignorance and passion : it is not deceived by the prattle of the child, but is not offended by it. The knowledge that existence can manifest but cannot retain the good reconciles us at once to living and to dying. That, I think, is the wisdom of the cross.

There is a folly of the cross also, when the knowledge or half-knowledge that life must be suffering, until it is cleared of the love of life, erects suffering into an end in itself, which is insane and monstrous. I suspect, however, that in asceticism as actually preached and practised there is less of this idolatry of suffering than the outsider imagines, who lying amid his cushions severely reproves those who indulge in a penance. There is an asceticism which may be loved for its simplicity, its clean poverty and cold water, hygienic like mountain air ; but flagellations and blood and night-long wailings are not an end in themselves ; no saint expects to carry them with him into heaven ; at best they are a homoeopathic cure for the lusts of the flesh. Their purpose, if not their effect, is freedom and peace. I wish Protestants, who find their ascetic discipline in hard work, were equally clear about its object. From the worship of instrumentalities, whether penitential or worldly, the cross redeems us : in draining the cup of suffering it transcends suffering, and in being raised above the earth it lifts us out of it. My instinct is to go and stand under the cross, with the monks and the crusaders, far away from these Jews and Protestants who adore the world and who govern it.

There is a mystical folly also among the Indians, when they assign a positive bliss to pure Being ; this, too, is substance-worship. Identity with substance is deemed blessed because beneath the vicissitudes of illusion, substance remains always solid, safe, and real. Certainly substance, if there is such a thing, must be safe, real, and solid ; for we understand by substance whatever is constant in change. Hence the desire to escape from illusion and from suffering hails a return to the indistinction of substance as a positive salvation ; remember that you are dust, return to the infinite from which you came, and nothing ominous can threaten you any more, the dust and the infinite are safe. But changeless substance, being unconscious, cannot be blissful ; the attribution of divine bliss to it is an illusion of contrast, and, like so much philosophy, mere rhetoric turned into a revelation. What verbal mirage is this, to see happiness in fixity ? Substance may be conceived logically, and then it means pure Being ; or it may be conceived psychologically, and then it means absorption in the sense of pure Being ; or it may be conceived physically as matter, a name for the constant quantities in things that are traceably transformed into one another. Pure Being and the contemplation of pure Being seem at first sight very different from matter ; but they may be a dramatic impersonation of matter, viewed from the inside, and felt as blind intensity and solidified ignorance. No one calls matter blessed when viewed externally, although it is then that its best qualities, its fertility and order, come into view : yet half mankind have fallen to worshipping matter in envy of its internal condition, and to trying to fall back into it, because it is the negation (and yet the cause !) of all their troubles. The idea of an intense nothing hypnotizes them, it is the sovereign anaesthetic ; and they forget that this intense nothing, by its fruitfulness in the realm of illusion, has generated all their desires, including this desperate desire to be nothing, which turns that nothingness, by a last illusion, into a good.

If to be saved were merely to cease, we should all be saved by a little waiting : and I say this advisedly, without forgetting that the Indians threaten us with reincarnation. It is a myth to which I have no objection, because only selfishness persuades me that if I am safe, all is well. What difference does it make in reality whether the suffering and ignominy of life fall to what I call myself or to what I call another man ? The only trouble is that the moral redemption which is proposed to us as a means of safety instead of death, touches the individual only, just as death does. Christ and Buddha are called saviours of the world ; I think it must be in irony, for the world is just as much in need of salvation as ever. Death and insight and salvation are personal. The world springs up un-regenerate every morning in spite of all the Tabors and Calvaries of yesterday. What can save the world, without destroying it, is self-knowledge on the part of the world, not of course reflective self-knowledge (for the world is not an animal that can think) but such a regimen and such a philosophy established in society as shall recognize truly what the world is, and what happiness is possible in it. The force that has launched me into this dream of life does not care what turns my dream takes nor how long it troubles me. Nature denies at every moment, not indeed that I am troubled and dreaming, but that there are any natural units like my visions, or anything anomalous in what I hate, or final in what I love. Under these circumstances, what is the part of wisdom ? To dream with one eye open ; to be detached from the world without hostility to it; to welcome fugitive beauties and pity fugitive sufferings without forgetting for a moment how fugitive they are; and not to lay up treasures, except in heaven.

How charming is divine philosophy, when it is really divine, when it descends to earth from a higher sphere, and loves the things of earth without needing or collecting them! What the gay Aristippus said of his mistress: I possess, I am not possessed, every spirit should say of an experience that ruffles it like a breeze playing on the summer sea. A thousand ships sail over it in vain, and the worst of tempests is in a teapot. This once acknowledged and inwardly digested, life and happiness can honestly begin. Nature is innocently fond of puffing herself out, spreading her peacock feathers, and saying, What a fine bird am I! And so she is; to rave against this vanity would be to imitate it. On the contrary, the secret of a merry carnival is that Lent is at hand. Having virtually renounced our follies, we are for the first time able to enjoy them with a free heart in their ephemeral purity. When laughter is humble, when it is not based on self-esteem, it is wiser than tears. Conformity is wiser than hot denials, tolerance wiser than priggishness and puritanism. It is not what earnest people renounce that makes me pity them, it is what they work for. No possible reform will make existence adorable or fundamentally just. Modern England has worked too hard and cared too much; so much tension is hysterical and degrading; nothing is ever gained by it worth half what it spoils. Wealth is dismal and poverty cruel unless both are festive. There is no cure for birth and death save to enjoy the interval. The easier attitudes which seem more frivolous are at bottom infinitely more spiritual and profound than the tense attitudes; they are nearer to understanding and to renunciation; they are nearer to the cross. Perhaps if England had remained Catholic it might have remained merry; it might still dare, as Shakespeare dared, to be utterly tragic and also frankly and humbly gay. The world has been too much with it; Hebraic religion and German philosophy have confirmed it in a deliberate and agonized worldliness. They have sanctioned, in the hard-working and reforming part of the middle classes, an unqualified respect for prosperity and success; life is judged with all the blindness of life itself. There is no moral freedom. In so far as minds are absorbed in business or in science they all inevitably circle about the same objects, and take part in the same events, combining their thoughts and efforts in the same "world's work." The world, therefore, invades and dominates them; they lose their independence and almost their distinction from one another. Their philosophy accordingly only exaggerates a little when it maintains that their individual souls are all manifestation of a single spirit, the Earth-spirit. They hardly have any souls they can call their own, that may be saved out of the world, or that may see and judge the world from above.

Death is the background of life much as empty space is that of the stars; it is a deeper thing always lying behind, like the black sky behind the blue. In the realm of existence death is indeed nothing; only a word for something negative and merely notional—the fact that each life has limits in time and is absent beyond them. But in the realm of truth, as things are eternally, life is a little luminous meteor in an infinite abyss of nothingness, a rocket fired on a dark night; and to see life, and to value it, from the point of view of death is to see and to value it truly. The foot of the cross—I dare not say the cross itself—is a good station from which to survey existence. In the greatest griefs there is a tragic calm; the fury of the will is exhausted, and our thoughts rise to another level; as the shrill delights and the black sorrows of childhood are impossible in old age. People sometimes make crosses of flowers or of gold; and I like to see the enamelled crucifix richly surrounded with scrolls, and encrusted with jewels; without a touch of this pagan instinct the religion of the cross would not be healthy nor just. In the skirts of Mount Calvary lies the garden of the resurrection: I do not refer to any melodramatic resurrection, such as is pictured in Jewish and Christian legend, but to one which actually followed quietly, sweetly, in the light of a purer day, in the cloister, in the home, in the regenerate mind. After renouncing the world, the soul may find the world more amiable, and may live in it with

a smile and a mystic doubt and one foot in eternity. Vanity
is innocent when recognized to be vain, and is no longer
a disgrace to the spirit. The happiness of wisdom may
at first seem autumnal, and the shadow of the cross the
shadow of death ; but it is healing shadow ; and presently,
in the hollow where the cross was set, the scent of violets
surprises us, and the crocuses peep out amongst the
thorns. The dark background which death supplies brings
out the tender colours of life in all their purity. Far be it
from me to suggest that existence is the better because
non-existence precedes and follows it ; certainly, if man
was immortal his experience could not include tradition,
parentage, childhood, love, nor old age ; nevertheless, from
the point of view of both bodily and intellectual instincts
immortality would be far better. But since, as a matter
of fact, birth and death actually occur, and our brief
career is surrounded by vacancy, it is far better to live in
the light of the tragic fact, rather than to forget or deny
it, and build everything on a fundamental lie. Death
does not say to life that life is nothing, or does not exist,
or is an illusion ; that would be wild talk, and would show
that the inspiration we had drawn from death was as little
capable of doing justice to life, as life itself is, when mindless,
of discovering death, or learning anything from it. What
the environing presence of death teaches is merely that
life has such and such limits and such and such a course,
whether it reflects on its course or not, whether it recognizes
its limits or ignores them. Death can do nothing to our
lives except to frame them in, to show them off with a
broad margin of darkness and silence ; so that to live in
the shadow of death and of the cross is to spread a large
nimbus of peace around our littleness.

25

TIPPERARY

WHAT a strange pleasure there is sometimes in seeing
what we expected, or hearing what we knew was a fact !
The dream then seems really to hold together and truth

to be positively true. The bells that announced the
Armistice brought me no news ; a week sooner or a week
later they had to ring. Certainly if the purpose of the
war had been conquest or victory, nobody had achieved
it ; but the purposes of things, and especially of wars,
are imputed to them rhetorically, the impulses at work
being too complicated and changeful to be easily surveyed ;
and in this case, for the French and the English, the moving
impulse had been defence ; they had been sustained through
incredible trials by the awful necessity of not yielding.
That strain had now been relaxed ; and as the conduct
of men is determined by present forces and not by future
advantages, they could have no heart to fight on. It
seemed enough to them that the wanton blow had been
parried, that the bully had begged for mercy. It was
amusing to hear him now. He said that further bloodshed
this time would be horrible ; his tender soul longed to
get home safely, to call it quits, and to take a long breath
and plan a new combination before the next bout. His
collapse had been evident for days and months ; yet
these bells that confirmed the fact were pleasant to hear.
Those mean little flags, hung out here and there by private
initiative in the streets of Oxford, had almost put on a
look of triumph ; the very sunlight and brisk autumnal
air seemed to have heard the tidings, and to invite the
world to begin to live again at ease. Certainly many a
sad figure and many a broken soul must slink henceforth
on crutches, a mere survival ; but they, too, will die off
gradually. The grass soon grows over a grave.

So musing, I suddenly heard a once familiar strain,
now long despised and out of favour, the old tune of
Tipperary. In a coffee-house frequented at that hour
some wounded officers from the hospital at Somerville
were singing it, standing near the bar ; they were breaking
all rules, both of surgeons and of epicures, and were having
champagne in the morning. And good reason they had
for it. They were reprieved, they should never have to
go back to the front, their friends—such as were left—
would all come home alive. Instinctively the old grumbling, good-natured, sentimental song, which they used to
sing when they first joined, came again into their minds.

It had been indeed a long, long way to Tipperary. But they had trudged on and had come round full circle ; they were in Tipperary at last.

I wonder what they think *Tipperary* means—for this is a mystical song. Probably they are willing to leave it vague, as they do their notions of honour or happiness or heaven. Their soldiering is over ; they remember, with a strange proud grief, their comrades who died to make this day possible, hardly believing that it ever would come ; they are overjoyed, yet half ashamed, to be safe themselves ; they forget their wounds ; they see a green vista before them, a jolly, busy, sporting, loving life in the old familiar places. Everything will go on, they fancy, as if nothing had happened.

Good honest unguided creatures ! They are hardly out of the fog of war when they are lost in the fog of peace. If experience could teach mankind anything, how different our morals and our politics would be, how clear, how tolerant, how steady ! If we knew ourselves, our conduct at all times would be absolutely decided and consistent ; and a pervasive sense of vanity and humour would disinfect all our passions, if we knew the world. As it is, we live experimentally, moodily, in the dark ; each generation breaks its egg-shell with the same haste and assurance as the last, pecks at the same indigestible pebbles, dreams the same dreams, or others just as absurd, and if it hears anything of what former men have learned by experience, it corrects their maxims by its first impressions, and rushes down any untrodden path which it finds alluring, to die in its own way, or become wise too late and to no purpose. These young men are no rustics, they are no fools ; and yet they have passed through the most terrible ordeal, they have seen the mad heart of this world riven and un-masked, they have had long vigils before battle, long nights tossing with pain, in which to meditate on the spectacle ; and yet they have learned nothing. The young barbarians want to be again at play. If it were to be only cricket or boating, it would be innocent enough ; but they are going to gamble away their lives and their country, taking their chances in the lottery of love and of business and of politics, with a sporting chance thrown in, perhaps,

of heaven. They are going to shut out from view everything except their topmost instincts and easy habits, and
to trust to luck. Yet the poor fellows think they are
safe ! They think that the war—perhaps the last of all
wars—is over !

Only the dead are safe ; only the dead have seen the
end of war. Not that non-existence deserves to be called
peace ; it is only by an illusion of contrast and a pathetic
fallacy that we are tempted to call it so. The church has
a poetical and melancholy prayer, that the souls of the
faithful departed may rest in peace. If in that sigh there
lingers any fear that, when a tomb is disturbed, the unhappy ghost is doomed to walk more often abroad, the
fear is mad ; and if it merely expresses the hope that
dead men's troubles are over, the wish is superfluous ;
but perhaps we may gloss the old superstition, and read
into it the rational aspiration that all souls in other spheres,
or in the world to come upon earth, might learn to live
at peace with God and with things. That would be something worth praying for, but I am afraid it is asking too
much. God—I mean the sum of all possible good—is
immutable ; to make our peace with him it is we, not
he, that must change. We should need to discover, and
to pursue singly, the happiness proper to our nature,
including the accidents of race and sex and the very real
advantages of growing old and of not living for ever ;
and we should need to respect without envying all other
forms of the good. As to the world of existence, it is
certainly fluid, and by judicious pressure we may coax
some parts of it into greater conformity with our wills ;
yet it is so vast, and crawls through such ponderous,
insidious revolutions, all so blind and so inimical to one
another, that in order to live at peace with things we
should need to acquire a marvellous plasticity, or a splendid
indifference. We should have to make peace with the fact
of war. It is the stupid obstinacy of our self-love that
produces tragedy, and makes us angry with the world.
Free life has the spirit of comedy. It rejoices in the
seasonable beauty of each new thing, and laughs at its
decay, covets no possessions, demands no agreement, and
strives to sustain nothing in being except a gallant spirit

of courage and truth, as each fresh adventure may re-
new it.

This gallant spirit of courage and truth, you young
men had it in those early days when you first sang
Tipperary ; have you it still, I wonder, when you repeat
the song ? Some of you, no doubt. I have seen in some
of you the smile that makes light of pain, the sturdy
humility that accepts mutilation and faces disability
without repining or shame ; armless and legless men are
still God's creatures, and even if you cannot see the sun
you can bask in it, and there is joy on earth—perhaps the
deepest and most primitive joy—even in that. But others
of you, though you were driven to the war by contagious
example, or by force, are natural cowards ; you are perhaps
superior persons, intellectual snobs, and are indignant
at having been interrupted in your important studies and
made to do useless work. You are disgusted at the
stupidity of all the generals, and whatever the Government does is an outrage to your moral sense. You were
made sick at the thought of the war before you went to
it, and you are sicker of it now. You are pacifists, and you
suspect that the Germans, who were not pacifists, were
right after all. I notice you are not singing *Tipperary*
this morning ; you are too angry to be glad, and you
wish it to be understood that you can't endure such a
vulgar air. You are willing, however, to sip your champagne with the rest ; in hospital you seem to have come
forward a little socially ; but you find the wine too dry
or too sweet, and you are making a wry face at it.

Ah, my delicate friends, if the soul of a philosopher may
venture to address you, let me whisper this counsel in your
ears : Reserve a part of your wrath ; you have not seen
the worst yet. You suppose that this war has been a
criminal blunder and an exceptional horror ; you imagine
that before long reason will prevail, and all these inferior
people that govern the world will be swept aside, and your
own party will reform everything and remain always in
office. You are mistaken. This war has given you your
first glimpse of the ancient, fundamental, normal state of
the world, your first taste of reality. It should teach you
to dismiss all your philosophies of progress or of a governing

reason as the babble of dreamers who walk through one world mentally beholding another. I don't mean that you or they are fools ; heaven forbid. You have too much mind. It is easy to behave very much like other people and yet be possessed inwardly by a narcotic dream. I am sure the flowers—and you resemble flowers yourselves, though a bit wilted—if they speculate at all, construct idealisms which, like your own, express their inner sensibility and their experience of the weather, without much resemblance to the world at large. Their thoughts, like yours, are all positings and deductions and asseverations of what ought to be, whilst the calm truth is marching on unheeded outside. No great harm ensues, because the flowers are rooted in their places and adjusted to the prevailing climate. It doesn't matter what they think. You, too, in your lodgings in Chelsea, quite as in Lhassa or in Mount Athos, may live and die happy in your painted cells. It is the primitive and the ultimate office of the mind to supply such a sanctuary. But if you are ever driven again into the open, if the course of events should be so rapid, that you could catch the drift of it in your short life (since you despise tradition), then you must prepare for a ruder shock. There is eternal war in nature, a war in which every cause is ultimately lost and every nation destroyed. War is but resisted change ; and change must needs be resisted so long as the organism it would destroy retains any vitality. Peace itself means discipline at home and invulnerability abroad—two forms of permanent virtual war ; peace requires so vigorous an internal regimen that every germ of dissolution or infection shall be repelled before it reaches the public soul. This war has been a short one, and its ravages slight in comparison with what remains standing : a severe war is one in which the entire manhood of a nation is destroyed, its cities razed, and its women and children driven into slavery. In this instance the slaughter has been greater, perhaps, only because modern populations are so enormous ; the disturbance has been acute only because the modern industrial system is so dangerously complex and unstable ; and the expense seems prodigious because we were so extravagantly rich. Our society was a sleepy glutton who thought himself immortal and squealed inexpressibly, like a stuck pig, at the first prick of the sword. An ancient city would have thought this war, or one relatively as costly, only a normal incident ; and certainly the Germans will not regard it otherwise.

Existence, being a perpetual generation, involves aspiration, and its aspiration envelops it in an atmosphere of light, the joy and the beauty of being, which is the living heaven ; but for the same reason existence, in its texture, involves a perpetual and a living hell—the conflict and mutual hatred of its parts, each endeavouring to devour its neighbour's substance in the vain effort to live for ever. Now, the greater part of most men's souls dwells in this hell, and ends there. One of their chief torments is the desire to live without dying—continual death being a part of the only possible and happy life. We wish to exist materially, and yet resent the plastic stress, the very force of material being, which is daily creating and destroying us. Certainly war is hell, as you, my fair friends, are fond of repeating ; but so is rebellion against war. To live well you must be victorious. It is with war as with the passion of love, which is a war of another kind : war at first against the beloved for favour and possession ; war afterwards against the rest of the world for the beloved's sake. Often love, too, is a torment and shameful ; but it has its laughing triumphs, and the attempt to eliminate it is a worse torture, and more degrading. When was a coward at peace ? Homer, who was a poet of war, did not disguise its horrors nor its havoc, but he knew it was the shield of such happiness as is possible on earth. If Hector had not scoured the plain in his chariot, Paris could not have piped upon the slopes of Ida, nor sported with his sheep and his goddesses upon the green. The merchants of Crete or Phoenicia could not have drawn up their black keels upon the beach, if the high walls of Ilium had not cast their protecting shadow on their bales of merchandise, their bags of coin, and their noisy bargaining. When Hector was no more and the walls were a heap of dust, all the uses of peace vanished also : ruin and utter meanness came to inhabit that land, and still inhabit it. Nor is war, which makes peace possible, without occasions in which a free spirit, not too much attached to existence, may come into its own. Homer shows us how his heroes could gather even from battle a certain harvest of tenderness and nobility, and how above their heads, half seen through the clouds of dust and of pain, flew the winged chariots of the gods, and music mingled with their banquet.

Be sad if you will, there is always reason for sadness, since the good which the world brings forth is so fugitive and bought at so great a price ; but be brave. If you think happiness worth enjoying, think it worth defending. Nothing you can lose by dying is half so precious as the readiness to die, which is man's charter of nobility ; life would not be worth having without the freedom of soul and the friendship with nature which that readiness brings. The things we know and love on earth are, and should be, transitory ; they are, as were the things celebrated by Homer, at best the song or oracle by which heaven is revealed in our time. We must pass with them into eternity, not in the end only but continually, as a phrase passes into its meaning ; and since they are part of us and we of them, we should accompany them with a good grace : it would be desolation to survive. The eternal is always present, as the flux of time in one sense never is, since it is all either past or future ; but this elusive existence in passing sets before the spirit essences in which spirit rests, and which can never vary ; as a dramatic poet creates a character which many an actor afterwards on many a night may try to enact. Of course the flux of matter carries the poets away too ; they become old-fashioned, and nobody wishes any longer to play their characters ; but each age has its own gods. Time is like an enterprising manager always bent on staging some new and surprising production, without knowing very well what it will be. Our good mother Psyche, who is a convolution of this material flux, breeds us accordingly to mindlessness and anxiety, out of which it is hard for our youthful intellect to wean itself to peace, by escaping into the essential eternity of everything it sees and loves. So long as the world goes round we shall see Tipperary only, as it were, out of the window of our troop-train. Your heart and mine may remain there, but it's a long, long way that the world has to go.

26

SKYLARKS

THERE is a poet in every nice Englishman ; there is a
little fund of free vitality deep down in him which the
exigencies of his life do not tap and which no art at his
command can render articulate. He is able to draw upon
it, and to drink in the refreshment and joy of inner freedom,
only in silent or religious moments. He feels he is never
so much himself as when he has shed for the time being
all his ordinary preoccupations. That is why his religion
is so thin or (as he might say) so pure : it has no relevance
to any particular passions or events ; a featureless background, distant and restful, like a pale clear sky. That is
why he loves nature, and country life, and hates towns and
vulgar people ; those he likes he conceives emasculated,
sentimentalized, and robed in white. The silent poet
within him is only a lyric poet. When he returns from
those draughts of rare and abstract happiness, he would
find it hard to reconcile himself to the world, or to himself,
did he not view both through a veil of convention and
make-believe ; he could not be honest about himself and
retain his self-respect ; he could not be clear about other
people and remain kind. Yet to be kind to all, and true
to his inner man, is his profound desire ; because even if
life, in its unvarnished truth, is a gross medley and a cruel
business, it is redeemed for him, nevertheless, by the perfect
beauty of soul that here and there may shine through it.
Hamlet is the classic version of this imprisoned spirit ; the
skylark seems a symbol of what it would be in its freedom.

Poor larks ! Is the proportion of dull matter in their
bodies, I wonder, really less than in ours ? Must they not
find food and rear their young ? Must they not in their
measure work, watch, and tremble ? Cold, hunger, and
disease probably beset them more often and more bitterly
than they do most of us. But we think of them selfishly,
as of actors on the stage, only in the character they wear
when they attract our attention. As we walk through the
fields we stop to watch and to listen to them performing in
the sky, and never think of their home troubles ; which

they, too, seem for the moment to have eluded ; at least they have energy and time enough left over from those troubles for all this luxury of song. It is this glorious if temporary emancipation, this absolute defiant emphasis laid with so much sweetness on the inner life that the poet in every nice Englishman loves in the lark ; it seems to reveal a brother-spirit more fortunate than oneself, almost a master and a guide.

Larks made even Shelley envious, although no man ever had less reason to envy them for their gift, either in its rapture or in its abstraction. Even the outer circumstances of Shelley's life were very favourable to inspiration and left him free to warble as much and as ardently as he chose ; but perhaps he was somewhat deceived by the pathos of distance and fancied that in Nephelococcygia bad birds and wicked traditions were less tyrannous than in parliamentary England. He seems to have thought that human nature was not really made for puddings and port wine and hunting and elections, nor even for rollicking at universities and reading Greek, but only for innocent lyrical ecstasies and fiery convictions that nevertheless should somehow not render people covetous or jealous or cruelly disposed, nor constrain them to prevent any one from doing anything that any one might choose to do. Perhaps in truth the cloisters of Oxford and the streets of London are quite as propitious to the flights of which human nature is really capable as English fields are to the flights of larks ; there is food in them for thought. But Shelley was impatient of human nature ; he was horrified to find that society is a web of merciless ambitions and jealousies, mitigated by a quite subsidiary kindness ; he forgot that human life is precarious and that its only weapon against circumstances, and against rival men, is intelligent action, intelligent war. The case is not otherwise with larks, on the fundamental earthly side of their existence ; yet because their flight is bodily, because it is a festive outpouring of animal vitality, not of art or reflection, it suggests to us a total freedom of the inner man, a freedom which is impossible.

In the flight of larks, however, by a rare favour of fortune, all seems to be spontaneity, courage, and trust,

even within this material sphere ; nothing seems to be
adjustment or observation. Their life in the air is a sort
of intoxication of innocence and happiness in the blind
pulses of existence. They are voices of the morning,
young hearts seeking experience and not remembering
it ; when they seem to sob they are only catching their
breath. They spring from the ground as impetuously
as a rocket or the jet of a fountain, that bursts into a
shower of sparks or of dew-drops ; they circle as they rise,
soaring through veil after veil of luminous air, or dropping
from level to level. Their song is like the gurgling of
little rills of water, perpetual through its delicate variations,
and throbbing with a changed volume at every change in
the breeze. Their rapture seems to us seraphic, not merely
because it descends to us invisibly from a luminous height,
straining our eyes and necks—in itself a cheap sublimity—
but rather because the lark sings so absolutely for the mad
sake of singing. He is evidently making high holiday,
spending his whole strength on something ultimate and
utterly useless, a momentary entrancing pleasure which
(being useless and ultimate) is very like an act of worship
or of sacrifice. Sheer life in him has become pure. That
is what we envy ; that is what causes us, as we listen, to
draw a deeper breath, and perhaps something like tears to
come to our eyes. He seems so triumphantly to attain
what all our labours end by missing, yet what alone would
justify them : happiness, selflessness, a moment of life
lived in the spirit. And we may be tempted to say to
ourselves : Ah, if I could only forget, if I could cease to
look before and after, if the pale cast of thought did not
make a slave of me, as well as a coward !

Vital raptures such as the lark's are indeed not unknown
even to man, and the suggestion of them powerfully allures
the Englishman, being as he is a youth morally, still
impelled to sport, still confident of carrying his whole
self forward into some sort of heaven, whether in love,
in politics, or in religion, without resigning to nature the
things that are nature's nor hiding in God the things that
are God's. Alas, a sad lesson awaits him, if he ever grows
old enough to learn it. Vital raptures, unless long training
or a miracle of adaptation has antecedently harmonized

them with the whole orchestration of nature, necessarily come to a bad end. Dancing and singing and love and sport and religious enthusiasm are mighty ferments : happy he who vents them in their season. But if ever they are turned into duties, pumped up by force, or made the basis of anything serious, like morals or science, they become vicious. The wild breath of inspiration is gone which hurried them across the soul like a bright cloud. Inspiration, as we may read in Plato between the lines, inspiration is animal. It comes from the depths, from that hearth of Hestia, the Earth-Mother, which conservative pagans could not help venerating as divine. Only art and reason, however, are divine in a moral sense, not because they are less natural than inspiration (for the Earth-Mother with her seeds and vapours is the root of everything) but because they mount towards the ultimate heaven of order, beauty, intellectual light, and the achievement of eternal dignities. In that dimension of being even featherless bipeds can soar and sing with a good grace. But space is not their element ; airmen, now that we have them, are only a new sort of sailor. They fly for the sake of danger and of high wages ; it is a boyish art, with its romantic glamour soon tarnished, and only a material reward left for all its skill and hardships. The only sublimity possible to man is intellectual ; when he would be sublime in any other dimension he is merely fatuous and bombastic. By intelligence, so far as he possesses it, a man sees things as they are, transcends his senses and his passions, uproots himself from his casual station in space and time, sees all things future as if they were past, and all things past as for ever present, at once condemns and forgives himself, renounces the world and loves it. Having this inner avenue open to divinity, he would be a fool to emulate the larks in their kind of ecstasy.

His wings are his intelligence ; not that they bring ultimate success to his animal will, which must end in failure, but that they lift his failure itself into an atmosphere of laughter and light, where is his proper happiness. He cannot take his fine flight, like the lark, in the morning, in mad youth, in some irresponsible burst of vitality, because life is impatient to begin : that sort of thing is

the fluttering of a caged bird, a rebellion against circumstance and against commonness which is a sign of spirit,
but not spirit in its self-possession, not happiness nor a
school of happiness. The thought which crowns life at
its summit can accompany it throughout its course, and
can reconcile us to its issue. Intelligence is Homeric in
its pervasive light. It traces all the business of nature,
eluding but not disturbing it, rendering it in fact more
amiable than it is, and rescuing it from vanity.

Sense is like a lively child always at our elbow, saying,
Look, look, what is that ? Will is like an orator, indignantly
demanding something different. History and fiction and
religion are like poets, continually recomposing the facts
into some tragic unity which is not in them. All these
forms of mind are spiritual, and therefore materially
superfluous and free ; but their spirit is pious, it is attentive
to its sources, and therefore seems to be care-laden and
not so gloriously emancipated as the music of larks, or
even of human musicians ; yet thought is pure music in
its essence, and only in its subject-matter retrospective
and troubled about the facts. It must indeed be troubled
about them, because in man spirit is not a mere truant,
as it seems to be in the lark, but is a faithful chronicler of
labour and wisdom. Man is hard-pressed ; long truancies
would be fatal to him. He is tempted to indulge in them
—witness his languages and pyramids and mythologies ;
yet his margin of safety is comparatively narrow, and he
cannot afford to spend such relatively prodigious amounts
of energy in mere play as the lark does with a light heart
and in the grand manner. There are words to man's
music ; he gives names to things ; he tries to catch the
rhythm of his own story, or to imagine it richer and more
sublime than it is. His festivals are heavy with pathos ;
they mark the events on which his existence turns—
harvests, funerals, redemptions, wooings, and wars.
When he disregards all these tiresome things, he becomes
a fop or a fanatic. There is no worthy transport for him
except sane philosophy—a commentary, not a dream.
His intelligence is most intense and triumphant when
there is least waste in his life ; for if hard thinking sometimes makes the head ache, it is because it comes hard,

not because it is thinking ; our fuddled brain grates and
repeats itself in that it *can't* think.   But if your business
is in order, it requires no further pains to understand it.
Intelligence is the flower of war and the flower of love.
Both, in the end, are comprehension.   How miraculously
in our happy moments we understand, how far we jump,
what masses of facts we dominate at a glance !   There is
no labour then, no friction or groping, no anxious jostling
against what we do not know, but only joy in this intricate
outspread humorous world, intoxication as ethereal as the
lark's, but more descriptive.   If his song is raised above
the world for a moment by its wantonness and idle rapture,
ours is raised above it essentially by its scope.   To look
before and after is human ;   it would not be sincere nor
manly in us not to take thought for the morrow and not to
pine for what is not.   We must start on that basis, with
our human vitality (which is art) substituted for the
vegetative prayerfulness of the lily, and our human scope
(which is knowledge of the world) substituted for the
outpourings of larks.

On this other plane we could easily be as happy as the
larks, if we were as liberal.   Men when they are civilized
and at ease are liberal enough in their sports, and willing
to *desipere in loco*, like kittens, but it is strange how
barbarous and illiberal, at least in modern times, they
have remained about thought.   They wish to harness
thought like a waterfall, or like the blind Samson, to
work for them night and day, in the treadmill of their
interests or of their orthodoxy.   Fie upon their stupidity
and upon their slavishness !   They do not see that when
nature, with much travail, brings something living to
birth, inevitable thought is there already, and gratis,
and cannot possibly be there before.   The seething of the
brain is indeed as pragmatic as the habit of singing and
flying, which in its inception doubtless helped the larks to
survive, as even the whiteness of the lily may have done
through the ministry of insects which it attracted ;   but
even material organs are bound to utility by a very loose
tie.   Nature does not shake off her baroque ornaments
and her vices until they prove fatal, and she never thinks
of the most obvious invention or pressing reform, until

some complication brings her, she knows not how, to try the experiment. Nature, having no ulterior purpose, has no need of parsimony or haste or simplicity. Much less need she be niggardly of spirit, which lays no tax upon her, and consumes no energy, but laughs aloud, a marvel and a mystery to her, in her very heart. All animal functions, whether helpful or wasteful, have this fourth dimension in the realm of spirit—the joy, or the pain, or the beauty that may be found in them. Spirit loads with a lyric intensity the flying moment in which it lives. It actually paints the lily and casts a perfume on the violet ; it turns into vivid presences a thousand forms which, until its flame lighted them up, were merged in the passive order and truth of things, like the charms of Lucy by the springs of Dove, before Wordsworth discovered them. The smile of nature is not ponderable ; and the changing harmonies of nature, out of which spirit springs, are like the conjunctions or eclipses of planets, facts obvious enough to sense in their specious simplicity, yet materially only momentary positions of transit for wayfarers bound each on his own errand. The songs of larks are like shooting stars that drop downwards and vanish ; human intelligence is a part of the steadier music of the spheres.

27

AT HEAVEN'S GATE

SKYLARKS, if they exist elsewhere, must be homesick for England. They need these kindly mists to hide and to sustain them. Their flexible throats would soon be parched, far from these vaporous meadows and hedgerows rich in berries and loam. How should they live in arid tablelands, or at merciless altitudes, where there is nothing but scorching heat or a freezing blizzard ? What space could they find for solitude and freedom in the tangle of tropical forests, amongst the monkeys and parrots ? What reserve, what tenderness, what inward springs of happiness could they treasure amid those gross harlot-like flowers ? No, they are the hermits of this mild atmosphere, fled to its wilderness of gentle light. Well may they leave

it to eagles to rush against the naked sun, as if its round
eye challenged them to single combat : not theirs the stupid
ferocity of passion against fact, anger against light, swiftness against poise, beak and talons against intangible fire.
Larks may not be very clever, but they are not so foolish
as to be proud, or to scream hoarsely against the nature
of things. Having wings and voluble throats they play
with them for pure pleasure ; they are little artists and little
gentlemen ; they disdain to employ their faculties for their
mere utility, or only in order to pounce down to the earth,
whenever they spy a dainty morsel, or to return to sulk
shivering on some solitary crag, their voracity but half
appeased, like eagles dreaming of their next victim. Of
course, even the most playful songster must eat, and
skylarks no doubt keep an eye open for worms, and their
nest calls them back to terrene affections ; but they are as
forgetful of earth as they can be, and insatiable craving
does not stamp itself on their bent necks, as if they were
vultures, nor strain their feathers of iron. No more are
they inspired by sentimental pangs and love-sick like the
nightingale ; they do not hide in the labyrinthine shade
of ilex or cypress, from there to wail in the melancholy
moonlight, as it were a seductive serenade addressed to
mortal lovers. No, the trilling of larks is not for mankind.
Like English poets they sing to themselves of nature, in-
articulately happy in a bath of light and freedom, sporting
for the sake of sport, turning what doubts they may have
into sweetness, not asking to see or to know anything
ulterior. They must needs drink the dew amongst these
English fields, peeping into the dark little hearts and
flushed petals of these daisies, like the heart and cheeks
of an English child, or into these buttercups, yellow like
his Saxon hair. They could hardly have built their nests
far from this maze of little streams, or from these narrow
dykes and ditches, arched with the scented tracery of
limes and willows. They needed this long, dull, chilly
winter in which to gather their unsuspected fund of yearning and readiness for joy ; so that when high summer
comes at last they may mount with virgin confidence and
ardour through these sunlit spaces, to pour their souls out
at heaven's gate.

At heaven's gate, but not in heaven. The sky, as these larks rise higher and higher, grows colder and thinner ; if they could rise high enough, it would be a black void. All this fluid and dazzling atmosphere is but the drapery of earth ; this cerulean vault is only a film round the oceans. As these choristers pass beyond the nether veils of air, the sun becomes fierce and comfortless ; they freeze and are dazzled ; they must hurry home again to earth if they would live. They must put fuel in their little engines : after all it was flesh and blood in them that were praising the Lord. And accordingly, down they drop to their nests and peck about, anxious and silent ; but their song never comes down. Up there they leave it, in the glittering desert it once ravished, in what we call the past. They bore their glad offering to the gate and returned empty ; but the gladness of it, which in their palpitation and hurry they only half guessed, passed in and is a part of heaven. In the home of all good, from which their frail souls fetched it for a moment, it is still audible for any ear that ever again can attune itself to that measure. All that was loved or beautiful at any time, or that shall be so hereafter, all that never was but that ought to have been, lives in that paradise, in the brilliant treasure-house of the gods.

How many an English spirit, too modest to be heard here, has now committed its secret to that same heaven ! Caught by the impulse of the hour, they rose like larks in the morning, cheerily, rashly, to meet the unforeseen, fatal, congenial adventure, the goal not seen, the air not measured, but the firm heart steady through the fog or blinding fire, making the best of what came, trembling but ready for what might come, with a simple courage which was half joy in living and half willingness to die. Their first flight was often their last. What fell to earth was only a poor dead body, one of a million ; what remained above perhaps nothing to speak of, some boyish sally or wistful fancy, less than the song of a lark for God to treasure up in his omniscience and eternity. Yet these common brave fools knew as well as the lark the thing that they could do, and did it ; and of other gifts and other adventures they were not envious. Boys and free men are always a little inclined to flout what is not the goal of their present desires, or is beyond their present scope; spontaneity in them has its ebb-flow in mockery. Their tight little selves are too vigorous and too clearly determined to brood much upon distant things; but they are true to their own nature, they know and love the sources of their own strength. Like the larks, those English boys had drunk here the quintessence of many a sunlit morning; they had rambled through these same fields, fringed with hedges and peeping copse and downs purple with heather; these paths and streams had enticed them often; they had been vaguely happy in these quiet, habitable places. It was enough for them to live, as for nature to revolve; and fate, in draining in one draught the modest cup of their spirit, spared them the weary dilution and waste of it in the world. The length of things is vanity, only their height is joy.

Of myself also I would keep nothing but what God may keep of me—some lovely essence, mine for a moment in that I beheld it, some object of devout love enshrined where all other hearts that have a like intelligence of love in their day may worship it; but my loves themselves and my reasonings are but a flutter of feathers weaker than a lark's, a prattle idler than his warblings, happy enough if they too may fly with him and die with him at the gate of heaven.

LATER SOLILOQUIES

1918–1921

28

SOCIETY AND SOLITUDE

O solitudo, sola beatitudo, Saint Bernard said ; but might he not have said just as well, *O societas, sola felicitas* ? Just as truly, I think ; because when a man says that the only happiness is this or that, he is like a lover saying that Mary Jane is the one woman in the world. She may be truly the one woman for him, though even that is not probable ; but he cannot mean to assert that she is the only woman living, nor to deny that each of the others might be the one woman for somebody. Now, when a Hegelian philosopher, contradicting Saint Bernard, says that society is his be-all and end-all, that he himself is nothing but an invisible point at which relations cross, and that if you removed from him his connection with Hegel, with his university, his church, his wife, and his publishers, there would be nothing left, or at best a name and a peg to hang a gown on, far be it from me to revise his own analysis of his nature ; society may be the only felicity and the only reality for him. But that cannot annul the judgement of Saint Bernard. He had a great mind and a great heart, and he knew society well ; at least, he accepted the verdict which antiquity had passed on society, after a very long, brilliant, and hearty experience of it ; and he knew the religious life and solitude as well ; and I can't help thinking that he, too, must have been right in his self-knowledge, and that solitude must have been the only happiness for him.

Nevertheless, the matter is not limited to this confronting of divers honest judgements, or confessions of moral experience. The natures expressed in these judgements have a long history, and are on different levels ; the one may be derived from the other. Thus it is evident that the beatific solitude of Saint Bernard was filled with a kind of society ; he devoted it to communion with the Trinity, or to composing fervent compliments to the Virgin Mary. It was only the society to be found in inns and hovels, in castles, sacristies, and refectories, that he thought it happiness to avoid. That the wilderness to which hermits flee must be peopled by their fancy, could have been foreseen by any observer of human nature. Tormenting demons or ministering angels must needs appear, because man is rooted in society and his instincts are addressed to it ; for the first nine months, or even years, of his existence he is a parasite ; and scarcely are these parental bonds a little relaxed, when he instinctively forms other ties, that turn him into a husband and father, and keep him such all his days. If ever he finds happiness in solitude, it can only be by lavishing on objects of his imagination the attentions which his social functions require that he should lavish on something. Without exercising these faculties somehow his nature would be paralysed ; there would be no fuel to feed a spiritual flame. All Saint Bernard could mean, then, is that happiness lies in this substitution of an ideal for a natural society, in converse with thoughts rather than with things. Such a substitution is normal, and a mark of moral vigour ; we must not be misled into comparing it with a love of dolls or of lap-dogs. Dolls are not impersonal, and lap-dogs are not ideas : they are only less rebellious specimens of the genus thing ; they are more portable idols. To substitute the society of ideas for that of things is simply to live in the mind ; it is to survey the world of existences in its truth and beauty rather than in its personal perspectives, or with practical urgency. It is the sole path to happiness for the intellectual man, because the intellectual man cannot be satisfied with a world of perpetual change, defeat, and imperfection. It is the path trodden by ancient philosophers and modern saints or poets ; not, of course, by modern writers on philosophy (except Spinoza), because these have not been philosophers in the vital sense ; they have practised no spiritual discipline, suffered no change of heart, but lived on exactly like other professors, and exerted themselves

to prove the existence of a God favourable to their own
desires, instead of searching for the God that happens to
exist. Certainly this path, in its beginnings, is arduous,
and leaves the natural man somewhat spare and haggard ;
he seems to himself to have fasted for forty days and forty
nights, and the world regards his way of living afterwards
as rather ghostly and poor. But he usually congratulates
himself upon it in the end ; and of those who persevere
some become saints and some poets and some philosophers.

Yet why, we may ask, should happiness be found
exclusively in this ideal society where none intrudes ?
If the intellectual man cannot lay up his treasures in a
world of change, the natural man can perfectly well
satisfy his instincts within it ; and why shouldn't the
two live amicably together in a house of two stories ?
I can see no essential reason ; but historically natural
society long ago proved a moral failure. It could not
harmonize nor decently satisfy even the instincts on which
it rests. Hence the philosophers have felt bound not only
to build themselves a superstructure but to quit the
ground floor—materially, if possible, by leading a monastic
life, religiously in any case by not expecting to find much
except weeping and wailing in this vale of tears. We may
tax this despair with being premature, and call such a
flight into an imaginary world a desperate expedient ;
at any time the attempts of the natural man to live his
comic life happily may be renewed, and may succeed.
Solitude peopled with ideas might still remain to employ
the mind ; but it would not be the only beatitude.

Yet the insecurity of natural society runs deeper, for
natural society itself is an expedient and a sort of refuge
of despair. It, too, in its inception, seemed a sacrifice and
a constraint. The primitive soul hates order and the
happiness founded on order. The barbarous soul hates
justice and peace. The belly is always rebelling against
the members. The belly was once all in all ; it was a
single cell floating deliciously in a warm liquid ; it had
no outer organs ; it thought it didn't need them. It
vegetated in peace ; no noises, no alarms, no lusts, no
nonsense. Ah, veritably solitude was blessedness then !
But it was a specious solitude and a precarious blessedness,

resting on ignorance. The warm liquid might cool, or might
dry up ; it might breed all sorts of enemies ; presently
heaven might crack and the cell be cleft in two. Happy
the hooded microbe that put forth feelers in time, and
awoke to its social or unsocial environment ! I am not
sure that, beneath the love of ideal society, there was not
in Saint Bernard a lingering love of primeval peace, of
seminal slumber ; that he did not yearn for the cell bio-
logical as well as for the cell monastic. Life, mere living,
is a profound ideal, pregnant with the memory of a possible
happiness, the happiness of protoplasm ; and the advocate
of moral society must not reckon without his host. He has
a rebellious material in hand ; his every atom is instinct
with a life of its own which it may reassert, upsetting his
calculations and destroying his organic systems. Only the
physical failure of solitude drove the spirit at first into
society, as the moral failure of society may drive it later
into solitude again. If any one said, then, that happiness
lies only in society, his maxim would be no less sincere and
solid than Saint Bernard's, but it would not be so profound.
For beneath natural society, in the heart of each of its
members, there is always an intense and jealous solitude,
the sleep of elemental life which can never be wholly broken ;
and above natural society there is always another solitude
—a placid ethereal wilderness, the heaven of ideas—
beckoning the mind.

29

IMAGINATION

MEN are ruled by imagination : imagination makes them
into men, capable of madness and of immense labours.
We work dreaming. Consider what dreams must have
dominated the builders of the Pyramids—dreams geometrical, dreams funereal, dreams of resurrection, dreams of
outdoing the pyramid of some other Pharaoh ! What
dreams occupy that fat man in the street, toddling by
under his shabby hat and bedraggled rain-coat ? Perhaps
he is in love ; perhaps he is a Catholic, and imagines
that early this morning he has partaken of the body and

blood of Christ ; perhaps he is a revolutionist, with the millennium in his heart and a bomb in his pocket. The spirit bloweth where it listeth ; the wind of inspiration carries our dreams before it and constantly refashions them like clouds. Nothing could be madder, more irresponsible, more dangerous than this guidance of men by dreams. What saves us is the fact that our imaginations, groundless and chimerical as they may seem, are secretly suggested and controlled by shrewd old instincts of our animal nature, and by continual contact with things. The shock of sense, breaking in upon us with a fresh irresistible image, checks wayward imagination and sends it rebounding in a new direction, perhaps more relevant to what is happening in the world outside.

When I speak of being governed by imagination, of course I am indulging in a figure of speech, in an ellipsis ; in reality we are governed by that perpetual latent process within us by which imagination itself is created. Actual imaginings—the cloud-like thoughts drifting by—are not masters over themselves nor over anything else. They are like the sound of chimes in the night ; they know nothing of whence they came, how they will fall out, or how long they will ring. There is a mechanism in the church tower ; there was a theme in the composer's head ; there is a beadle who has been winding the thing up. The sound wafted to us, muffled by distance and a thousand obstacles, is but the last lost emanation of this magical bell-ringing. Yet in our dream it is all in all ; it is what first entertains and absorbs the mind. Imagination, when it chimes within us, apparently of itself, is no less elaborately grounded ; it is a last symptom, a rolling echo, by which we detect and name the obscure operation that occasions it ; and not this echo in its aesthetic impotence, but the whole operation whose last witness it is, receives in science the name of imagination, and may be truly said to rule the human world.

This extension of names is inevitable although unfortunate, because language and perception are poetical before they become scientific, if they ever do ; as Aristotle observes that the word anger is used indifferently for two different things : dialectically, or as I call it, imaginatively, for the desire for revenge, but physically for a boiling of the humours. And utterly different as these two things are in quality, no great inconvenience results from giving them the same name, because historically they are parts of the same event. Nature has many dimensions at once, and whenever we see anything happen, much else is happening there which we cannot see. Whilst dreams entertain us, the balance of our character is shifting beneath : we are growing while we sleep. The young think in one way, the drunken in another, and the dead not at all ; and I imagine—for I have imagination myself—that they do not die because they stop thinking, but they stop thinking because they die. How much veering and luffing before they make that port ! The brain of man, William James used to say, has a hair-trigger organization. His life is terribly experimental. He is perilously dependent on the oscillations of a living needle, imagination, that never points to the true north.

There are books in which the footnotes, or the comments scrawled by some reader's hand in the margin, are more interesting than the text. The world is one of these books. The reciprocal interference of magnetic fields (which I understand is the latest conception of matter) may compose a marvellous moving pattern ; but the chief interest to us of matter lies in its fertility in producing minds and presenting recognizable phenomena to the senses ; and the chief interest of any scientific notion of its intrinsic nature lies in the fact that, if not literally true, it may liberate us from more misleading conceptions. Did we have nothing but electrical physics to think of, the nightmare would soon become intolerable. But a hint of that kind, like a hasty glance into the crater of a volcano, sends a wholesome shudder through our nerves ; we realize how thin is the crust we build on, how mythical and remote from the minute and gigantic scale of nature are the bright images we seem to move among, all cut out and fitted to our human stature. Yet these bright images are our natural companions, and if we do not worship them idolatrously nor petrify them into substances, forgetting the nimble use of them in mental discourse, which is where they belong, they need not be more misleading to us, even for scientific purposes, than are words or any other symbols.

It is fortunate that the material world, whatever may be its intrinsic structure or substance, falls to our apprehension into such charming units. There is the blue vault of heaven, there are the twinkling constellations, there are the mountains, trees, and rivers, and above all those fascinating unstable unities which we call animals and persons ; magnetic fields I am quite ready to believe them, for such in a vast vague way I feel them to be, but individual bodies they will remain to my sensuous imagination, and dramatic personages to my moral sense. They, too, are animate : they, too, compose a running commentary on things and on one another, adding their salacious footnotes to the dull black letter of the world. Many of them are hardly aware of their own wit ; knowing they are but commentators, they are intent on fidelity and unconscious of invention. Yet against their will they gloss everything, willy - nilly we are all scholiasts together. Heaven forbid that I should depreciate this prodigious tome of nature, or question in one jot or tittle the absolute authority of its Author ; but it is like an encyclopaedia in an infinite number of volumes, or a directory with the addresses of everybody that ever lived. We may dip into it on occasion in search of some pertinent fact, but it is not a book to read ; its wealth is infinite, but so is its monotony ; it is not composed in our style nor in our language, we could not have written one line of it. Yet the briefest text invites reflection, and we may spin a little homily out of it in the vernacular for our own edification.

In the *Mahabharata*, a learned friend tells me, a young champion armed for the combat and about to rush forward between the two armies drawn up in battle array, stops for a moment to receive a word of counsel from his spiritual adviser—and that word occupies the next eighteen books of the epic ; after which the battle is allowed to proceed. These Indian poets had spiritual minds, they measured things by their importance to the spirit, not to the eye. They despised verisimilitude and aesthetic proportion ; they despised existence, the beauties of which they felt exquisitely nevertheless, and to which their imagination made such stupendous additions. I honour their courage in bidding the sun stand still, not that they might thoroughly vanquish an earthly enemy, but that they might wholly clarify their own soul. For this better purpose the sun need not stand still materially. For the spirit, time is an elastic thing. Fancy is quick and brings the widest vistas to a focus in a single instant. After the longest interval of oblivion and death, it can light up the same image in all the greenness of youth ; and if cut short, as it were at Pompeii, in the midst of a word, it can, ages after, without feeling the break, add the last syllable. Imagination changes the scale of everything, and makes a thousand patterns of the woof of nature, without disturbing a single thread. Or rather—since it is nature itself that imagines—it turns to music what was only strain ; as if the universal vibration, suddenly ashamed of having been so long silent and useless, had burst into tears and laughter at its own folly, and in so doing had become wise.

30

THE WORLD'S A STAGE

NATURE, like a theatre, offers a double object to the mind. There is in the first place the play presented, the overt spectacle, which is something specious and ideal ; and then there is something material and profound lying behind and only symbolically revealed, namely, the stage, the actors, and the author. The playful spectacular sort of reality we can pretty well dominate and exhaust, if we are attentive ; indeed the prospect, in its sensuous and poetic essence, is plastic to attention, and alters its character according to the spectator's station and faculty ; a poetic theme develops as interest in it is aroused, and offers different beauties and different morals to every new critic. The instrumentalities, on the contrary, which bring this spectacle before us, whether they be material or personal, are unfathomable. They are events, not ideas. Even putting together all that carpenters and chemists, biographers and psychologists, might learn about these events, we could never probe them to the bottom.

In the beginning, as for a child at his first pantomime,

the play's the thing ; and a human audience can never
quite outgrow this initial illusion, since this world is a
theatre nobody can visit twice. If we could become
habitués, old theatre-goers amongst the worlds, we might
grow more discriminating ; on the whole we might enjoy
the performances just as much or even more, perhaps ;
yet less breathlessly. We should see more and believe
less. The pleasure of seeing is one, and the pleasure of
believing is quite another ; the first liberates our senses
and fills the present with light ; the second directs our
conduct and relieves our anxiety or doubts about the past
and future. When the spectator bethinks himself of
destiny as well as of beauty, his sensibility becomes tragic,
it becomes intelligence. Every picture is then regarded
as a sign for the whole situation which has generated
it or which it forebodes. The given image, for intelligence,
expresses a problematic fact ; and intelligence invents
various grammatical forms and logical categories by which
to describe its hidden enemy or fascinating prey. So
spontaneous and dogmatic is the intellect in this interpretation of the scene that the conceived object (however
abstractly sketched) is unhesitatingly judged to be, as we
say, the real thing : it alone works and acts, whilst the
given image is either disregarded altogether or despised as
a mere word or phantasm of sense, such as only fools
would stop to gaze at. And it is very true, whatever
desperate efforts empiricism may make to deny it, that
every figure crossing the stage of apprehension is a symbol,
or may become a symbol ; they all have some occasion
and arise out of some deeper commotion in the material
world. The womb of nature is full of crowding events,
to us invisible ; the ballet has machinery behind its vistas
and its music ; the dancers possess a character and fate
in the daylight quite foreign to these fays and shepherds
before the footlights : what to us is a pirouette to them
is a twitch or a shilling. Shame to the impious egotism
that would deny it, and, in order to spare itself the tension
of faith and the labour of understanding, would pretend
to find in experience nothing but a shadowy tapestry, a
landscape without a substance. To its invisible substance
the spectacle owes not only its existence but its meaning,

since our interest in the scene is rooted in a hidden life within us, quite as much as the shifts and colours of the scenery are rooted in tricks of the stage. Nevertheless the roots of things are properly and decently hidden under ground, and it is as childish to be always pulling them up, to make sure that they exist, as it is to deny their existence. The flowers are what chiefly interests a man of taste ; the spectacle is what liberal-minded people have come to see. Every image has its specific aspect and aesthetic essence, more or less charming in itself ; the sensualist, the poet, the chronicler of his passing visions must take them at their face value, and be content with that. Fair masks, like flowers, like sunsets, like melodies wrung out of troubled brains and strung wire, cover for us appropriately the anatomical face of nature ; and words and dogmas are other masks, behind which we, too, can venture upon the stage ; for it is life to give expression to life, transmuting diffused movements into clear images. How blind is the zeal of the iconoclasts, and how profoundly hostile to religious impulse ! They pour scorn upon eyes that see not and a mouth that cannot speak ; they despise a work of art or of thought for being finished and motion-less ; as if the images of the retina were less idols than those of the sculptor, and as if words, of all things, were not conventional signs, grotesque counterfeits, dead messengers, like fallen leaves, from the dumb soul. Why should one art be contemptuous of the figurative language of another ? Jehovah, who would suffer no statues, was himself a metaphor.

31

MASKS

WHEN we are children we love putting on masks to astonish our elders ; there is a lordly pleasure in puzzling those harmless giants who are not in the secret. We ourselves, of course, know that it is only a disguise ; and when presently we pull it off, their surprise at recognizing us is something deliciously comic. Yet, at bottom, this compulsory return to nature is a little sad ; our young empiricism would like to take appearances more seriously. To an unsophisticated mind every transformation seems as credible as it is interesting ; there is always danger and hope of anything. Why should people hesitate to believe something intrinsically so plausible as that Johnny should have acquired a bull's head, or that little Alice should suddenly develop a red nose and furious mustachios ? That is just the sort of thing that would happen if this stupid world were only more natural ; but the trouble with old people is that their minds have become stagnant, dominated as they are by precedent and prejudice ; it is too much of an exertion for them to imagine anything but what they have always seen. Even when they tell us about religion, which is so full of exciting and lovely things that we know *must* be true, they seem to be trying to remember something they have read or heard of, and quite spoil the story ; they don't seem to understand at all, as we do, why it all happens. They are terrible believers in substance, and can hardly lend themselves to the wayward game of experience. This after all wouldn't matter so much ; it is not worth while playing with people who don't relish games. The subtlest part of the pleasure is being blindfolded on purpose and feeling lost when you know you are not lost. Empiricism would be agony if any one was so silly as really to forget his material status and to become the sport of his passing ideas. But masks are great fun in themselves, and when you are fundamentally sane it is pleasant to play the madman and to yield to the eloquence of an imagined life ; and it is intolerable to have the game spoiled by some heavy-footed person who constantly reminds you of the discovered facts and will not lend himself to the spirit of your fiction, which is the deepest part of your own spirit. No one would be angry with a man for unintentionally making a mistake about a matter of fact ; but if he perversely insists on spoiling your story in the telling of it, you want to kick him ; and this is the reason why every philosopher and theologian is justly vexed with every other. When we are children the accident and fatality of having been born human are recent and only half welcome ; we still feel a little hurt at being so arbitrarily confined to one miserable career and forced to remain always consistent ; we still see the equal antecedent propriety of being anybody or anything else. Masks afford us the pleasing excitement of revising our so accidental birth-certificate and of changing places in spirit with some other changeling.

Nevertheless the game soon tires. Although children are no believers in substance, they are substances themselves without knowing it. The mask refuses to grow on to their flesh : it thwarts their rising impulses. Play-acting is seldom worth the commitments it involves ; your part, after a few enthusiastic rehearsals, turns out not really to suit you. It seemed at first to open up splendid adventures and give you a chance to display your unsuspected passions and powers ; but now you begin to think your speeches ridiculous and your costume unbecoming. You must pull off the mask to see clearly and to breathe freely ; you are overheard indulging in asides that are out of character, and swearing in the unvarnished vernacular ; and when the performance at last is over, what a relief to fling away your wig and your false beard, and relapse into your honest self ! There is no place like home, although there may be better places ; and there is no face like one's own, for comfort to the wearer.

The Englishman likes to be comfortable, and he hates masks. It is pleasant to be straightforward, as it is to be clean. Mere façades offend him so much that he actually manages to build houses without them ; they have creepers, they have chimneys, they have bow-windows, they have several doors, but they have no front. His Empire, too, for all its extent and complexity, presents no imposing façade to the world ; it seems to elude observation and to be everywhere apologizing for its existence. Its enemies, on the contrary, both at home and abroad, are blatancy itself, always parading their heroisms and their ambitions ; and one wonders how a power so hated, so hesitant, and so involuntary can last at all. But it has a certain plastic invulnerability ; you pommel it and trample on it here, and its strength turns out to have lain in quite another quarter. It is like the sort of man who serves it, a pale languid youth, sprawling on cushions, and lisping a

little when he cares to take his pipe out of his mouth at
all ; but what is your surprise when, something having
happened, he gets up and knocks you down. Nothing
had prepared you for that ; no philosophical eloquence
or resounding *coup d'état* : he is perhaps a little surprised
himself at his energy. He blushes if by chance any warm
gesture or expression has escaped him ; he feels that it
misrepresents his average sentiment ; the echo of it sounds
hollow in his ear, and just because it was so spontaneous
he detests it as if it had been a lie. The passing grimaces
of passion, the masks of life, are odious to him ; yet he
is quite happy to be deceived and to be masked by a thick
atmosphere of convention, if only this atmosphere is
temperate and sustained. He will be loyal to any nonsense
that seems to justify his instincts and that has got a
domestic stamp ; but elaborate original lies are not in
his nature ; he has no histrionic gift. Intrigue requires
a clear perception of the facts, an insight into other
people's motives, and a power of sustained simulation ;
he is not clever at any of these things. Masks, wigs,
cowls, and stays are too troublesome ; if you are not
always on the watch, the beastly things will fall off. He
prefers to dress his personage more constitutionally ; the
dyes he uses must be all indelible, such as religion and
education can supply. These, with the habit of his set or
profession, are his lifelong make-up and his second nature ;
his only mask is the imperturbed expression which time and
temperance have chiselled in his face.

32

THE TRAGIC MASK

MASKS are arrested expressions and admirable echoes of
feeling, at once faithful, discreet, and superlative. Living
things in contact with the air must acquire a cuticle,
and it is not urged against cuticles that they are not hearts ;
yet some philosophers seem to be angry with images for
not being things, and with words for not being feelings.
Words and images are like shells, no less integral parts of

nature than are the substances they cover, but better addressed to the eye and more open to observation. I would not say that substance exists for the sake of appearance, or faces for the sake of masks, or the passions for the sake of poetry and virtue. Nothing arises in nature for the sake of anything else ; all these phases and products are involved equally in the round of existence, and it would be sheer wilfulness to praise the germinal phase on the ground that it is vital, and to denounce the explicit phase on the ground that it is dead and sterile. We might as justly despise the seed for being merely instrumental, and glorify the full-blown flower, or the conventions of art, as the highest achievement and fruition of life. Substance is fluid, and, since it cannot exist without some form, is always ready to exchange one form for another ; but sometimes it falls into a settled rhythm or recognizable vortex, which we call a nature, and which sustains an interesting form for a season. These sustained forms are enshrined in memory and worshipped in moral philosophy, which often assigns to them a power to create and to reassert themselves which their precarious status is very far from justifying. But they are all in all to the mind : art and happiness lie in pouring and repouring the molten metal of existence through some such tenable mould.

Masks are accordingly glorious things ; we are instinctively as proud of designing and wearing them as we are of inventing and using words. The blackest tragedy is festive ; the most pessimistic philosophy is an enthusiastic triumph of thought. The life which such expressions seem to arrest or to caricature would be incomplete without them ; indeed, it would be blind and abortive. It is no interruption to experience to master experience, as tragedy aspires to do ; nor is it an interruption to sink into its episodes and render them consummate, which is the trick of comedy. On the contrary, without such playful pauses and reflective interludes our round of motions and sensations would be deprived of that intellectual dignity which relieves it and renders it morally endurable—the dignity of knowing what we are doing, even if it be foolish in itself, and with what probable issue. Tragedy, the knowledge of death, raises us to that height. In fancy and for a moment it brings our mortal wills into harmony with our destiny, with the wages of existence, and with the silence beyond. These discoveries of reason have fixed the expression of the tragic mask, half horror and half sublimity. Such is the countenance of man when turned towards death and eternity and looking beyond all his endeavours at the Gorgon face of the truth. This is not to say that it is less human, or less legitimate, to look in other directions and to make other faces. But whether the visage we assume be a joyful or a sad one, in adopting and emphasizing it we define our sovereign temper. Henceforth, so long as we continue under the spell of this self-knowledge, we do not merely live but act ; we compose and play our chosen character, we wear the buskin of deliberation, we defend and idealize our passions, we encourage ourselves eloquently to be what we are, devoted or scornful or careless or austere ; we soliloquize (before an imaginary audience) and we wrap ourselves gracefully in the mantle of our inalienable part. So draped, we solicit applause and expect to die amid a universal hush. We profess to live up to the fine sentiments we have uttered, as we try to believe in the religion we profess. The greater our difficulties the greater our zeal. Under our published principles and plighted language we must assiduously hide all the inequalities of our moods and conduct, and this without hypocrisy, since our deliberate character is more truly ourself than is the flux of our involuntary dreams. The portrait we paint in this way and exhibit as our true person may well be in the grand manner, with column and curtain and distant landscape and finger pointing to the terrestrial globe or to the Yorick-skull of philosophy ; but if this style is native to us and our art is vital, the more it transmutes its model the deeper and truer art it will be. The severe bust of an archaic sculpture, scarcely humanizing the block, will express a spirit far more justly than the man's dull morning looks or casual grimaces. Every one who is sure of his mind, or proud of his office, or anxious about his duty assumes a tragic mask. He deputes it to be himself and transfers to it almost all his vanity. While still alive and subject, like all existing things, to the undermining flux of his own substance, he has crystallized his soul into an idea, and more in pride than in sorrow he has offered up his life on the altar of the Muses. Self-knowledge, like any art or science, renders its subject-matter in a new medium, the medium of ideas, in which it loses its old dimensions and its old pace. Our animal habits are transmuted by conscience into loyalties and duties, and we become " persons " or masks. Art, truth, and death turn everything to marble.

That life should be able to reach such expression in the realm of eternal form is a sublime and wonderful privilege, but it is tragic, and for that reason distasteful to the animal in man. A mask is not responsive ; you must not speak to it as to a living person, you must not kiss it. If you do, you will find the cold thing repulsive and ghastly. It is only a husk, empty, eyeless, brittle, and glazed. The more comic its expression the more horrible it will prove, being that of a corpse. The animal in man responds to things according to their substance, edible, helpful, or plastic ; his only joy is to push his way victoriously through the material world, till a death stops him which he never thought of and, in a sense, never experiences. He is not in the least interested in picturing what he is or what he will have been ; he is intent only on what is happening to him now or may happen to him next. But when the passions see themselves in the mirror of reflection, what they behold is a tragic mask. This is the escutcheon of human nature, in which its experience is emblazoned. In so far as men are men at all, or men of honour, they militate under this standard and are true to their colours. Whatever refuses to be idealized in this way, they are obliged to disown and commit to instant oblivion. It will never do for a mind merely to live through its passions or its perceptions ; it must discern recognizable objects, in which to centre its experience and its desires ; it must choose names and signs for them, and these names and symbols, if they are to perform their function in memory and intercourse, must be tightly conventional. What could be more unseemly than a fault in grammar, or in many a case more laughable and disconcerting ? Yet any solecism, if it were once stereotyped and made definitely significant, would become an idiom : it would become a good verbal mask. What is not covered in this way by some abiding symbol can never be recovered ; the dark flood of existence carries it down bodily. Only in some word or conventional image can the secret of one moment be flashed to another moment ; and even when there is no one ready to receive the message, or able to decipher it, at least the poet in his soliloquy has uttered his mind and raised his monument in his own eyes ; and in expressing his life he has found it.

33

THE COMIC MASK

THE clown is the primitive comedian. Sometimes in the exuberance of animal life a spirit of riot and frolic comes over a man ; he leaps, he dances, he tumbles head over heels, he grins, shouts, or leers, possibly he pretends to go to pieces suddenly, and blubbers like a child. A moment later he may look up wreathed in smiles, and hugely pleased about nothing. All this he does hysterically, without any reason, by a sort of mad inspiration and irresistible impulse. He may easily, however, turn his absolute histrionic impulse, his pure fooling, into mimicry of anything or anybody that at the moment happens to impress his senses ; he will crow like a cock, simper like a young lady, or reel like a drunkard. Such mimicry is virtual mockery, because the actor is able to revert from those assumed attitudes to his natural self ; whilst his models, as he thinks, have no natural self save that imitable attitude, and can never disown it ; so that the clown feels himself immensely superior, in his rôle of universal satirist, to all actual men, and belabours and rails at them unmercifully. He sees everything in caricature, because he sees the surface only, with the lucid innocence of a child ; and all these grotesque personages stimulate him, not to moral sympathy, nor to any consideration of their fate, but rather to boisterous sallies, as the rush of a crowd, or the hue and cry of a hunt, or the contortions of a jumping-jack might stimulate him. He is not at all amused intellectually ; he

is not rendered wiser or tenderer by knowing the predicaments into which people inevitably fall ; he is merely
excited, flushed, and challenged by an absurd spectacle.
Of course this rush and suasion of mere existence must
never fail on the stage, nor in any art ; it is to the drama
what the hypnotizing stone block is to the statue, or
shouts and rhythmic breathing to the bard ; but such
primary magical influences may be qualified by reflection,
and then rational and semi-tragic unities will supervene.
When this happens the histrionic impulse creates the idyl
or the tragic chorus ; henceforth the muse of reflection
follows in the train of Dionysus, and the revel or the rude
farce passes into humane comedy.

Paganism was full of scruples and superstitions in matters
of behaviour or of *cultus*, since the *cultus* too was regarded
as a business or a magic craft ; but in expression, in
reflection, paganism was frank and even shameless ; it felt
itself inspired, and revered this inspiration. It saw nothing
impious in inventing or recasting a myth about no matter
how sacred a subject. Its inspiration, however, soon fell
into classic moulds, because the primary impulses of nature,
though intermittent, are monotonous and clearly defined,
as are the gestures of love and of anger. A man who is
unaffectedly himself turns out to be uncommonly like other
people. Simple sincerity will continually rediscover the
old right ways of thinking and speaking, and will be perfectly
conventional without suspecting it. This classic iteration
comes of nature, it is not the consequence of any revision
or censorship imposed by reason. Reason, not being
responsible for any of the facts or passions that enter into
human life, has no interest in maintaining them as they
are ; any novelty, even the most revolutionary, would
merely afford reason a fresh occasion for demanding a
fresh harmony. But the Old Adam is conservative ; he
repeats himself mechanically in every child who cries and
loves sweets and is imitative and jealous. Reason, with
its tragic discoveries and restraints, is a far more precarious
and personal possession than the trite animal experience
and the ancestral grimaces on which it supervenes ; and
automatically even the philosopher continues to cut his
old comic capers, as if no such thing as reason existed. The

wiseacres too are comic, and their mask is one of the most
harmlessly amusing in the human museum ; for reason,
taken psychologically, is an old inherited passion like any
other, the passion for consistency and order ; and it is just
as prone as the other passions to overstep the modesty of
nature and to regard its own aims as alone important. But
this is ridiculous ; because importance springs from the
stress of nature, from the cry of life, not from reason and
its pale prescriptions. Reason cannot stand alone ; brute
habit and blind play are at the bottom of art and morals,
and unless irrational impulses and fancies are kept alive,
the life of reason collapses for sheer emptiness. What
tragedy could there be, or what sublime harmonies rising
out of tragedy, if there were no spontaneous passions to
create the issue, no wild voices to be reduced to harmony ?
Moralists have habitually aimed at suppression, wisely
perhaps at first, when they were preaching to men of
spirit ; but why continue to harp on propriety and
unselfishness and labour, when we are little but labour-
machines already, and have hardly any self or any passions
left to indulge ? Perhaps the time has come to suspend
those exhortations, and to encourage us to be sometimes
a little lively, and see if we can invent something worth
saying or doing. We should then be living in the spirit of
comedy, and the world would grow young. Every occasion
would don its comic mask, and make its bold grimace at
the world for a moment. We should be constantly original
without effort and without shame, somewhat as we are in
dreams, and consistent only in sincerity ; and we should
gloriously emphasize all the poses we fell into, without
seeking to prolong them.

Objections to the comic mask—to the irresponsible,
complete, extreme expression of each moment—cut at the
roots of all expression. Pursue this path, and at once you
do away with gesture : we must not point, we must not
pout, we must not cry, we must not laugh aloud ; we
must not only avoid attracting attention, but our
attention must not be obviously attracted ; it is silly
to gaze, says the nursery-governess, and rude to stare.
Presently words, too, will be reduced to a telegraphic
code. A man in his own country will talk like the laconic

tourist abroad ; his whole vocabulary will be *Où ? Combien ? All right ! Dear me !* Conversation in the quiet home will dispense even with these phrases ; nothing will be required but a few pragmatic grunts and signals for action. Where the spirit of comedy has departed, company becomes constraint, reserve eats up the spirit, and people fall into a penurious melancholy in their scruple to be always exact, sane, and reasonable, never to mourn, never to glow, never to betray a passion or a weakness, nor venture to utter a thought they might not wish to harbour for ever.

Yet irony pursues these enemies of comedy, and for fear of wearing a mask for a moment they are hypocrites all their lives. Their very reserve becomes a pose, a convention imposed externally, and their mincing speech turns to cant. Sometimes this evasion of impulsive sentiment fosters a poignant sentimentality beneath. The comedy goes on silently behind the scenes, until perhaps it gets the upper hand and becomes positive madness ; or else it breaks out in some shy, indirect fashion, as among Americans with their perpetual joking. Where there is no habitual art and no moral liberty, the instinct for direct expression is atrophied for want of exercise ; and then slang and a humorous perversity of phrase or manner act as safety-valves to sanity ; and you manage to express yourself in spite of the censor by saying something grotesquely different from what you mean. That is a long way round to sincerity, and an ugly one. What, on the contrary, could be more splendidly sincere than the impulse to play in real life, to rise on the rising wave of every feeling and let it burst, if it will, into the foam of exaggeration ? Life is not a means, the mind is not a slave nor a photograph : it has a right to enact a pose, to assume a *panache*, and to create what prodigious allegories it will for the mere sport and glory of it. Nor is this art of innocent make-believe forbidden in the Decalogue, although Bible-reading Anglo-Saxondom might seem to think so. On the contrary, the Bible and the Decalogue are themselves instances of it. To embroider upon experience is not to bear false witness against one's neighbour, but to bear true witness to oneself. Fancy is playful and may be misleading to those who try to take it for literal fact ; but literalness is impossible in any utterance of spirit, and if it were possible it would be deadly. Why should we quarrel with human nature, with metaphor, with myth, with impersonation ? The foolishness of the simple is delightful ; only the foolishness of the wise is exasperating.

34

CARNIVAL

In this world we must either institute conventional forms of expression or else pretend that we have nothing to express ; the choice lies between a mask and a fig-leaf. Art and discipline render seemly what would be unseemly without them, but hypocrisy hides it ostentatiously under something irrelevant, and the fig-leaf is only a more ignominious mask. For the moment it is certainly easier to suppress the wild impulses of our nature than to manifest them fitly, at the right times and with the proper fugitive emphasis ; yet in the long run suppression does not solve the problem, and meantime those maimed expressions which are allowed are infected with a secret misery and falseness. It is the charm and safety of virtue that it is more natural than vice, but many moralists do their best to deprive it of this advantage. They seem to think it would lose its value if they lost their office. Their precepts, as distinguished from the spontaneous appreciations of men, are framed in the interests of utility, and are curiously out of sympathy with the soul. Precept divides the moral world materially into right and wrong things ; but nothing concrete is right or wrong intrinsically, and every object or event has both good and bad effects in the context of nature. Every passion, like life as a whole, has its feet in one moral climate and its head in another. Existence itself is not a good, but only an opportunity. Christians thank God for their creation, preservation, and all the blessings of this life, but life is the condition and source of all evil, and the Indians thank Brahma or Buddha for lifting them out of it. What metaphysical psychologists call Will is the great original sin, the unaccountable and irrational interest which the spirit takes, when it is incarnate, in one thing happening rather than another ; yet this mad interest is the condition of generosity and of every virtue. Love is a red devil at one end of its spectrum and an ultra-violet angel at the other end.

Nor is this amphibious moral quality limited to the passions ; all facts and objects in nature can take on opposite moral tints. When abstracted from our own presence and interests, everything that can be found or imagined is reduced to a mere essence, an ideal theme picked out of the infinite, something harmless, marvellous, and pure, like a musical rhythm or geometrical design. The whole world then becomes a labyrinth of forms and motions, a castle in the clouds built without labour and dissolved without tears. The moment the animal will reawakes, however, these same things acquire a new dimension ; they become substantial, not to be created without effort nor rent without resistance ; at the same time they become objects of desire and fear ; we are so engrossed in existence that every phenomenon becomes questionable and ominous, and not so much a free gift and manifestation of its own nature as a piece of good or bad news. We are no longer surprised, as a free spirit would be, at the extraordinary interest we take in things turning out one way rather than another. We are caught in the meshes of time and place and care ; and as the things we have set our heart on, whatever they may be, must pass away in the end, either suddenly or by a gentle transformation, we cannot take a long view without finding life sad, and all things tragic. This aspect of vanity and self-annihilation, which existence wears when we consider its destiny, is not to be denied or explained away, as is sometimes attempted in cowardly and mincing philosophies. It is a true aspect of existence in one relation and on a certain view ; but to take this long view of existence, and look down the avenues of time from the station and with the emotions of some particular moment, is by no means inevitable, nor is it a fair and sympathetic way of viewing existence. Things when they are actual do not lie in that sort of sentimental perspective, but each is centred in itself ; and in this intrinsic aspect existence is nothing tragic or sad, but rather something joyful, hearty, and merry. A buoyant and full-blooded soul has quick senses and miscellaneous sympathies : it changes with the changing world ; and when not too much starved or thwarted by circumstances, it finds all things vivid and comic. Life is free play fundamentally and would like to be free play altogether. In youth anything is pleasant to see or to do, so long as it is spontaneous, and if the conjunction of these things is ridiculous, so much the better : to be ridiculous is part of the fun.

Existence involves changes and happenings and is comic inherently, like a pun that begins with one meaning and ends with another. Incongruity is a consequence of change ; and this incongruity becomes especially conspicuous when, as in the flux of nature, change is going on at different rates in different strands of being, so that not only does each thing surprise itself by what it becomes, but it is continually astonished and disconcerted by what other things have turned into without its leave. The mishaps, the expedients, the merry solutions of comedy, in which everybody acknowledges himself beaten and deceived, yet is the happier for the unexpected posture of affairs, belong to the very texture of temporal being ; and if people repine at these mishaps, or rebel against these solutions, it is only because their souls are less plastic and volatile than the general flux of nature. The individual grows old and lags behind ; he remembers his old pain and resents it when the world is already on a new tack. In the jumble of existence there must be many a knock and many a grief ; people living at cross purposes cannot be free from malice, and they must needs be fooled by their pretentious passions. But there is no need of taking these evils tragically. At bottom they are gratuitous, and might have been avoided if people had not pledged their hearts to things beyond their control and had not entrenched themselves in their illusions. At a sufficient remove every drama seems pathological and makes much ado about what to other people is nothing. We are interested in those vicissitudes, which we might have undergone if placed under the given circumstances ; but we are happy to have escaped them. Thus the universe changes its hues like the chameleon, not at random but in a fashion which moral optics can determine, as it appears in one perspective or another ; for everything in nature is lyrical in its ideal essence, tragic in its fate, and comic in its existence.

Existence is indeed distinguishable from the platonic essences that are embodied in it precisely by being a conjunction of things mutually irrelevant, a chapter of accidents, a medley improvised here and now for no reason, to the exclusion of the myriad other farces which, so far as their ideal structure is concerned, might have been performed just as well. This world is contingency and absurdity incarnate, the oddest of possibilities masquerading momentarily as a fact. Custom blinds persons who are not naturally speculative to the egregious character of the actual, because custom assimilates their expectations to the march of existing things and deadens their power to imagine anything different. But wherever the routine of a barbaric life is broken by the least acquaintance with larger ways, the arbitrariness of the actual begins to be discovered. The traveller will first learn that his native language is not the only one, nor the best possible, nor itself constant ; then, perhaps, he will understand that the same is true of his home religion and government. The naturalist will begin by marvelling at the forms and habits of the lower animals, while continuing to attribute his own to their obvious propriety ; later the heavens and the earth, and all physical laws, will strike him as paradoxically arranged and unintelligible ; and ultimately the very elements of existence — time, change, matter, habit, life cooped in bodies—will reveal themselves to him in their extreme oddity, so that, unless he has unusual humility and respect for fact, he will probably declare all these actual things to be impossible and therefore unreal. The most profound philosophers accordingly deny that any of those things exist which we find existing, and maintain that the only reality is changeless, infinite, and indistinguishable into parts ; and I call them the most profound philosophers in spite of this obvious folly of theirs, because they are led into it by the force of intense reflection, which discloses to them that what exists is unintelligible and has no reason for existing ; and

since their moral and religious prejudices do not allow
them to say that to be irrational and unintelligible is the
character proper to existence, they are driven to the
alternative of saying that existence is illusion and that
the only reality is something beneath or above existence.
That real existence should be radically comic never occurs
to these solemn sages ; they are without one ray of humour
and are persuaded that the universe too must be without
one.   Yet there is a capital joke in their own systems,
which prove that nothing exists so strenuously, that
existence laughs aloud in their vociferations and drowns
the argument.   Their conviction is the very ghost which it
rises to exorcise ; yet the conviction and the exorcism
remain impressive, because they bear witness to the
essential strangeness of existence to the spirit.   Like
the Ghost in *Hamlet* this apparition, this unthinkable
fact, is terribly disturbing and emphatic ; it cries to us
in a hollow voice, " Swear ! " and when in an agony of
concern and affection we endeavour to follow it, " 'Tis
here ! 'Tis here ! 'Tis gone ! "   Certainly existence can
bewitch us ; it can compel us to cry as well as to laugh ;
it can hurt, and that is its chief claim to respect.   Its
cruelty, however, is as casual as its enchantments ; it is
not cruel on purpose but only rough, like thoughtless boys.
Coarseness—and existence is hopelessly coarse—is not an
evil unless we demand refinement.   A giggling lass that
peeps at us through her fingers is well enough in her sphere,
but we should not have begun by calling her Dulcinea.
Dulcinea is a pure essence, and dwells only in that realm.
Existence should be met on its own terms ; we may dance
a round with it, and perhaps steal a kiss ; but it tempts
only to flout us, not being dedicated to any constant love.
As if to acknowledge how groundless existence is, everything that arises instantly backs away, bowing its excuses,
and saying, " My mistake ! "   It suffers from a sort of
original sin or congenital tendency to cease from being.
This is what Heraclitus called $\Delta i \kappa \eta$, or just punishment ;
because, as Mephistopheles long afterwards added, *alles
was entsteht ist wert dass es zugrunde geht*—whatsoever
arises deserves to perish ; not of course because what
arises is not often a charming creation, but because it has

no prerogative to exist not shared by every Cinderella-like essence that lies eternally neglected in that limbo to which all things intrinsically belong—the limbo of unheard melodies and uncreated worlds. For anything to emerge from that twilight region is inexplicable and comic, like the popping up of Jack-in-the-box ; and the shock will amuse us, if our wits are as nimble as nature and as quick as time. We too exist ; and existence is a joy to the sportive side of our nature, itself akin to a shower of sparks and a patter of irrevocable adventures. What indeed could be more exhilarating than such a rout, if only we are not too exacting, and do not demand of it irrelevant perfections ? The art of life is to keep step with the celestial orchestra that beats the measure of our career, and gives the cue for our exits and our entrances. Why should we willingly miss anything, or precipitate anything, or be angry with folly, or in despair at any misadventure ? In this world there should be none but gentle tears, and fluttering tip-toe loves. It is a great Carnival, and amongst these lights and shadows of comedy, these roses and vices of the playhouse, there is no abiding.

35

QUEEN MAB

NATURE, which is far more resourceful than logic, has found a way out of the contradiction between the human need for expression and the British distaste for personal outbursts. This way is rambling fiction. When out of shyness, or because they have shocked each other, the inner man and the outer man are not on speaking terms, loud language and vehement gestures are incompatible with depth of feeling. What lies deep must in such a case remain unexpressed, and will seem inexpressible. A man's heart will be revealed, even to himself, only in long stretches of constant endeavour and faithful habit : towards the end of his life he may begin to discern his ruling motives. In the meantime, however, his fancy may have played at self-revelation ; he may have indulged

in day-dreams and romantic transformations of himself,
as boys do ; and without pledging his real person too much
he may have made trial of candour, or, if need be, of
extravagance, in imaginary substitutes for himself, thus
trying the paces of his inner man without cheapening his
secret feelings or publishing them in common and second-
hand terms.   Such a man will talk little about himself ;
his opinions and preferences will not be very explicit,
but he will privily nurse and develop them by endless
variations played upon them in fancy, as he reads or perhaps
writes a book of fiction by his chimney corner.   He will
dream of what Queen Mab makes other people dream.

Romantic fiction is a bypath of expression ; it meanders
through fields of possible experience that stretch harmlessly
between the highroads of actual lives, far from the precipices
of private and public passions.   The labyrinth is infinite,
but the path chosen in it is always traceable by a sort of
Ariadne's thread spun out of the poet's heart.   He means
to forget himself and to feign some charming monster in
some picturesque landscape, the more exotic the better ;
but in doing so he obeys the dream-impulses of his own
soul, and recasts or corrects the images supplied by his
experience.   His very extravagances and hectic concentration of fancy betray him ; they manifest his impatience,
his affections, his potentialities ; for he paints what he
can conceive and what fascinates him in conceiving it.
That which he might have been, and was not, comforts
him.   Such a form of self - expression, indirect, bashful,
and profoundly humorous, being play rather than art,
is alone congenial to the British temperament ; it is the
soul of English literature.   Like English politics and
religion, it breathes tolerance, plasticity, waywardness,
infinitude ; it is tender and tentative, shapeless and guile-
less.   Its straggling march forms a vast national soliloquy,
rich in casual touches, in alternatives, in contrasts, in
suspended themes ; the plot grows out of the episodes, it
is always being remodelled and always to be continued.
The facts, though much talked of in detail, are never faced
as a whole, nor is the soul ever gathered together to
pronounce upon them ; the whole procedure is a subterfuge, and may be easily disparaged by people with other

gifts and aspirations. Intelligence certainly does not dominate it ; its conclusions, when it reaches conclusions, are false, and its methods cumbrous ; and foreigners who adopt them are catching only the vices of their model. But its virtues are transcendent ; if the mind of England is wrapped in mists, it is touched with ethereal colours ; and who shall measure the benign influences, the lights, the manliness, the comforts, the moral sanity that have spread from it through the world ? Its very incapacities are full of promise ; it closes no doors ; it is the one fountain of kindly liberty on earth. The Englishman's prejudices are so obviously prejudices as to be almost innocent, and even amiable ; his consecrated formulas (for of course he has them) are frankly inadequate and half humorous ; he would not have you suppose he has said his all, nor his last word. He is jealous of preserving, far from public observation or censure, the free play of his potential sentiments ; from thence he will occasionally fetch some scrap of a word, or let slip some hint of emotion ; he will only murmur or suggest or smile his loves. Everybody dislikes a caricature of himself ; and the Englishman feels (I think justly) that any figure a man can cut in other people's eyes is a caricature. Therefore, if there is anything in him, he fears to betray it ; and if there is nothing in him, he fears to betray that ; and in either case he is condemned to diffidence and shyness. He wishes you to let him alone ; perhaps if you do he may presently tell you, about quite another imaginary person, some vivid and tender story.

This story may be a fairy tale or it may be a piece of realistic fiction, in which the experiences of sundry characters, as different as possible from oneself and from one another, are imagined and lived through. The author may fairly say that these creations are not masks for his own person ; it is expressly not his own feelings that he is evoking and developing. He is fancying other feelings ; and yet, as this fancy and the magic life it constitutes are necessarily his own, his mind is being secretly agitated and relieved by these fictions ; and his sensibility, instead of being sublimated into some ultimate tragic passion, is diffused over a thousand picturesque figures and adventures

with which he acknowledges no moral kinship, save such
as is requisite for a lively interest in them and a minute
portrayal. It is only by accident that any of his poetic
offspring may resemble their parent. What cares he what
curious eye may note their deformity ? *He* need not blush
for them. He may even be bent on unmasking and fiercely
condemning them, as a scrupulous penitent is bent on
ferreting out and denouncing his real or fancied sins. In
the most searching truth of fiction there is accordingly
no indiscretion ; the author's inmost and least avowable
feelings may be uttered through it without reserve. Like
a modest showman behind the curtain of his booth, he
manipulates his marionettes and speaks for them in a
feigned voice, by a sort of ventriloquy. Here is no religious
tragedy, no distilled philosophy, no overarching cosmic
myth. The scale is pleasantly small and the tone familiar,
though the sum of the parts may fade into the infinite.
We do not find in this complicated dream any life greater
than our own or less accidental. We do not need to outgrow ourselves in order to understand it ; no one summons
us to pause, to recant, to renounce any part of our being.
On the contrary, we simply unwind our own reel ; we play
endlessly at living, and in this second visionary life we
survive all catastrophes, and we exchange one character
for another without carrying over any load of memory
or habit or fate. We seem still to undergo the vicissitudes
of a moral world, but without responsibility.

Queen Mab is a naughty sprite, full of idle curiosity
and impartial laughter. When she flutters over the
roofs of cities, she is no angel with a mission, coming to
sow there some chosen passion or purpose of her own ;
nor does she gather from those snoring mortals any
collective sentiment or aspiration, such as a classic muse
might render articulate, or such as religion or war or
some consecrated school of art might embody. She steals
wilily like a stray moonbeam into every crack and dark
old corner of the earth. Her deft touch, as she pretends,
sets all men dreaming, each after his own heart ; but like
other magicians, she is a fraud. Those garden fancies
about her fairy equipage are all a joke to amuse the
children ; her wings are, in reality, far finer than gossamer,

and the Equivocation she rides on is nimbler than any
grasshopper. All she professes to spy out or provoke is
her own merry invention. Her wand really works no
miracle and sets no sleeper dreaming ; on the contrary,
it is rather an electric spark from the lover's brain or the
parson's nose, as she tickles it, that quickens her own
fancy, and hatches there an interminable brood of exquisite
oddities, each little goblin perfectly ridiculous, each quite
serious and proud of its little self, each battling bravely
for its little happiness. Queen Mab is the genius proper
to the art of a nation whose sensibility is tender, but
whose personal life is drab and pale. To report, however
poetically, the events and feelings they have actually
experienced would be dull, as dull as life ; their imagination
craves entertainment with something richer, more wayward,
more exciting. Every one is weary of his own society ;
the lifelong company of so meagre and warped a creature
has become insufferable. We see that the passions of
Mercutio are potentially deep and vivid ; but they have
been crossed by fortune, and on fortune his kindly humour
mockingly takes its revenge, by feigning no end of parodies
and escapades for the ineffable bright mischiefs lurking
in his bosom. Queen Mab is the frail mothlike emanation
of such a generous but disappointed mind ; her magic
lies in the ironical visions which, like the dust of the poppy,
she can call forth there. A Cinderella at home, she becomes
a seer in her midnight travels. Hence Table Rounds and
Ivanhoes ; hence three-volume novels about Becky Sharps
and David Copperfields. These imagined characters are
often alive, not only because the scene in which they move
may be well indicated, with romantic absorption in the
picturesque aspects of human existence, but also because
their minds are the author's mind dreaming ; they skirt
the truth of his inner man ; in their fancifulness or their
realism they retain a secret reference to the deepest impulses
in himself.

English lovers, I believe, seldom practise what in Spain
is called conjugating the verb ; they do not spend hours
ringing the changes on I love, you love, we love. This,
in their opinion, would be to protest too much. They
prefer the method of Paolo and Francesca : they will

sit reading out of the same book, and when they come to the kissing, she will say, " How nice that is ! " and he will reply, " Isn't it ? " and the story will supply the vicarious eloquence of their love. Fiction and poetry, in some supposititious instance, report for the Englishman the bashful truth about himself ; and what English life thereby misses in vivacity, English literature gains in wealth, in tenderness, in a rambling veracity, and in preciousness to the people's heart.

36

A CONTRAST WITH SPANISH DRAMA

In classical Spanish drama the masks are few. The characters hardly have individual names. The lady in Calderon, for instance, if she is not Beatriz will be Leonor, and under either name so superlatively beautiful, young, chaste, eloquent, devoted, and resourceful, as to be indistinguishable from her namesakes in the other plays. The hero is always exaggeratedly in love, exaggeratedly chivalrous, and absolutely perfect, save for this heroic excess of sensitiveness and honour. The old father is always austere, unyielding, perverse, and sublime. All the maids in attendance possess the same roguishness, the same genius for intrigue and lightning mendacity ; whilst the valet, whether called Crispin or Florin, is always a faithful soul and a coward, with the same quality of rather forced humour. No diversity from play to play save the diversity in the fable, in the angle at which the stock characters are exhibited and the occasion on which they versify ; for they all versify in the same style, with the same inexhaustible facility, abundance, rhetorical finish, and lyric fire.

Why this monotony ? Did Spanish life afford fewer contrasts, less individuality of character and idiom, than did the England of Shakespeare ? Hardly : in Spain the soldier of fortune, the grandee, peasant, monk, or prelate, the rogue, beggar, and bandit were surely as highly characterized as anything to be then found in England ; and Spanish women in their natural ardour of affection, in their ready speech and discretion, in their dignity and religious consecration, lent themselves rather better, one would think, to the making of heroines than did those comparatively cool and boylike young ladies whom Shakespeare transmuted into tragic angels. I think we may go further and say positively that it was Spain rather than England that could have shown the spectacle of " every man in his humour."

Even in the days before Puritanism English character was English ; it tended to silent independence and outward reserve, preferring to ignore its opposite rather than to challenge it. In pose and expression the Spaniard is naturally more theatrical and pungent ; and his individuality itself is stiffer. No doubt, in society, he will simulate and dissimulate as an Englishman never would ; but he is prompted to this un-English habit by the very fixity of his purposes ; all his courtesy and loyalty are ironical, and inwardly he never yields an inch. He likes if possible to be statuesque ; he likes to appeal to his own principles and character, and to say, " Sir, whatever you may think of it, that is the sort of man I am." He has that curious form of self-love which inclines to parade even its defects, as a mourner parades his grief. He admits readily that he is a sinner, and that he means to remain one ; he composes his countenance proudly on that basis ; whereas when English people say they are miserable sinners (which happens only in church) they feel perhaps that they are imperfect or unlucky, and they may even contemplate being somewhat different in future ; but it never occurs to them to classify themselves as miserable sinners for good, with a certain pride in their class, deliberately putting on the mask of Satan or the cock's feather of Mephistopheles and saying to all concerned, " See what a very devil I am ! " The Englishman's sins are slips ; he feels he was not himself on those occasions, and does not think it fair to be reminded of them. Though theology may sometimes have taught him that he is a sinner fundamentally, such is not his native conviction ; the transcendental ego in him cannot admit any external standard to which it ought to have conformed. The Spaniard is metaphysically humbler, knowing himself to be a creature of accident and fate ;

yet he is dramatically more impudent, and respects himself more than he respects other people. He laughs at kings ; and as amongst beggars it is etiquette to whine, and ostentatiously to call oneself blind, old, poor, crippled, hungry, and a brother of yours, so amongst avowed sinners it may become a point of pride to hold, as it were, the record as a liar, a thief, an assassin, or a harlot. These rôles are disgraceful when one is reduced to them by force of circumstances or for some mean ulterior motive, but they recover their human dignity when one wears them as a chosen mask in the comedy of life. The pose, at that angle, redeems the folly, and the façade the building. Nor is this a lapse into sheer immorality ; there is many a primitive or animal level of morality beneath the conventional code ; and often crime and barbarism are as proud of themselves as virtue, and no less punctilious. If there is effrontery in such a rebellion, there may be also sincerity, courage, relief, profound truth to one's own nature. Hence the eloquence of romanticism. Passion and wilfulness (which romanticists think are above criticism) cannot be expected to understand that, if they merged and subsided into a harmony, the life distilled out of their several deaths would be infinitely more living and varied than any of them, and would be beautiful and perfect to boot ; whereas the romantic chaos which they prolong by their obstinacy is the most hideous of hells. But avowed sinners and proud romanticists insist on preserving and on loving hell, because they insist on loving and preserving themselves.

It was not, then, moral variety that was lacking in Spain, always a romantic country, but only interest in moral variety. This lack of interest was itself an expression of romantic independence, intensity, and pride. The gentleman with his hand always on the hilt of his sword, lest some whiff from anywhere should wound his vanity, or the monk perpetually murmuring *memento mori*, closed his mind to every alien vista. Of course he knew that the world was full of motley characters : that was one of his reasons for holding it at arm's length. What were those miscellaneous follies to him but an offence or a danger ? Why should he entertain his leisure in depicting or idealizing them ? If some psychological zoologist cared to discant

on the infinity of phenomena, natural or moral, well and
good ; but how should such things charm a man of honour,
a Christian, or a poet ? They might indeed be referred to
on occasion, as fabulists make the animals speak, with a
humorous and satirical intention, as a sort of warning and
confirmation to us in our chosen path ; but an appealing
poet, for such tightly integrated minds, must illustrate
and enforce their personal feelings. Moreover, although
in words and under the spell of eloquence the Spaniard
may often seem credulous and enthusiastic, he is dis-
illusioned and cynical at heart ; he does not credit the
existence of motives or feelings better than those he has
observed, or thinks he has observed. His preachers
recommend religion chiefly by composing invectives against
the world, and his political writers express sympathy with
one foreign country only out of hatred for another, or
perhaps for their own. The sphere of distrust and indifference begins for him very near home ; he has little
speculative sympathy with life at large ; he is cruel to
animals ; he shrugs his shoulders at crime in high places ;
he feels little responsibility to the public, and has small
faith in time and in work. This does not mean in the
least that his character is weak or his morality lax within
its natural range ; his affections are firm, his sense of
obligation deep, his delicacy of feeling often excessive ;
he is devoted to his family, and will put himself to any
inconvenience to do a favour to a friend at the public
expense. There are definite things to which his sentiments
and habits have pledged him : beyond that horizon
nothing speaks to his heart.

Such a people will not go to the play to be vaguely
entertained, as if they were previously bored. They
are not habitually bored ; they are full to the brim of their
characteristic passions and ideas. They require that the
theatre should set forth these passions and ideas as
brilliantly and convincingly as possible, in order to be
confirmed in them, and to understand and develop them
more clearly. Variety of plot and landscape they will
relish, because nothing is easier for them than to imagine
themselves born in the purple, or captive, or in love, or in
a difficult dilemma of honour ; and they will be deeply

moved to see some constant spirit, like their own, buffeted by fortune, but even in the last extremity never shaken. The whole force of their dramatic art will lie in leading them to dream of themselves in a different, perhaps more glorious, position, in which their latent passions might be more splendidly expressed. These passions are intense and exceptionally definite ; and this is the reason, I think, for the monotony of Spanish music, philosophy, and romantic drama. All eloquence, all issues, all sentiments, if they are not to seem vapid and trivial, must be such as each man can make his own, with a sense of enhanced vitality and moral glory. The lady, if he is to warm to her praises, must not be less divine than the one he loves, or might have loved ; the hero must not fall short of what, under such circumstances, he himself would have wished to be. The language, too, must always be worthy of the theme : it cannot be too rapturous and eloquent. Unless his soul can be fired by the poet's words, and can sing them, as it were, in chorus, he will not care to listen to them. But he will not tire of the same cadences or the same images — stars, foam, feathers, flowers — if these symbols, better than any others, transport him into the ethereal atmosphere which it is his pleasure to breathe.

The Spanish nation boils the same peas for its dinner the whole year round ; it has only one religion, if it has any ; the pious part of it recites the same prayers fifty or one hundred and fifty times daily, almost in one breath ; the gay and sentimental part never ceases to sing the same *jotas* and *malagueñas*. Such constancy is admirable. If a dish is cheap, nutritious, and savoury on Monday, it must be so on Tuesday, too ; it was a ridiculous falsehood, though countenanced by some philosophers, which pretended that always to feel (or to eat) the same thing was equivalent to never feeling (or eating) anything. Nor does experience of a genuine good really have any tendency to turn it into an evil, or into an indifferent thing ; at most, custom may lead people to take it for granted, and the thoughtless may forget its value, until, perhaps, they lose it. Of course, men and nations may slowly change their nature, and consequently their rational preferences ;

but at any assigned time a man must have some moral complexion, or if he has none, not much need be said about him.

But there is another point to be considered. Need human nature's daily food be exclusively the Spanish pea? Might it not just as well be rice, or polenta, or even beef and bacon? Much as I admire my countrymen's stomachs for making a clear choice and for sticking to it, I rather pity them for the choice they have made. That hard yellow pea is decidedly heavy, flatulent, and indigestible. I am sure Pythagoras would not have approved of it; possibly it is the very bean he abhorred. Against the *jota* and the *malagueña* I can say nothing; I find in them I know not what infinite, never-failing thrill and inimitable power, the power which perfection of any kind always has; yet what are they in comparison to all the possibilities of human music? Enjoyment, which some people call criticism, is something aesthetic, spontaneous, and irresponsible; the aesthetic perfection of anything is incommensurable with that of anything else. But there is a responsible sort of criticism which is political and moral, and which turns on the human advantage of possessing or loving this or that sort of perfection. To cultivate some sorts may be useless or even hostile to the possible perfection of human life. Spanish religion, again, is certainly most human and most superhuman; but its mystic virtue to the devotee cannot alter the fact that, on a broad view, it appears to be a romantic *tour de force*, a desperate illusion, fostered by premature despair and by a total misunderstanding of nature and history. Finally, those lyrical ladies and entranced gentlemen of the Spanish drama are like filigree flowers upon golden stems; they belong to a fantastic ballet, to an exquisite dream, rather than to sane human society. The trouble is not that their types are few and constant, but that these types are eccentric, attenuated, and forced. They would not be monotonous if they were adequate to human nature. How vast, how kindly, how enveloping does the world of Shakespeare seem in comparison! We seem to be afloat again on the tide of time, in a young, green world; we are ready to tempt new fortunes, in the hope of reaching better things

than we know. And this is the right spirit ; because
although the best, if it had been attained, would be all-
sufficient, the best is not yet.

37
THE CENSOR AND THE POET

THERE is an important official of the inner man who in the
latest psychology is called the Censor ; his function is to
forbid the utterance, in the council chamber within us, of
unparliamentary sentiments, and to suppress all reports
not in the interest of our moral dignity. By relegating
half our experience to oblivion and locking up our unseemly
passions in solitary dungeons, the Censor composes a
conventional personage that we may decently present to
the world. It is he, whilst we are sane and virtuous, that
regulates our actions. It had occurred to me sometimes
that the Censor was only another name for our old friend
Reason ; but there is a great difference. This is no censor
of the noble Roman sort, like Cato Major ; he makes no
attempt to purify the republic from within ; he is not
concerned with moral health, honest harmony, and the
thorough extirpation of hopeless rebels. He is concerned
only with appearances and diplomatic relations ; his old
name was not Reason but Vanity or Self-love. He is
merely the head of the government propaganda, charged
with preventing inconvenient intelligence of our psychological home politics from reaching foreign powers or
weakening the *moral* of our fighting force. He is the
father of shams. He invents those masterly methods of
putting our best foot forward, and sustaining the illusion
that we are always actuated by becoming and avowable
motives. He it is that dictates the polite movements by
which we show that we prefer the comfort of others to our
own. He causes us to put on mourning for those who have
left us legacies. He persuades us that we believe in the
religion of our ancestors, in the science of the day, in the
national cause, and in the party cry. He leads us to admire
the latest art, or the most ancient ; he enables us to be

pleased with every fashion in turn, or perhaps to sigh at its ugliness, if we are conscious of being the best-dressed persons in the room. He induces us to follow the doings of the royal family with affectionate awe, to love our relations, to prefer Bach to Offenbach, and always to have had a good time when we leave a friend's house. The Censor sends our children to the best schools, to prove what sacrifices we are willing to make for their good, and to relieve us of further responsibility in regard to them. He directs that considerations of wealth shall control our careers, our friendships, and our manners ; and this is perhaps the greatest sham of all the shams he has set up : that money is an expression of happiness and a means to it. What opens the way to happiness, if our character does not render happiness impossible, is freedom, and some security against want is usually necessary for that ; but wealth, and the necessity of being fashionable if one is rich, take away freedom. A genuine love for the pleasant surroundings and the facilities which riches afford is often keener in the outsider, who peeps in at the gate, than in the master or his children who perhaps, if the Censor would let them, would prefer their low acquaintance and their days afield. But the Censor-ridden inner man cannot break his harness. He is groomed and reined in like a pony at the circus : at the crack of the whip the neck must be bent, the tail switched, the trained feet must retrace the circle in the sawdust, or tap the velvet barrier. So we prance to our funeral, the last sham of all, after the Censor has made our wills for us ; whereupon somebody else's Censor gives us the finishing touches by praising our character, and nailing down the coffin.

The untutored passions which the Censor keeps down are themselves remarkable dissemblers. That old propensity to allegory, which is now condemned in literature, seems to rule unchecked in dreams. Invention in dreams, as in mythology, is far-fetched, yet spontaneous. What it sets immediately before us is a third or a fourth transformation of the fundamental fact. It hides the fact, without misrepresenting it ; the orchestration of the theme, the alien images in which allegory dresses it up, are suggested by some subtle affinity, some instinctive choice, which is perfectly automatic and innocent ; the Psyche could find no simpler way of bringing her agitations to consciousness.   Just as we cannot see a material object more clearly than by seeing exactly how it looks (though that may not be at all how it is), so we cannot express a feeling more sincerely than by rehearsing all the images, all the metaphors, which it suggests to us.   Passion when aroused to speech is rich in rhetorical figures.   When we assert inaccurately that a man is a cur we depart from observation only to register sentiment ; we express truly the niche he fills in our thoughts.   Dramatic poetry is an excursus in this direction ; it reports the echoes which events produce in a voluminous inner sensibility ; it throws back our perception of what is going on into the latent dream which this perception has for its background : for a perception, apart from its object, is only one feature in a dream, momentarily more salient than the rest.   These natural harlequins, the passions, are perfectly sincere in their falsehoods and indirections :   their fancy is their only means of expressing the facts.   To be more literal would require training, and a painful effort ; it would require the art of reading and discounting dreams, whilst these simple poets have only the gift of dreaming.   When Juliet dreams (it is a desperate poetic little dream created by her passion) that she will cut up Romeo into bits and make stars of him, the image is extravagant ; yet if the fundamental theme is, as I suppose, that every atom of Romeo is precious, this mad but natural passion for the bits, even, of what she loves, is expressed truly.   But this sort of sincere fiction, though it may put the Censor to sleep if he does not quite understand what it signifies, is the very opposite of his own shams ; it is exuberance and these are suppression.   If the Censor could have got at Juliet in time, she would have expressed herself quite differently. Wiping her prospective tears he would have said, " What is Romeo's body to me ?   Our spirits will be reunited in heaven ! "   This would have been a sham ; because we should now not be led to understand that Juliet loved the eyes and the hands and the lips of Romeo—which was the fact to be expressed—but on the contrary her idolatrous infatuation would have been hushed up, and something else, an empty convention contradicting her true feeling, would have been substituted for it.

The Censor may not be useless to the poet in the end, because the need of shamming develops sensitiveness in some directions, as in that, for instance, of self-consciousness. The vigour of art in England may depend on the possibility of using the fineness of perception which reticence enhances in order to invent new metaphors and allegories by which to express the heart. Could a vigorous English art, for instance, ever give expression to the erotic passion which, according to this latest psychology, plays such a great part in the Psyche ? The comic vein of English writers commonly stops short at the improper. This is doubtless a wise modesty on their part, because every artist is a moralist, though he need not preach ; like Orpheus he tames the simple soul to his persuasive measures ; he insinuates his preferences and his principles, he teaches us what to love : and to discover what we truly love is the whole of ethics. Now if any passion were sinful and really shameful in itself, it ought not to enter at all into human life, either through the door of art or through any other door. Conceivably a perfect expression might still be given to it technically, although even this is improbable if the artist had a bad conscience and a leering eye ; but this expression, good only from an abstracted point of view, would be on the whole an evil experience and an evil possession. If the early Christians and the Puritans and a whole cloud of mystics and ascetics everywhere have been right in thinking the flesh essentially sinful, the Censor must not be allowed to flinch ; on the contrary, he must considerably extend his operations. If you renounce the flesh you must renounce the world ; things called indecent or obscene are inextricably woven into the texture of human existence ; there can be no completely honest comedy without them. Life itself would have to be condemned as sinful ; we should deny that anything harmonious, merry, or sweet could be made of it, either in the world or on the stage. If we made any concession to art at all, on the same grounds as to matrimony, it would be only in favour of tragedy, which should show us that all we think most amiable is an illusion, ending in torments and in nothingness. Wedlock itself would be sanctioned only grudgingly, as a concession to human frailty, lest a worse thing be ; and we should marry, if at all very sadly, with fear and trembling and strictly for the sake of children. Marriage would then not be the happy-go-lucky, tender, faithful, humorous, trying fatality which nature has made of it, and which comedy describes.

Perhaps the emancipated plebeians of the future will expect their comic poets to play upon sensuality as upon something altogether innocent and amiable : comic, too, because all reality is comic, and especially a phase of it where illusion, jollity, conceit, mishap, and chagrin follow one another in such quick alternation. If this subject could be passed by the Censor, and treated judiciously, it would enrich the arts and at the same time disinfect the mind in one of its most troubled and sullen moods, by giving it a merry expression. In the *Arabian Nights* I find something of this kind ; but erotic art in Europe, even in antiquity, seems to have been almost always constrained and vicious. A man who is moralized politically, as Europeans are, rather than religiously or poetically like Orientals, cannot treat natural things naturally. He respects the uttered feelings of others more than his own feelings unuttered, and suppresses every manifestation of himself which a spectator might frown upon, even if behind the Censor's back everybody would rejoice in it. So long as this social complication lasts public art and the inner life have to flow separately, the one remains conventional the other clouded and incoherent. If poets under these circumstances tried to tell the whole truth, they would not only offend the public but do a grave injustice to their theme, and fail to make it explicit, for want of discipline and grace of expression. It is as well that the Censor, by imposing silence, keeps them from attempting the impossible.

38

THE MASK OF THE PHILOSOPHER

AMONGST tragic masks may be counted all systems of
philosophy and religion. So long as they are still plastic
in the mind of their creator, they seem to him to wear
the very lineaments of nature. He cannot distinguish
the comic cast of his own thought ; yet inevitably it shows
the hue and features of his race ; it has its curious idiom
and constitutional grammar, its quite personal rhetoric,
its ridiculous ignorances and incapacities, and when his
work is finished and its expression set, and other people
behold it, it becomes under his name one of the stock
masks or *dramatis personae* of the moral world.   In it
every wrinkle of his soul is eternalized, its old dead passion
persisted in, its open mouth, always with the same *rictus*,
bawling one deaf thought for ever.   Even to himself, if
he could have seen his mind at a distance, it would have
appeared limited and foreign, as to an old man the verses
of his youth, or like one's own figure seen unexpectedly
in a mirror and mistaken at first for another person.   His
own system, as much as those of others, would have
seemed to him a mask for the truth, partial, over-emphatic,
exaggerating one feature and distorting another, and
above all severed from the context of nature, as a picture
in a frame, where much may be shown with a wonderfully
distilled beauty, yet without its substance, and without its
changeful setting in the moving world.   Yet this fate is
in part a favour.   A system, like a tell-tale glass, may reveal
by a trick of reflection many a fact going on behind one's
back.   By it the eye of the mind travels where experience
cannot penetrate ; it turns into a spectacle what was
never open to sight, and it disentangles things seen from
the personal accidents of vision.   The mask is greater than
the man.   In isolating what was important and pertinent
in his thoughts, it rescues his spirit from the contamination
of all alien dyes, and bequeaths it to posterity such as it
would have wished to be.

39

THE VOYAGE OF THE *SAINT CHRISTOPHER*

THE voyage of Peter's Bark in search of another world has been less fortunate than that of Columbus. There have been mutinies on board ; the other world is not yet found. Soon after this good ship, the *Saint Christopher*, was launched from her Phoenician home-port, she had a strange experience very like that which legend attributes to her namesake, the sainted ferryman. Her freight at the beginning seemed to be of the lightest—only living Hopes and daily Miracles ; and the crossing was to be very brief, the other shore being plainly visible at a stone's throw. But that promised land turned out to be a mirage, lying across the mouth of the port, which really opened out into a vast ocean. Meantime the cargo too was strangely transformed ; for whilst the Hopes and Miracles were still reputed to be on board, they were hidden from sight and smothered in a litter of Possessions. These included a great load of Books, a heavy fund of Traditions, and a multitude of unruly passengers, with their clamorous wives and children, and all sorts of provender. So over-weighted, the *Saint Christopher* sank down until the waves almost covered her deck ; but she was staunch, like the wading saint when his light burden grew heavier and heavier, and she laboured on.

Not only was this ship named after a saint—which in so old a ship is no wonder—but incredible as it may seem, her captain was a saint too—Saint Simon or (since these vague roving people often have an *alias*) Saint Peter. He had been a fisherman by profession, and had only become a saint late in life ; a fact which explained his good seamanship and his bad language. Besides, he did not pretend to be a saint except in his official capacity, as captain, and in matters of science and navigation : in his private life he was frankly not impeccable, and deprecated any strict scrutiny of it as not to the point. Not only might there have been some blemishes in his early career, but even when in command he might have his faults. People enjoy doing what they can do well from long habit ; and he was perhaps too fond of fishing, of cursing, and of commanding.

These foibles once brought upon him a serious mutiny. A large part of the crew, imitating his expressive speech, cried, " Damn the captain ! " and took to the boats, saying the ship was rotten and water-logged. They carried away with them most of the Hopes, whilst scrupulously leaving the Miracles alone. In their boats and rafts they pulled ahead in all directions, covering the sea with specks for a long distance ; and the captain, after running down and sinking a few of them in his towering rage, got used to their existence, made things shipshape again on board, and fell to observing them, not without some chucklings of humour, rowing and splashing about, quarrelling and never getting anywhere, but often merely drifting and quietly fishing, much in his own old manner.

The worst mutiny in the *Saint Christopher*, however, was of quite another kind. The remaining crew had no objection to the captain—they were human themselves— and no desire to paddle their own canoes. But they got thoroughly weary of sailing day after day into the same sunset, decided that there was no El Dorado, and insisted clamorously on putting the ship about. But in what direction ? Some were for going home ; they said all talk of another world was nonsense, that those Hopes and Miracles were worthless, and that the only thing to do was to return to the old country and live there in the old way, making the best of it. But the majority said that such an acknowledgment of defeat and error would be ignominious ; and that life at home, never really happy, would now be doubly intolerable. They would never have set out on so problematical an expedition, had they found life possible in their native seats. But it had been horrible. They remembered with a shudder the cruelties and vanities of their ancestral heathenism. They were adventurers and mariners by nature. They might be now bewildered for a moment and discouraged in their explorations, but the impulse to hope for the better and to try the unknown was ineradicable in their breast.

In some of them, indeed, this brave impulse was so

vigorous, that they now had a sudden intuition of the romantic principle of life, and harangued their companions as follows :

" What need, O shipmates, to sail for *any* port ? The sailor is not a land animal. How we chafed and stifled when we lived on *terra firma*, pent in those horrible stone dungeons called houses and churches, and compelled to till those inert and filthy clods, year in and year out—a most stupefying existence ! Let us sail for the sake of sailing. It was not in putting forth into this infinite sea that we were ill-advised, but only in imagining that we could reach an opposite shore, and that the sea was not infinite but hemmed about by dead land. That was a gross illusion. In reality there is no *terra firma* at all, but only ships and rafts more or less extensive, covered over with earth and trees, riding on the water. Fancy deceived us, when we supposed that our Earth was anchored in some deeper earth. It floats and drifts upon a bottomless flood, and will dissolve into it. Do not dream of any backward voyage, or of reaching home. You will never find that old home again ; it exists no longer. But this good ship of ours, with its wind-blown sails, can never sink and can never stop. If the banners and crosses, which we still fly in deference to custom, have lost their meaning for us, other symbols will take their place. We must not confuse our infinite task with the illusions that may first have prompted us to undertake it. A brave and an endless life awaits us, battling with the storms of winter ; in the summer days, leaping over the waves with the dolphins and the porpoises ; in the watches of the night hailing the ever - new constellations which, as we sail onward, will rise to greet us, and pass over our heads. For ocean is a river that flows unendingly, and the stars and clouds are exhalations attendant upon it ; they rise and soar in great circles perpetually before its course, like loosed doves before the bounding shell of Galatea."

These words were not at all relished by the majority of those who listened to them. They were stay-at-homes by temperament, who had embarked only in the hope of gain, or of finding peace and plenty in some softer climate. They were alarmed and disgusted at what they had just heard, and not being quite sure that it was false, they denied it with some irritation.

"What folly," they cried, "what nonsense you are talking. Of course it is the land that is infinite, since it is much better than the sea ; and the sea is no river, or its water would be fresh, and you know how brackish and bitter it is : indeed, but for the rain we have collected in pans and hogsheads, we should already have died of thirst. This sea is nothing but a stagnant lake in the midst of the green earth, one of the myriad salt ponds studded all over it ; and as for this leaky little ship, which we were induced to embark in only by fraud, it is not really seaworthy. The planks and cordage are already rotting, and how shall we replace them, unless we speedily sight land—and God grant it may be a civilized country ! And look there ! Is not that land on the horizon ! Through the clearing mists I can discern a lighthouse, quite distinctly; and beyond lies a low shore, overhung with smoke. Something tells me this is the New Atlantis described by Bacon. A prosperous and populous city, full of docks and factories, where we shall find everything needful—warehouses, shops, inns, theatres, baths, even churches and chapels of every sect and denomination. What joy ! "

This sight was so welcome to those heartsick passengers, that they could not wait for the ship to make fast, though they steered her straight for the coast, but jumped overboard and eagerly swam ashore. Their example was contagious. The other party could not bear to be left behind without experiencing the new life, whatever it might bring. They reflected that as the land was really a part of the sea, it was not bad seamanship sometimes to run aground, that in leaving the ship they would, in a higher sense, be continuing their voyage, and that they would not be true to the supreme principle of their philosophy, which was absolute free-will, if they did not often change their principles in minor matters. The chief point was to experience everything. They did not regret the past, as did their narrow-minded positivistic friends, simply because it had involved hardships and errors. Hardships and errors were blessings, if you could only outgrow them ; and they, in their splendid vitality, knew how to outgrow everything. Sacred history, classic fable, chivalry, and the cure of one's soul had, in that former age, proved absorbing themes for the fancy, and had exquisitely modulated the emotions ; but the fountain of those emotions had always been their own breast, and since after such dramatic adventures their breast remained deeply unsatisfied, it was time to look again narrowly into its depths to discover some newer and truer way of expressing it. Why should not the development of material arts be the next phase in their career ? They would not be less free amid the gusts and the billows of politics than they had been in their marine adventure ; commerce would offer them glorious opportunities to exercise their willpower and their invention ; infinite vistas, here too, were open before them : cities always more populous, possessions always more varied, instruments always more wonderful, and labour always more intense.

The romantic party accordingly joined the lovers of material progress in their new city, called Mechanapolis : but the old opposition in their temperaments remained undiminished. The lovers of adventure wanted machines in order to make war, and the lovers of thrift wanted peace in order to make other machines.

Meantime Peter the captain, with much grumbling and shaking of his grey beard, had got the old *Saint Christopher* afloat again, and accompanied still by a faithful boatswain and cook, and some nondescript recruits that he had got together, set out again to sea, in search of that other land beyond the ocean which is called heaven. And every evening with a trembling finger he pointed to it in the setting sun, not seeing that heaven was above his head.

40

CLASSIC LIBERTY

WHEN ancient peoples defended what they called their liberty, the word stood for a plain and urgent interest of theirs : that their cities should not be destroyed, their territory pillaged, and they themselves sold into slavery.

For the Greeks in particular liberty meant even more than this. Perhaps the deepest assumption of classic philosophy is that nature and the gods on the one hand and man on the other, both have a fixed character ; that there is consequently a necessary piety, a true philosophy, a standard happiness, a normal art. The Greeks believed, not without reason, that they had grasped these permanent principles better than other peoples. They had largely dispelled superstition, experimented in government, and turned life into a rational art. Therefore when they defended their liberty what they defended was not merely freedom to live. It was freedom to live well, to live as other nations did not, in the public experimental study of the world and of human nature. This liberty to discover and pursue a natural happiness, this liberty to grow wise and to live in friendship with the gods and with one another, was the liberty vindicated at Thermopylae by martyrdom and at Salamis by victory.

As Greek cities stood for liberty in the world, so philosophers stood for liberty in the Greek cities. In both cases it was the same kind of liberty, not freedom to wander at hazard or to let things slip, but on the contrary freedom to legislate more precisely, at least for oneself, and to discover and codify the means to true happiness. Many of these pioneers in wisdom were audacious radicals and recoiled from no paradox. Some condemned what was most Greek : mythology, athletics, even multiplicity and physical motion. In the heart of those thriving, loquacious, festive little ant-hills, they preached impassibility and abstraction, the unanswerable scepticism of silence. Others practised a musical and priestly refinement of life, filled with metaphysical mysteries, and formed secret societies, not without a tendency to political domination. The cynics railed at the conventions, making themselves as comfortable as possible in the rôle of beggars and mocking parasites. The conservatives themselves were radical, so intelligent were they, and Plato wrote the charter of the most extreme militarism and communism, for the sake of preserving the free state. It was the swan-song of liberty, a prescription to a diseased old man to become young again and try a second life of superhuman virtue. The old man preferred simply to die.

Many laughed then, as we may be tempted to do, at all those absolute physicians of the soul, each with his panacea. Yet beneath their quarrels the wranglers had a common faith. They all believed there was a single solid natural wisdom to be found, that reason could find it, and that mankind, sobered by reason, could put it in practice. Mankind has continued to run wild and like barbarians to place freedom in their very wildness, till we can hardly conceive the classic assumption of Greek philosophers and cities, that true liberty is bound up with an institution, a corporate scientific discipline, necessary to set free the perfect man, or the god, within us.

Upon the dissolution of paganism the Christian church adopted the classic conception of liberty. Of course, the field in which the higher politics had to operate was now conceived differently, and there was a new experience of the sort of happiness appropriate and possible to man ; but the assumption remained unchallenged that Providence, as well as the human soul, had a fixed discoverable scope, and that the business of education, law, and religion was to bring them to operate in harmony. The aim of life, salvation, was involved in the nature of the soul itself, and the means of salvation had been ascertained by a positive science which the church was possessed of, partly revealed and partly experimental. Salvation was simply what, on a broad view, we should see to be health, and religion was nothing but a sort of universal hygiene.

The church, therefore, little as it tolerated heretical liberty, the liberty of moral and intellectual dispersion, felt that it had come into the world to set men free, and constantly demanded liberty for itself, that it might fulfil this mission. It was divinely commissioned to teach, guide, and console all nations and all ages by the self-same means, and to promote at all costs what it conceived to be human perfection. There should be saints and as many saints as possible. The church never admitted, any more than did any sect of ancient philosophers, that its teaching might represent only an eccentric view of the world, or that its guidance and consolations might be suitable only at one stage of human development. To waver in the pursuit of the orthodox ideal could only betray frivolity and want of self-knowledge. The truth of things and the happiness of each man could not lie elsewhere than where the church, summing up all human experience and all divine revelation, had placed it once for all and for everybody. The liberty of the church to fulfil its mission was accordingly hostile to any liberty of dispersion, to any radical consecutive independence, in the life of individuals or of nations.

When it came to full fruition this orthodox freedom was far from gay ; it was called sanctity. The freedom of pagan philosophers too had turned out to be rather a stiff and severe pose ; but in the Christian dispensation this austerity of true happiness was less to be wondered at, since life on earth was reputed to be abnormal from the beginning, and infected with hereditary disease. The full beauty and joy of restored liberty could hardly become evident in this life. Nevertheless a certain beauty and joy did radiate visibly from the saints ; and while we may well think their renunciations and penances misguided or excessive, it is certain that, like the Spartans and the philosophers, they got something for their pains. Their bodies and souls were transfigured, as none now found upon earth. If we admire without imitating them we shall perhaps have done their philosophy exact justice. Classic liberty was a sort of forced and artificial liberty, a poor perfection reserved for an ascetic aristocracy in whom heroism and refinement were touched with perversity and slowly starved themselves to death.

Since those days we have discovered how much larger the universe is, and we have lost our way in it. Any day it may come over us again that our modern liberty to drift in the dark is the most terrible negation of freedom. Nothing happens to us as we would. We want peace and make war. We need science and obey the will to believe, we love art and flounder among whimsicalities, we believe in general comfort and equality and we strain every nerve to become millionaires. After all, antiquity must have been right in thinking that reasonable self-direction must rest on having a determinate character and knowing what it is, and that only the truth about God and happiness, if we somehow found it, could make us free. But the truth is not to be found by guessing at it, as religious prophets and men of genius have done, and then damning every one who does not agree. Human nature, for all its substantial fixity, is a living thing with many varieties and variations. All diversity of opinion is therefore not founded on ignorance ; it may express a legitimate change of habit or interest. The classic and Christian synthesis from which we have broken loose was certainly premature, even if the only issue of our liberal experiments should be to lead us back to some such equilibrium. Let us hope at least that the new morality, when it comes, may be more broadly based than the old on knowledge of the world, not so absolute, not so meticulous, and not chanted so much in the monotone of an abstracted sage.

41

GERMAN FREEDOM

THERE is a fine theory of Hegel's that the universe exists in order to realize freedom. In Oriental despotisms, he tells us, only one man was free. In ancient republican cities a minority, the aristocracy of citizens, obtained freedom. Now at last freedom has extended to all ; not, however, as we might fondly suppose, in free and casual America, but under the perfect organization of the Prussian monarchy. For freedom in the mouth of German philosophers has a very special meaning. It does not refer to any possibility of choice nor to any private initiative. It means rather that sense of freedom which we acquire when we do gladly and well what we should have to do anyhow, as when in passing from a close room into the open air we say we breathe freely at last. German freedom is like the freedom of the angels in heaven who see the face of God and cannot sin. It lies in such a deep love and understanding of what is actually established that you would not have it other- wise ; you appropriate and bless it all and feel it to be the providential expression of your own spirit. You are enlarged by sympathy with your work, your country, and the universe, until you are no longer conscious of the least distinction between the Creator, the state, and yourself. Your compulsory service then becomes perfect freedom.

For liberal freedom, for individualism, these philosophers have a great contempt. They say a man is nothing but the sum of his relations to other things, and if he should throw off one after another these constitutive bonds, he would find his private residuum of a self to be a mathematical point and a naked cipher, incapable of willing or of choosing anything. And they further say that a dutiful soul is right in feeling that the world it accepts and co-operates with is its own work ; for, according to their metaphysics, the world is only an idea which each man makes after his own image, and even as you are, so is the world you imagine you live in. Only a foolish recalcitrant person, who does not recognize the handiwork of his own spirit about him, rebels against it, and thereby cancels his natural freedom ; for everywhere he finds contradictions and closed doors and irksome necessities, being divided against himself and constantly bidding his left hand undo what his right hand is doing. So that, paradoxical as it may seem, it is only when you conform that you are free, while if you rebel and secede you become a slave. Your spiritual servitude in such a case would only be manifesting itself in a phenomenal form if the government should put you in prison.

The national expression of this kind of freedom is what the Germans call *Kultur*, a word not well understood in other countries. Every nation has certain characteristic institutions, certain representative writers and statesmen, past and present, certain forms of art and industry, a certain type of policy and moral inspiration. These are its *Kultur*, its national tradition and equipment. When by education the individual is brought to understand all these things, to share their spirit and life, and to be able to carry them forward faithfully, then he has absorbed the *Kultur* in his own person. *Kultur* is transmitted by systematic education. It is not, like culture, a matter of miscellaneous private attainments and refined tastes, but, rather, participation in a national purpose and in the means of executing it. The adept in this *Kultur* can live freely the life of his country, possessing its secret inspiration, valuing what it pursues and finding his happiness in those successes which he can help it to attain. *Kultur* is a lay religion, which includes ecclesiastical religion and assigns to it its due place.

German *Kultur* resembles the polity of ancient cities and of the Christian church in that it constitutes a definite, authoritative, earnest discipline, a training which is practical and is thought to be urgent and momentous. It is a system to be propagated and to be imposed. It is all-inclusive and demands entire devotion from everybody. At the same time it has this great advantage over the classic systems, that it admits variations. At Sparta, in Plato's Republic, and in the Catholic church the aims and constitution of society were expected to remain always the same. The German ideal, on the contrary, not only admits evolution, but insists upon it. Like music, it is essentially a form of movement. According to the philosophers, however, the form of this movement is fixed by the absolute genius of the composer, and prescribes the way in which the changes shall go on. Evolution thus introduces life into this ideal, but does not admit ambiguities. In this sense the German law of progression is as inexorable as the classic model of form.

The more reasonable theorists of German *Kultur* introduce another qualification, which, if admitted, is of the greatest importance, namely, that German *Kultur* is not to be extended to other nations. Some make a special point of contrasting the universal claims of the Roman and Napoleonic empires and of the Catholic church with the aspirations of German genius, which, they say, is infinite inwardly, being capable of endless growth and modification by men of Teutonic blood, yet is limited externally or in space, in that it is not communicable to other races. Non-Teutons should never be summoned, therefore, to acquire the German spirit, which they would only pollute. Their proper rôle is rather to stand by, no doubt overawed and filled with admiration, but left without hope or fear of being assimilated. Yet as the church could admit that there might be unconscious and virtual Christians among the heathen, who might by exception be saved, so there may be sporadic manifestations of Teutonic genius in unforeseen quarters. Shakespeare, Dante, and Christ were virtual and unconscious Germans.

There is, of course, a less indulgent Germanism, which has on its side the authority of Fichte and Hegel, the enthusiasm of the pan-Germans and that lust for boundless ascendancy which enterprise and war naturally foster in anybody who has carried them on passionately and successfully. According to this stricter view, the whole world is to be subjugated and purified by the German nation, which alone inherits the undefiled language and religion of Eden, and must assign to the remaining creole races, descended from savages and ultimately perhaps from monkeys or devils, such tasks as they are capable of. The masters, being by nature generous and kind, will allow their slaves, after their work is done, to bask in despicable happiness, since happiness is all that slaves are capable of living for ; but they will be proudly commanded by a race of hard, righteous, unhappy, heroic German experts, with blue eyes fixed on the eternal ideal.

The admission that German *Kultur* is merely national, which might seem to promise peace and goodwill, may be turned in this way into a sinister claim to absolute dominion. The ancients and the church had supposed that all men, though endowed with talent and goodness in the most various degrees, had qualitatively the same nature. The same passions, the same arts, and the same salvation were proper to them all. The servant, in furthering the aims of his betters, served what his own soul potentially loved and was capable of appropriating ; there could be religion and love in his subordination. Reciprocally the master could feel respect and affection for his servants, who were his wards and his god-children. The best things in classic life—religion, poetry, comradeship, moral sagacity—were shared by the humblest classes and expressed their genius. The temple, the church, the agora, the theatre, Socrates, and the saints were of the people.

German *Kultur*, on the contrary, boasts that it is not the expression of diffused human nature, but the product of a special and concentrated free will. It is therefore incommunicable, unrepresentative. It is not felt by any one else to realize his ideal, but seems foreign to him, forced and unamiable. Every nation loves its idiosyncrasies and, until it reflects, thinks its own balance of faculties, like its language, more natural than other people's. But the prophets of Germanism have turned this blameless love of home and its sanctities into a deliberate dogma that everything German has a divine superiority. This dogma they have foisted on a flattered and trustful nation, with the command to foist it on the rest of the world. The fatuity of this is nothing new, many nations and religions having shared it in their day, and we could afford to laugh at it, if by direct and indirect coercion it did not threaten to trespass upon our liberties.

What is universally acceptable in German *Kultur* is what it contains that is not German but human, what with praiseworthy docility it has borrowed from the ancients, from Christianity, from the less intentional culture of its modern neighbours. The Teutonic accent which these elements have acquired is often very engaging ; it adds to them a Gothic charm for the lack of which mankind would be the poorer. But the German manner, in art, in philosophy, in government, is no better—in its broad appeal to human nature we may fairly say it is worse—than the classic manner which it hopes to supersede. It is avowedly a product of will, arbitrary, national, strained ; it is not superior to what other nations possess or may create but only different, not advanced but eccentric. To study it and use it for a stimulus may be profitable in times and places of spiritual famine or political chaos, but to impose it as normal, not to say as supreme, would be a plain invasion of human liberty.

42

LIBERALISM AND CULTURE

MODERN reformers, religious and political, have usually retained the classic theory of orthodoxy, namely, that there is one right or true system—democracy and free thought, for instance—which it is the reformer's duty to establish in the place of prevalent abuses. Certainly Luther and Calvin and the doctrinaires of the French revolution only meant to substitute one orthodoxy for another, and what they set forth they regarded as valid for all men and forever. Nevertheless they had a greater success in discrediting the received system than in establishing their own, and the general effect of their reforms was to introduce the modern conception of liberty, the liberty of liberalism.

This consists in limiting the prescriptions of the law to a few points, for the most part negative, leaving it to the initiative and conscience of individuals to order their life and conversation as they like, provided only they do not interfere with the same freedom in others. In practice liberal countries have never reached this ideal of peaceful anarchy, but have continued to enforce state education, monogamy, the vested rights of property, and sometimes military service. But within whatever limits, liberty is understood to lie in the individual being left alone, so that he may express his personal impulses as he pleases in word and action.

A philosopher can readily see that this liberal ideal implies a certain view about the relations of man in the universe. It implies that the ultimate environment, divine or natural, is either chaotic in itself or undiscoverable by human science, and that human nature, too, is either radically various or only determinable in a few essentials, round which individual variations play *ad libitum*. For this reason no normal religion, science, art, or way of happiness can be prescribed. These remain always open, even in their foundations, for each man to arrange for himself. The more things are essentially unsettled and optional, the more liberty of this sort there may safely be in the world and the deeper it may run.

Man, however, is a gregarious animal, and much more so in his mind than in his body. He may like to go alone for a walk, but hates to stand alone in his opinions. And he is so imitative that what he thinks he most wishes to do is whatever he sees other people doing. Hence if compulsory organization disappears a thousand free and private organizations at once take its place. Virginal liberty is good only to be surrendered at the right time to a right influence. A state in which government is limited to police duty must allow churches, universities (with millionaires to found them), public sports, private charities, masonic or monastic orders, and every other sort of party institution, to flourish within it unhindered ; otherwise that state would hardly be civilized and nothing of importance would ever be done in it. Yet the prevalence of such free associations will jeopardize the perfect liberty which individuals are supposed to enjoy. Private organizations are meddlesome ; if they cannot impose themselves by force, they insinuate themselves by propaganda, and no paternal government ever exerted so pervasive and indiscreet an influence as they know how to acquire. Fashions in speech or clothes are harder to evade than any laws, and religion, when it is chosen and sectarian, eats more into the soul than when it is established and conventional. In a society honeycombed by private societies a man finds his life supervised, his opportunities pre-empted, his conscience intimidated, and his pocket drained. Every one he meets informs him of a new duty and presents him with a new subscription list. At every turn he must choose between being incorporated or being ostracized. Indeed, the worst and most radical failure in his fabled liberty of choice is that he never had a choice about his environment or about his faculties, and has to take his luck as to his body, his mind, his position, his country, and his family. Even where he may cast a vote his vote is far from decisive. In electing a government, as in selecting a wife, only two or three candidates are commonly available, and the freeman's modest privilege is to declare hopefully which one he wants and then to put up with the one he gets.

If liberalism had been a primitive system, with no positive institutions behind it, it would have left human genius in the most depressed and forlorn condition. The organized part of life would have been a choice among little servitudes, and the free personal part would have been a blank. Fortunately, liberal ages have been secondary ages, inheriting the monuments, the feelings, and the social hierarchy of previous times, when men had lived in compulsory unison, having only one unquestioned religion, one style of art, one political order, one common spring of laughter and tears. Liberalism has come to remove the strain and the trammels of these traditions without as yet uprooting the traditions themselves. Most people retain their preliberal heritage and hardly remember that they are legally free to abandon it and to sample any and every other form of life. Liberalism does not go very deep; it is an adventitious principle, a mere loosening of an older structure. For that reason it brings to all who felt cramped and ill-suited such comfort and relief. It offers them an escape from all sorts of accidental tyrannies. It opens to them that sweet, scholarly, tenderly moral, critically superior attitude of mind which Matthew Arnold called culture.

Primitive, dragooned, unanimous ages cannot possess culture. What they possess is what the Germans call a *Kultur*, some type or other of manners, laws, implements, arts, religion. When these national possessions are perused and relished by some individual who does not take them for granted and who understands and judges them as if from outside, his acquaintance with them becomes an element in his culture; and if he is at home in many such forms of life and thought, his culture is the more perfect. It should ideally be culled from everywhere. Culture is a triumph of the individual over society. It is his way of profiting intellectually by a world he has not helped to make.

Culture requires liberalism for its foundation, and liberalism requires culture for its crown. It is culture that integrates in imagination the activities which liberalism so dangerously disperses in practice. Out of the public disarray of beliefs and efforts it gathers its private collection of curiosities, much as amateurs stock their museums with fragments of ancient works. It possesses a wealth of vicarious experience and historical insight which comforts it for having nothing of its own to contribute to history. The man of culture abounds in discriminating sentiments; he lives under the distant influence of exalted minds; his familiar thoughts at breakfast are intimate appreciations of poetry and art, and if his culture is really mellow, he sometimes smiles a little at his own culture.

Culture came into the modern world with the renaissance, when personal humours and remote inspiration broke in upon the consecrated mediaeval mind. Piety and learning had their intrinsic charms, but, after all, they had been cultivated for the sake of ulterior duties and benefits, and in order to appropriate and hand down the revealed wisdom which opened the way to heaven. Culture, on the contrary, had no ulterior purpose, no forced unity. It was an aroma inhaled by those who walked in the evening in the garden of life. Far from being a means to religion, it threw religion also into the context of human experience, and touched its mysteries and quarrels with judgement and elegance. It liberated the studious mind from obligatory or national discipline, and as far as possible from all bonds of time, place, utility, and co-operation, kindling sympathies by preference with what was most exotic, and compensating the mind for the ignominious necessity of having to be, in practical matters, local and partisan. Culture was courteous, open, unconscious of self ; it was the joy of living every life but one's own. And its moral side—for everything has its moral side—lay in the just judgements it fostered, the clear sense it awakened of the different qualities and values of things. The scale of values established by the man of culture might sometimes be fanciful or frivolous, but he was always most scrupulous, according to his lights, in distinguishing the better from the worse. This conscientiousness, after all, is the only form of morality that a liberal society can insist upon.

The days of liberalism are numbered. First the horrors of competition discredited it, and now the trial of war, which it foolishly thought it could elude. The vogue of culture, too, has declined. We see that the man whose success is merely personal—the actor, the sophist, the millionaire, the aesthete—is incurably vulgar. The rightness of liberalism is exactly proportional to the diversity of human nature, to its vague hold on its ideals. Where this vagueness and play of variation stop, and they stop not far below the surface, the sphere of public organization should begin. It is in the subsoil of uniformity, of tradition,

of dire necessity that human welfare is rooted, together
with wisdom and unaffected art, and the flowers of culture
that do not draw their sap from that soil are only paper
flowers.

43

THE IRONY OF LIBERALISM

To the mind of the ancients, who knew something of such
matters, liberty and prosperity seemed hardly compatible,
yet modern liberalism wants them together. Liberals
believe that free inquiry, free invention, free association,
and free trade are sure to produce prosperity. I have no
doubt they are right in this ; the nineteenth century,
that golden age of liberalism, certainly saw a great increase
in wealth, in science, and in comforts. What the ancients
had before them was a different side of the question ;
they had no experience of liberalism ; they expected to be
state-ridden in their religion, their customs, and their
military service ; even in their personal and family morals
they did not begrudge the strictest discipline ; their states
needed to be intensely unified, being small and in constant
danger of total destruction. Under these circumstances
it seemed clear to them that prosperity, however it might
have been produced, was dangerous to liberty. Prosperity
brought power ; and when a people exercises control over
other peoples its government becomes ponderous even at
home ; its elaborate machinery cannot be stopped, and
can hardly be mended ; the imperial people becomes the
slave of its commitments. Moreover, prosperity requires
inequalities of function and creates inequalities of fortune ;
and both too much work and too much wealth kill liberty
in the individual. They involve subjection to *things* ;
and this is contrary to what the ancients, who had the
pride of noble animals, called freedom. Prosperity, both
for individuals and for states, means possessions ; and
possessions mean burdens and harness and slavery ; and
slavery for the mind, too, because it is not only the rich
man's time that is pre-empted, but his affections, his
judgement, and the range of his thoughts.

I often wonder, looking at my rich friends, how far their possessions are facilities and how far they are impediments. The telephone, for instance, is a facility if you wish to be in many places at once and to attend to anything that may turn up ; it is an impediment if you are happy where you are and in what you are doing. Public motor-vehicles, public libraries, and public attendants (such as waiters in hotels, when they wait) are a convenience, which even the impecunious may enjoy ; but private automobiles, private collections of books or pictures, and private servants are, to my thinking, an encumbrance : but then I am an old fogy and almost an ancient philosopher, and I don't count. I prize civilization, being bred in towns and liking to hear and to see what new things people are up to. I like to walk about amidst the beautiful things that adorn the world ; but private wealth I should decline, or any sort of personal possessions, because they would take away my liberty.

Perhaps what liberalism aspires to marry with liberty is not so much prosperity as progress. Progress means continued change for the better ; and it is obvious that liberty will conduce to progress in all those things, such as writing poetry, which a man can pursue without aid or interference from others : where aid is requisite and interference probable, as in politics, liberty conduces to progress only in so far as people are unanimous, and spontaneously wish to move in the same direction. Now what is the direction of change which seems progress to liberals ? A pure liberal might reply, The direction of liberty itself : the ideal is that every man should move in whatever direction he likes, with the aid of such as agree with him, and without interfering with those who disagree. Liberty so conceived would be identical with happiness, with spontaneous life, blamelessly and safely lived ; and the impulse of liberalism, to give everybody what he wants, in so far as that is possible, would be identical with simple kindness. Benevolence was one of the chief motives in liberalism in the beginning, and many a liberal is still full of kindness in his private capacity ; but politically, as a liberal, he is something more than kind. The direction in which many, or even most, people would

like to move fills him with disgust and indignation ; he
does not at all wish them to be happy, unless they can be
happy on his own diet ; and being a reformer and a
philanthropist, he exerts himself to turn all men into the
sort of men he likes, so as to be able to like them. It
would be selfish, he thinks, to let people alone. They
must be helped, and not merely helped to what they
desire—that might really be very bad for them—but helped
onwards, upwards, in the *right* direction. Progress could
not be rightly placed in a smaller population, a simpler
economy, more moral diversity between nations, and
stricter moral discipline in each of them. That would be
progress backwards, and if it made people happier, it
would not make the liberal so. Progress, if it is to please
him, must continue in the direction in which the nineteenth century progressed, towards vast numbers, material
complexity, moral uniformity, and economic interdepend-
ence. The best little boy, for instance, according to the
liberal ideal, desires to be washed, to go to school,
to do Swedish exercises, and to learn everything out of
books. But perhaps the individual little boy (and according to the liberal philosophy his individuality is sacred,
and the only judge of what is good or true for him is his
own consciousness) desires to go dirty, to make mud-pies
in the street, and to learn everything by experience or by
report from older boys. When the philanthropist runs
up to the rescue, this little ingrate snivels at him the
very principle of liberal liberty, " Let me alone." To
inform such an urchin that he does not know what is good
for him, that he is a slave to bad habits and devilish
instincts, that true freedom for him can only come of
correcting himself, until he has learned to find happiness
in virtue—plainly that would be to abandon liberalism,
and to preach the classical doctrine that the good is not
liberty but wisdom. Liberalism was a protest against
just such assumptions of authority. It emphatically
refused to pursue an eventual stoical freedom, absurdly
so called, which was to come when we had given up everything we really wanted—the mock freedom of service.
In the presence of the little boy liberal philosophy takes a
middle course. It is convinced—though it would not do

to tell him so prematurely—that he must be allowed to go dirty for a time, until sufficient experience of filth teaches him how much more comfortable it is to be clean ; also that he will go to school of his own accord if the books have pictures enough in them, and if the teacher begins by showing him how to make superior mud-pies. As to morals and religion, the boy and his companions will evolve the appropriate ones in time out of their own experience, and no others would be genuine.

Liberal philosophy, at this point, ceases to be empirical and British in order to become German and transcendental. Moral life, it now believes, is not the pursuit of liberty and happiness of all sorts by all sorts of different creatures ; it is the development of a single spirit in all life through a series of necessary phases, each higher than the preceding one. No man, accordingly, can really or ultimately desire anything but what the best people desire. This is the principle of the higher snobbery ; and in fact, all earnest liberals are higher snobs. If you refuse to move in the prescribed direction, you are not simply different, you are arrested and perverse. The savage must not remain a savage, nor the nun a nun, and China must not keep its wall. If the animals remain animals it is somehow through a failure of the will in them, and very sad. Classic liberty, though only a name for stubborn independence, and obedience to one's own nature, was too free, in one way, for the modern liberal. It accepted all sorts of perfections, animal, human, and divine, as final after their kind, each the seat of a sufficient virtue and happiness. It was polytheistic. Between master and slave, between man and woman, it admitted no moral advance or development ; they were, or might be, equally perfect. Inequality was honourable ; amongst the humblest there could be dignity and sweetness ; the higher snobbery would have been absurd, because if you were not content to be what you were now, how could you ever be content with any-thing ? But the transcendental principle of progress is pantheistic. It requires everything to be ill at ease in its own house ; no one can be really free or happy but all must be tossed, like herded emigrants, on the same compulsory voyage, to the same unhomely destination.

The world came from a nebula, and to a nebula it returns. In the interval, happiness is not to be found in being a fixed star, as bright and pure as possible, even if only for a season; happiness is to flow and dissolve in sympathy with one's higher destiny.

The notion of progress is thus merged with that of universal evolution, dropping the element of liberty and even of improvement. Nevertheless, in the political expression of liberalism, liberty took the first innings. Protestants began by asserting the right of private judgement in interpreting scripture; transcendentalists ended by asserting the divine right of the individual to impose his own spirit on everything he touched. His duty to himself, which was also his deepest instinct, was to suck in from the widest possible field all that was congenial to him, and to reject, down to his very centre, whatever might thwart or offend. Sometimes he carried his consistency in egotism to the length of denying that anything he could not digest could possibly exist, or that the material world and foreign nations were more than ideal pawns in the game he played with himself for his self-development. Even when not initiated into these transcendental mysteries, he was filled with practical self-trust, the desire to give himself freedom, and the belief that he deserved it. There was no need of exploring anything he was not tempted to explore; he had an equal right to his opinion, whatever the limits of his knowledge; and he should be coerced as little as possible in his action. In specific matters, for the sake of expediency, he might be willing to yield to the majority; but only when his vote had been counted, and as a sort of insurance against being disturbed in his residual liberty.

There was a general conviction behind all these maxims, that tradition corrupts experience. All sensation—which is the test of matters of fact—is somebody's sensation; all reasoning is somebody's reasoning, and vitally persuasive as it first comes; but when transmitted the evidence loses its edge, words drop their full meaning, and inert conventions falsify the insights of those who had instituted them. Therefore, reform, revision, restatement are perpetually required: any individual, according to this view, who

honestly corrected tradition was sure to improve upon it.
Whatsoever was not the fresh handiwork of the soul and
true to its present demand was bad for that soul.   A
man without traditions, if he could only be materially
well equipped, would be purer, more rational, more
virtuous than if he had been an heir to anything. *Weh dir,
dass du ein Enkel bist !* Blessed are the orphans, for they
shall deserve to have children ; blessed the American !
Philosophy should be transcendental, history romantic and
focussed in one's own country, politics democratic, and
art individual and above convention.   Variety in religious
dogma would only prove the truth—that is, the inwardness
—of inspiration.

   Yet if this transcendental freedom had been the whole
of liberalism, would not the animals, such of them at
least as are not gregarious, have been the most perfect
liberals ?   Are they not ruled wholly from within ?   Do
they not enjoy complete freedom of conscience and of
expression ?   Does Mrs. Grundy interfere with their
spontaneous actions ?   Are they ever compelled to fight
except by their own impulse and in their private interest ?
Yet it was not the ideal of liberalism to return to nature ;
far from it.   It admonished the dogs not to bark and bite,
even if, in the words of the sacred poet, " it is their nature
to."   Dogs, according to transcendental philosophy, ought
to improve their nature, and to behave better.   A chief
part of the liberal inspiration was the love of peace, safety,
comfort, and general information ;   it aimed at stable
wealth, it insisted on education, it venerated culture.   It
was wholly out of sympathy with the wilder instincts of
man, with the love of foraging, of hunting, of fighting, of
plotting, of carousing, or of doing penance.   It had an
acute, a sickening horror of suffering ;   to be cruel was
devilish and to be hardened to pain was brutal.   I am
afraid liberalism was hopelessly pre-Nietzschean ;   it was
Victorian ;   it was tame.   In inviting every man to be
free and autonomous it assumed that, once free, he would
wish to be rich, to be educated, and to be demure.   How
could he possibly fail to covet a way of life which, in the
eyes of liberals, was so obviously the best ?   It must have
been a painful surprise to them, and most inexplicable,

that hardly anybody who has had a taste of the liberal system has ever liked it.

What about liberty in love ? If there is one ingenuous and winged creature among the immortals, it is Eros ; the freer and more innocent love is, the more it will flutter, the farther it will range, and the higher it will soar. But at the touch of matter, of conditions, of consequences, how all its freedom shrivels, or turns into tragedy ! What prohibitions, what hypocrisies, what responsibilities, what sorrows ! The progress of civilization compels love to respect the limits set to it by earlier vows, by age, sex, class, race, religion, blood relationship, and even fictitious relationship ; bounds of which the impertinent Eros himself knows nothing. Society smothers the imp altogether in the long christening-clothes of domestic affection and religious duty. What was once a sensuous intoxication, a mystic rapture, an enchanted friendship, becomes all a question of money, of habit, of children. British liberalism has been particularly cruel to love ; in the Victorian era all its amiable impulses were reputed indecent, until a marriage certificate suddenly rendered them godly, though still unmentionable. And what liberty does even the latest radicalism offer to the heart ? Liberty to be divorced ; divorced at great expense, with shabby perjuries and public scandal, probably in order to be at once married again, until the next divorce. Was it not franker and nobler to leave love, as in Spain, to the poets ; to let the stripling play the guitar as much as he liked in the moonlight, exchange passionate glances, whisper daily at the lattice, and then, dressing the bride in black, to dismiss free fancy at the church door, saying : Henceforth let thy names be charity and fidelity and obedience ?

It is not politics that can bring true liberty to the soul ; that must be achieved, if at all, by philosophy ; but liberalism may bring large opportunities for achievement in a man's outward life. It intensifies—because it renders attainable—the lure of public distinction, of luxury, of love surrounded by refined pleasures. The liberal state stimulates the imagination of an ambitious man to the highest degree. Those who have a good start in the universal competition, or sharp wits, or audacity, will find plenty of prizes awaiting them. With the pride of wealth, when it is great, there comes the pride of munificence ; in the suburbs of wealth there is culture, and in its service there is science. When science can minister to wealth and intelligence to dominion, both can be carried on the shoulders of the plutocracy which dominates the liberal state ; and they can fill it with innumerable comforts and marvellous inventions. At the same time, nothing will hinder the weaker members of rich families from becoming clergymen or even scholars or artists ; or they may range over the five continents, hunt whatever wild beasts remain in the jungle, and write books about savages.

Whether these prizes offered by liberal society are worth winning, I cannot say from experience, never having desired them ; but the aspects of modern life which any one may observe, and the analytic picture of it which the novelists supply, are not very attractive. Wealth is always, even when most secure, full of itch and fear ; worry about health, children, religion, marriage, servants ; and the awful question of where to live, when one may live any-where, and yet all seems to depend on the choice. For the politician, politics are less important than his private affairs, and less interesting than bridge ; and he has always a party, or a wicked opposition, on which to throw the blame if his careless measures turn out badly. No one in office can be a true statesman, because a true statesman is consistent, and public opinion will never long support any consistent course. What the successful man in modern society really most cares about is love ; love for him is a curious mixture of sensuality, vanity, and friend-ship ; it lights up all the world of his thought and action with its secret and unsteady flame. Even when mutual and legal, it seems to be three-quarters anxiety and sorrow ; for if nothing worse happens to lovers, they grow old. I hear no laughter among the rich which is not forced and nervous. I find no sense of moral security amongst them, no happy freedom, no mastery over anything. Yet this is the very cream of liberal life, the brilliant success for the sake of which Christendom was overturned, and the dull peasantry elevated into factory-hands, shopkeepers, and chauffeurs.

When the lists are open to all, and the one aim of life is to live as much as possible like the rich, the majority must needs be discouraged. The same task is proposed to unequal strengths, and the competition emphasizes the inequality. There was more encouragement for mediocre people when happiness was set before them in mediocrity, or in excellence in some special craft. Now the mass, hopelessly out of the running in the race for wealth, falls out and drifts into squalor. Since there is liberty, the listless man will work as little and drink as much as he can ; he will crawl into whatever tenement he can get cheapest, seek the society in which least effort is demanded and least shame is felt, have as many children as improvidence sends him, let himself out, at a pinch, for whatever service and whatever wages he can obtain, drift into some syndicated servitude or some great migration, or sink in solitude into the deepest misery. He then becomes a denizen of those slimy quarters, under the shadow of railway bridges, breweries, and gas - works, where the blear lights of a public - house peer through the rain at every corner, and offer him the one joy remaining in life ; for joy is not to be mentioned in the same breath as the female prowling by the door, hardly less befuddled and bedraggled than the lurching idlers whom she endeavours to entice ; but perhaps God does not see all this, because a pall hangs over it perpetually of impenetrable smoke. The liberal system, which sought to raise the individual, has degraded the masses ; and this on so vast a scale and to so pitiable a degree, that the other element in liberalism, philanthropic zeal, has come again to the fore. Liberty go hang, say the new radicals ; let us save the people. Liberal legislation, which was to have reduced government to the minimum of police control, now has undertaken public education, social reform, and even the management of industry.

This happy people can read. It supports a press conforming to the tastes of the common man, or rather to such tastes as common men can have in common ; for the best in each is not diffused enough to be catered for in public. Moreover, this press is audaciously managed by some adventitious power, which guides it for its own purposes, commercial or sectarian. Superstitions old and

new thrive in this infected atmosphere ; they are now all
treated with a curious respect, as if nobody could have
anything to object to them. It is all a scramble of
prejudices and rumours ; whatever first catches the ear
becomes a nucleus for all further presumptions and
sympathies. Advertising is the modern substitute for
argument, its function is to make the worse appear the
better article. A confused competition of all propagandas
—those insults to human nature—is carried on by the
most expert psychological methods, which the art of
advertising has discovered ; for instance, by always
repeating a lie, when it has been exposed, instead of
retracting it. The world at large is deafened ; but each
propaganda makes its little knot of proselytes, and inspires
them with a new readiness to persecute and to suffer in
the sacred cause. The only question is, which propaganda
can first materially reach the greatest number of persons,
and can most efficaciously quench all the others. At
present, it looks as if the German, the Catholic, and the
communist propaganda had the best chances ; but these
three are divergent essentially (though against a common
enemy they may work for a while together, as they did
during this war), and they appeal to different weaknesses
of human nature ; they are alike, however, in being equally
illiberal, equally " *rücksichtlos* " and " *böse*," equally
regardless of the harm they may do, and accounting it
all an added glory, like baiting the devil. By giving a
free rein to such propagandas, and by disgusting the people
with too much optimism, toleration, and neutrality,
liberalism has introduced a new reign of unqualified ill-
will. Hatred and wilfulness are everywhere ; nations
and classes are called to life on purpose to embody them ;
they are summoned by their leaders to shake off the
lethargy of contentment and to become conscious of their
existence and of their terrible wrongs. These propagandas
have taken shape in the blue sky of liberalism, like so
many summer clouds ; they seem airships sailing under a
flag of truce ; but they are engines of war, and on the
first occasion they will hoist their true colours, and break
the peace which allowed them to cruise over us so leisurely.
Each will try to establish its universal ascendancy by force,

in contempt of personal freedom, or the voice of majorities. It will rely, against the apathy and vagueness of the million, on concentrated zeal in its adepts. Minorities everywhere have their way; and majorities, grown familiar with projects that at first shocked them, decide one fine morning that there may be no harm in them after all, and follow like sheep. Every trade, sect, private company, and aspiring nation, finding some one to lead it, asserts itself " ruthlessly " against every other. Incipient formations in the body politic, cutting across and subverting its old constitution, eat one another up, like different species of animals; and the combat can never cease except some day, perhaps, for lack of combatants. Liberalism has merely cleared a field in which every soul and every corporate interest may fight with every other for domination. Whoever is victorious in this struggle will make an end of liberalism; and the new order, which will deem itself saved, will have to defend itself in the following age against a new crop of rebels.

For myself, even if I could live to see it, I should not be afraid of the future domination, whatever it may be. One has to live in some age, under some fashion; I have found, in different times and places, the liberal, the Catholic, and the German air quite possible to breathe; nor, I am sure, would communism be without its advantages to a free mind, and its splendid emotions. Fanatics, as Tacitus said of the Jews or Christians, are consumed with hatred of the human race, which offends them; yet they are themselves human; and nature in them takes its revenge, and something reasonable and sweet bubbles up out of the very fountain of their madness. Once established in the world the new dispensation forms a ruling caste, a conventional morality, a standard of honour; safety and happiness soften the heart of the tyrant. Aristocracy knows how to kiss the ruddy cheeks of its tenants' children; and before mounting its thoroughbred horse at the park gates, it pats him with a gloved hand, and gives him a lump of sugar; nor does it forget to ask the groom, with a kindly interest, when he is setting out for the war. Poor flunkey! The demagogues will tell him he is a fool, to let himself be dragooned into a regiment, and marched off to endure untold privations, death, or ghastly wounds, all for some fantastic reason which is nothing to him. It is a hard fate ; but can this world promise anybody anything better ? For the moment he will have a smart uniform ; beers and lasses will be obtainable ; many comrades will march by his side ; and he may return, if he is lucky, to work again in his master's stables, lounge at the public-house, and bounce his children on his knee amongst the hollyhocks before his cottage. Would the demagogues give him better prospects, or prove better masters ? Would he be happier with no masters at all ? Consider the demagogues themselves, and their history. They found themselves in the extreme of misery ; but even this is a sort of distinction, and marks off a new species, seizing new weapons in the struggle for existence. The scum of the earth gathers itself together, becomes a criminal or a revolutionary society, finds some visionary or some cosmopolitan agitator to lead it, establishes its own code of ethics, imposes the desperate discipline of outlaws upon its members, and prepares to rend the free society that allowed it to exist. It is astonishing with what docility masses of Englishmen, supposed to be jealous of their personal liberty, will obey such a revolutionary junta, that taxes and commands them, and decrees when they shall starve and when they shall fight. I suspect that the working-people of the towns no longer have what was called the British character. Their forced unanimity in action and passion is like that of the ages of faith ; its inspiration, like that of early Christianity, comes from a few apostles, perhaps foreign Jews, men who in the beginning had visions of some millennium ; and the cohesion of the faithful is maintained afterwards by preaching, by custom, by persecution, and by murder. Yet it is intelligible that the most earnest liberals, who in so far as they were advocates of liberty fostered these conspiracies, in so far as they are philanthropists should applaud them, and feel the need of this new tyranny. They save liberal principles by saying that they applaud it only provisionally as a necessary means of freeing the people. But of freeing the people from what ? From the consequences of freedom.

44

JOHN BULL AND HIS PHILOSOPHERS

ENGLAND has been curiously served by her philosophers.
Personally and in their first intention they have usually
been sturdy Britons ; but their scope has seldom been
equal to their sagacity in particular matters, they have
not divined the ultimate drift of their ideas, and they
have often ended by adopting, a little blankly and doggedly,
some foreign or fantastic system, apparently most in-
expressive of John Bull.   Nevertheless the exotic tendency
in so many British philosophers, as in so many disaffected
British poets, is itself a mark of the British character.
The crust of convention has solidified too soon, and the
suppressed fires issue in little erratic streams that seem of
an alien substance.   In speculation as in other things the
Englishman trusts his inner man ; his impulse is to
soliloquize even in science.   At the same time his inner
man dislikes to be too articulate ; he is soon at a stand
in direct self - expression ; and as a poet may take to
describing nature or Italian passions, so a philosopher
may pick up some alien doctrine that comes to hand, and
that seems friendly to his mind ; not understanding it
very well, perhaps, in its native quality, but making it a
living companion in his own lucubrations, and a symbol
for what remains hidden but revered in his breast.   In
this way the Bible or Plato may serve him to found sects
upon exclusively expressing his own feelings ; or remaining
a plain Englishman to all practical purposes, he may
become, for his greater private satisfaction, a revolutionary
atheist, a spiritualist, a Catholic, or a Buddhist.   In such
strange allegiances something may be due to wayward
learning, or to genuine plasticity of mind and power to
feel as very different souls have felt in other climes ; but
a part is unmistakable helplessness and dire need, and a
part, perhaps, affectation.

When his own resources fail, however, the most obvious
easement and support for the English inner man are the
classical and Anglican traditions he has been bred in,
when these are not too nicely defined nor too slavishly

followed. Most characteristic is John Bull the theologian,
instinct with heresy and practising compromise ; but the
rationalistic John Bull is very like him in his alternative
way of securing the same supreme object of thinking what
he likes to think. In both cases he embraces his opinions
much more because they are wholesome and important
than because they are certain or clear. Opinions, he feels,
should be summary and safe ; they should express the
lessons of experience.

As he conceives it at first, experience does not merely
exist, it teaches. In a sporadic fashion it yields sound
satisfactions, clear warnings, plain facts. It admonishes
him to trust his senses, the reports of reputable travellers
and naturalists, Christianity, and the British constitution,
all when duly revised ; and on the other hand to shun
popery, scholastic quibbles, absolutism, and revolution.
But evidently experience could never teach him these
things if his inner man did not contribute its decided
cravings and aversions. His inner man detests dictation
and loves opportunity ; in ideas it prefers timeliness to
finality. Therefore, when his philosophers come upon
the scene they cannot appeal to him by coercive proofs,
nor by the impressive architecture of their systems, nor
by disentangling and setting clearly before him any
ultimate ideal. To win his ear they must rather drive
his current convictions home, nearer to their source in
himself ; they must invite him to concentrate his empiricism. For instance, he trusts his senses ; and the
philosophers can deeply interest him if they ask him
what, precisely, his senses vouch for. Is it external
things ? But can he actually see anything except colours,
or touch anything except resistances ? Can he feel anything except his own sensations ? By appealing to his
honesty, the sophists catch him in a trap, and he changes
his mind in trying to utter it. It will appear presently,
as he pursues his inquiry, that he has no knowledge of
those external things and events which he had been so
sure of ; they were mere empty notions, and his genuine
experience contained nothing but the pulses of his inner
life, changes in his ideas and vital temperature, which an
accurate autobiography might record. And the more

scrupulously he considers these pulses of his inner life the less and less will he find in them. He and his whole experience will soon be reduced to a series of sensations in single file, with nothing behind them. In reality even this is too much. Although the inertia of psychological conventions and the romantic habit of self-consciousness have kept him from perceiving it, even to this day, yet the fact that a sensation is occurring is not revealed by that sensation itself; no date, place, or relation to a mind is included in its deliverance, and no relation to anything before or beyond; so that the bare datum of sensation is an aesthetic being, not a mental one; an ideal term, not an event; a universal essence, not a particular fact; and immersion in sense or in absolute immediate experience, when animal faith and intelligence are taken away from it, would remove from us every vestige of the notion that anything exists or that anything happens. But without pushing analysis so far, the empirical philosophers left John Bull, when he listened to them, singularly bereft of those comfortable impedimenta with which he had expected to travel through life—without a body, without an environment, without a ground, or any natural perfection or destiny, for his moral being. He had loved exploration, and had looked forward with the flush of confidence to the knowledge and power which his discoveries would bring him; but now he saw that all discoveries were incalculable, arbitrary, and provisional, since they were not truly discoveries, but only developments.

Here was an odd transformation. The self-educated merchants and indignant reformers who, thumping their desks dogmatically, had appealed so roundly to the evidence of their senses, little expected that their philosophy was directed to turning them in the end into inarticulate sensualists, rapt in omphalic contemplation of their states of mind. Some academic idealists, disliking this result, which cast a slur on the pre-eminence of spirituality and learning, and yet not being willing or able to give up the method by which that result had been reached, sought to push the inquiry further, and to come out of the wood on quite the other side. My sensations, they said, since I can now survey the whole series they form, must all exist together in my present apprehension ; and as I cannot know them except in this single and present glance, they never can have existed out of it ; so that I am not really a series of sensations, but only the idea that I am a series of sensations ; in other words, I have become a single sensation instead of many. To make this clearer the same philosophers added that this single sensation or thought, which is what I really am, is also God. Experience now turned out not to be anything that goes on or happens or is endured ; it is the theme of an immutable divine contemplation and divine satisfaction. I am God in so far as I think and approve ; but the chequered experience which I supposed myself to be undergoing is merely imputed to myself by God and me in our thinking.

This second conclusion, like the first, has its value for some temperaments. It brings suddenly before us, as if it were an accomplished fact, the innate ideal of the intellect : to see the changing aspects of all things from above, in their true eternal relations. But this ideal, too, is utterly disparate from that practical experience and prevision which John Bull prizes so highly and thinks he possesses ; indeed, the sublimity of this view lies precisely in its tendency to freeze and submerge all experience, transmuting hard facts and anxious events into painted ships upon a painted ocean, and for our stumbling and unfinished progress substituting a bound volume of travels.

What false step could bring British philosophy, in its gropings, to conclusions so un-English that even those who feel compelled to propose them do so shamefacedly, with many euphemisms and convenient confusions, or even fail altogether to understand the tremendous paradoxes they are repeating ? It was a false step at which Hobbes halted, which Locke took unsuspectingly, and which sent Berkeley and Hume head over heels : the assumption that facts are known immediately. In reality none of the facts which the sturdy Briton feels that he knows—and they are the true facts of nature and of moral life—would be known to him if he were without tentative intelligence and instinctive animal faith ; indeed, without these the senses would have no virtue and would inform us of nothing ; and cows would not see grass nor horses hay, but only green or yellow patches, like rapt empirical philosophers. When Hobbes said that no discourse whatsoever can end in absolute knowledge of fact, he uttered a great truth, but he implied a great error, since he implied that sense—meaning the senseless sensations of idiots—could give such knowledge ; whereas the absolute datum in sense is just as ideal, and just as little a fact, as the deliverance of the most theoretical discourse ; and absolute knowledge—if we call such apprehension knowledge—can seize only some aesthetic or logical term, without any given date, place, or connection in experience. Empiricism in the end must substitute these ideal essences, on the ground that they are the only data, for the facts of nature —facts which animal reactions and the beliefs expressing them are requisite to discover, and which science defines by the cumulative use of reason. In making this substitution empiricism passes against its will into sensualism or idealism. Then John Bull and his philosophers part company : he sticks manfully to his confused conventional opinions, which after all give him a very tolerable knowledge of the facts ; while they go digging for an absolute knowledge of fact, which is impossible, in an intuitive cloudland where there are only aesthetic essences. Hence the bankruptcy of their enterprise. Immediate data are the counters of experience, but they are the money of empiricism.

45

OCCAM'S RAZOR

To many an Englishman the human head seems too luxuriant. With its quantities of superfluous words and ideas, it grows periodically hot and messy, and needs a thorough cropping and scrubbing. To this end, William of Occam long ago invented his razor : *entia non multiplicanda praeter necessitatem* ; a maxim calculated to shave the British inner man clean, and make a roundhead of him, not to say a blockhead. That everything is " nothing but " something else, probably inferior to it, became in time a sort of refrain in his politics and philosophy. He saw that reflection was constantly embroidering on the facts ; but did he suppose that the pattern of things was really simpler than that of ideas, or did he feel that, however elaborate things might be, thought at least might be simple ? At any rate, he aimed instinctively at economy of terms, retrenchment in belief, reduction of theory to the irreducible minimum. If theory was not useful, what was the use of it ? And certainly all that can be said for some theories is that perhaps they are useful ; and when ideas are merely useful, being worthless in themselves and absorbing human caloric, the less we require of them the better. Thought might then be merely a means to a life without thought, and belief a door to a heaven where no beliefs were expected ; all speech might be like the curt words one says to the waiter, in the hope of presently dining in silence ; and all looking might be looking out, as in crossing a crowded street, ending in the blessed peace of not having to look any more.

Occam's razor has gradually shorn British and German philosophy of the notions of substance and cause, matter and God, truth and the soul. Sometimes these terms were declared to stand for nothing whatever, because (as in the case of matter and substance) if I reduced myself to a state of artificial stupidity I might for a moment stop short of the conception of them. More often (as in the case of the soul) the term was declared to stand for something real, which, however, was " nothing but " something else. Of course, all words and thoughts stand for something else ; and the question is only whether we can find another word or thought that will express the reality better. Thus, if I said that the soul was " nothing but " a series of sensations, I should soon have to add that this series, to make up a soul, must arise in the same animal body, and must be capable of being eventually surveyed and recalled together ; while I should have to assign to some other obscure agency those unconscious vital functions which were formerly attributed to the soul in forming and governing the body, and breeding the passions ; functions without which my series of sensations would hardly be what it is. I am not confident that all this laboured psychology makes things much clearer in the end, or does not multiply entities without necessity ; since where I had simply spoken of the soul, I should now have to speak of sensations, series, possibility, synthesis, personal identity, the transcendental unity of apperception, and the unconscious mind. Something is doubtless gained by coining these modern and questionable expressions, since they indicate true complexities in the facts, while a poetic term like " soul " covers them only by pointing the finger of childish wonder at them, without analysis. Nature is far more complicated than any language or philosophy, and the more these refine, the closer they can fit. The anxiety of the honest Occam to stick to the facts, and pare his thoughts to the quick, had this justification in it, that sometimes our images and distinctions are misplaced. Grammar, usurping the rôle of physics, created metaphysics, the trouble with which is not at all that it multiplies entities, since no metaphysician can invent anything that did not lie from all eternity in the realm of essence, like the plot of unwritten novels, waiting for some one with wit enough to think of it. The trouble is rather that the metaphysician probably gives his favourite essences the wrong status. These beings may well be absent from the time and place to which he hastily assigns them ; they may even be incongruous altogether with what happens to exist anywhere. What happens to exist is perhaps what he thinks he is describing, or what, like Occam, he would like to describe if he could ; but he is probably not able. Yet that doesn't matter so much as he imagines. What happens to exist can take very good care of itself, and is quite indifferent to what people think of it ; and as for us, if we possess such cursory knowledge of the nearer parts of existence as is sufficient for our safety, there is no reason why we should attend to it too minutely : there's metal more attractive in discourse and in fiction. Mind, as Hobbes said, is fancy, and it is the things of fancy that greet us first and reward us best. They are far from being more absurd than the facts. In themselves, all things are equally unnecessary and equally possible ; for their own part, all are equally ready to be thought of or even to be born. It is only the routine of nature or the sluggish human imagination that refuses to admit most of them, as country people refuse to admit that foreign languages or manners might do as well as their own.

If God or nature had used Occam's razor and had hesitated to multiply beings without necessity, where should *we* be ? Far from practising economy, nature is prevented from overflowing into every sort of flourish and excrescence only by the local paucity of matter, or the pre-emption of it by other forms ; because forms, once embodied in matter, acquire all its inertia, and grow dreadfully stubborn and egotistical. Scrimpy philosophers little know whose stewards they are when they complain of lavishness in nature, or her lordly way of living ; her substance cannot be spent, nor its transformations exhausted. In sheer play, and without being able to help it, she will suddenly create organization, or memory, or intelligence, or any of those little vortices called passions, persons, or nations, which sustain themselves for a moment, hypostatizing their frail unity into some moral being— an interest or a soul. And as we are superfluous in the midst of nature, so is the best part of ourselves superfluous in us. Poetry, music and pictures, inspired and shaded by human emotion, are surely better worth having than the inarticulate experience they spring from. Even in our apprehension of the material world, the best part is the adaptation of it to our position and faculties, since this is what introduces boundaries, perspectives, comparison and beauty. It is only what exists materially that exists without excuse, whereas what the mind creates has some vital justification, and may serve to justify the rest. Hence the utility of Occam's razor itself, which may help us to arrive at a strict and spare account of what the world would be without us : a somewhat ironical speculation which is the subtlest product and last luxury of the scientific mind. Meantime the sensuous and rhetorical trappings of human knowledge, from which exact science abstracts, by no means disappear ; they remain to enrich the sphere of language and fancy, to which judicious people always felt that they belonged ; and this intellectual or literary realm is no less actual and interesting than any other, being a part of the moral radiation and exuberance of a living world.

46

EMPIRICISM

EXPERIENCE is a fine word, but what does it mean? It seems to carry with it a mixed sense of mastery and disappointment, suggesting knowledge of a sort with despair of better knowledge. Is it such contact with events as nobody can avoid, shocks and pressure endured from circumstances and from the routine of the world? But a cricket-ball has no experience, although it comes in contact with many hands, receives hard knocks, and plays its part in the vicissitudes of a protracted game. There are men in much the same case; they travel, they undergo an illness or a conversion, and after a little everything in them is exactly as it was before; πάθος with them is not μάθος; their natures are so faithful to the *a priori* and so elastic that they rebound from the evidence of sense and the buffets of fortune like a rubber bag full of wind; they pass through life with round eyes open, and a perpetual instinctive babble, and yet in the moral sense of the word they have no experience, not being mindful enough to acquire any. It would seem that to gather anything we must first pause, and that before we can have experience we must have minds.

Yet if we said that experience arose by the operation of mind, would not all the operations of mind be equally experience? Has not a maniac probably more and more vivid experience than a man of the world? Doubtless when people call their fancies or thoughts experience, they mean to imply that they have an external source, as " religious experience " is assumed to manifest divine intervention, and " psychical experience " to prove the self-existence of departed spirits. But these assumptions are not empirical; and evidently the religious or psychical experience itself, whatever its cause, is the only empirical fact in the case. Those who appeal to the *lessons* of experience are not empiricists, for these are lessons that only reason can learn. Experience, as practical people understand it, is not every sort of consciousness or memory, but only such as is addressed to the facts of nature and

controlled by the influence of those facts ; material contact
or derivation is essential to it.   Experience is both physical
and mental, the intellectual fruit of a material intercourse.
It presupposes animal bodies in contact with things, and
it presupposes intelligent minds in those bodies, keeping
count of the shocks received, understanding their causes,
and expecting their recurrence as it will actually take
place.   To these naturalistic convictions all those ought to
have clung who valued experience as a witness rather
than as a sensation ; without animals in a natural environment experience, as contrasted with fancy or intuition,
can neither be nor be conceived.   It means so much of
knowledge and readiness as is fetched from contact with
events by a teachable and intelligent creature ; it is a fund
of wisdom gathered by living in familiar intercourse with
things.

But such assumptions are an offence to the expert
empiricist.   The moment he comes upon the scene we
feel that all we thought experience had taught us is going
to be disproved.   " Do you admit," he begins by asking,
" that nothing can be more real than experience ? "   We
do admit it.   " And can you ever know anything that is
not experience ? "   Perhaps not ; and yet would experience
be very distinct or very significant if it was experience of
nothing ?   " Of nothing, indeed," he retorts, withering us
with a scornful glance and the consciousness of his masked
batteries ; " as if experience itself was nothing !   Experience
is everything ; and when you have experience of experience
what more could you ask for, even if you were Doctor
Faustus in person ?   What spurious little non-empirical
particle is this *of* of yours ?   And what illegitimate ghost
is this *something else* that experience should be *of* ?   Can
you, without confessing to an adulterous intercourse with
what is not experience, explain these natural but dis-
reputable members of your intellectual family ? "   We
cannot explain them, and we blush.   Yet why should
experience arise at all if there is no occasion for it ?
" Occasion ! " cries the empiricist ; " another illegal figment,
the old notion of cause !   Is it not notorious that causation
is nothing but the habit which some parts of experience
have of following upon others ?   How then should the

whole of it follow upon any part ? Experience cannot spring from anything, it cannot express anything, and it cannot know anything, because experience is all there is."

Here is a considerable retrenchment in the scope of our philosophy : no material world, no soul, and (in the proper sense of the words) no God and no knowledge. Retrenchment, however, is often a sign of wisdom, and the retrenching empiricist deserves to be followed, like the retrenching hermit, into his psychological wilderness, not with a vow never to return to the world, for that would be precipitate, but in the hope of sounding, in one direction, the depths of spiritual discipline and disillusion. And the empirical eremite can taste rare pleasures. All things, for him, become the appanage of the inner man ; and we need not wonder that the pensive Englishman is ready to be empirical in this sense and to become an idealist. The *lessons* of experience, if he was forced to take them seriously, might tend to dethrone his inner man and lead him to materialism ; but fortunately the lessons of experience, for an empiricist, can be nothing but little epicycles within it, or cross-references to its literal text ; they cannot spoil its intimate and romantic nature, which is to be no end of pulsations and no end of pictures. How dead would anything external or permanent be, even if we thought we could find it ! How abstract would be anything common to all times and places, how terrible a mocking truth that should overarch them for ever !

It is true that the romantic empiricist is not very radical ; he commonly stops short of any doubts on the validity of memory, with all the yarns it spins ; his past adventures and his growth are too fascinating for him to doubt their reality. Sometimes he even trusts a super-stitious prophecy, under the name of logical evolution, foretelling what his destiny is somehow compelled to be. At other times he prefers to leave the future ambiguous, so that the next step may lead him anywhere, perhaps to heaven, provided it is understood that his career, even there, is always to remain an unfinished voyage in an uncharted sea. In strictness, however, he has no right to this fond interest in himself. If he became a perfect empiricist he would trust experience only if it taught him absolutely nothing, even about his own past. This is hard for the flesh, and it may not be fair to ask an empiricist to be heroic in the interests of logic ; but if he could screw his courage up for the plunge, his spirit might find itself perfectly at home in the new situation. What he might have been or might have thought, he would dismiss as a dead issue ; he would watch only his present life as it flowed, and he would love exclusively what he was becoming. There is a sense of safety in being and not thinking which probably all the animals know, and there is a mystical happiness in accepting existence without understanding it ; but the sense of safety does not render the animals really safe, and the price they pay for living in the moment is that they carry nothing over from one moment to another except bare existence itself. The disadvantage of radical empiricism is that it shuts out experience.

47

THE BRITISH HEGELIANS

IT was formerly a matter of some surprise to me that there should be so many Hegelians in England, and in such places of influence. I could imagine how the system might have taken root in circles where the classic tradition was absent or enfeebled—in America, in Scotland, among the Dissenters or Jews in England itself ; but how could Oxford and Cambridge fail to see in that system the trail of the serpent ? How could they mistake it for a Christian or for a spiritual philosophy ? It is indeed, in form, an encyclopaedic system, and in that sense suitable to universities ; and it deifies knowledge such as an encyclopaedia can give, turning it into the sum total of reality, so that it flatters the self-sufficiency of pedants, or that of any reflective mind. But in Oxford and Cambridge knowledge is not everything ; they are more and less than universities ; the learning they cultivate is selective and pursued in the service of aristocratic liberty. I should not expect them to care much for a philosophy that was not poetic and devout. I sometimes fancy how the genuine Oxonians must have smiled to hear T. H. Green, in the early days of transcendentalism, talking about his spiritual principle in nature. By spiritual he meant mind-made ; he thought the world, remaining just as it is, could suddenly be proved to be spiritual if you could show that a mental synthesis was requisite to hold it together. But what possible advantage is it to the world to be held together by a mental synthesis, rather than by space or time or the truth of its constitution ? A synthesis of worthless facts does not render them severally better, nor itself a good. A spirit whose essential function was to create relations would be merely a generative principle, as the spider is to its web ; it would be no better than its work, unless perhaps it was spiritual enough to grow weary of that vain labour. Spiritual, for those who retain the language of Christendom, signifies free from the world and from the flesh, and addressed to the eternal and to the beautiful.

Everything, however, has its explanation, and in the matter of English Hegelism I think I begin to see it. In the first place, I was rashly identifying England with a figment of my dreams, with which I was in love : I saw in my mind's eye a manly and single-minded England, free, candid, poetical, akin to feudal France, beauty-loving like old Italy, the Benjamin of the Roman family of nations, adding to the dignity and disinterestedness of the Castilian character only a certain blond charm, a certain infusion of northern purity, and of sympathy with the wild and rural voices of nature. In this England, in which there was something Spartan and archaically Greek, the men were like Hippolytus and the women like Antigone. Naturally it was unintelligible to me that the system of Hegel should take root in such a nation. Persons with a ripe moral tradition are not attracted by sophistry. No argument, however specious, will convince them that the experience of man on earth makes up the whole universe, or the chief part of it ; much less will they allow fortune, under the pompous name of evolution, to dictate to them their moral allegiance. The chief force of the Hegelian system for those who are not metaphysicians lies in the criterion of progress which it imposes. This

criterion is not beauty in art, nor truth in philosophy,
nor justice in society, nor happiness in the individual
life : the criterion is simply the direction which the actual
movement happens to be taking. Hegel endeavours to
show in what way forms are inevitably passing into one
another. Thus his ethics begs defence of history, and his
history calls for aid on metaphysics. And what metaphysics ? A logic of moral fashions. Now it seemed to
me axiomatic that eager co-operation with whatever is
going on, or is bound to win, would be repulsive to a man
of honour. Nor could I conceive a true Englishman
taking kindly even to the grand side of this system, which
to me personally is rather attractive, I mean to its satirical
elevation. The English mind is tender and temperate :
it deprecates scorn. But Hegel, in his scathing moods, is
comparable to Heraclitus ; he mocks every opinion with
an opinion which refutes it, and every life with another
life which kills it. He has the wisdom of the serpent ;
but unlike Heraclitus, whose fabled tears were warm, he
has the heart of the serpent too. He despises finitude
because it is weak, as if an infinity of pervasive weakness
were strong, or a perpetual flux a victory for anything.
Laughing, I can't help thinking, up his sleeve, he suggests
that this flux itself is a victory for the spirit, meaning
by spirit the law by which he supposes that this flux is
controlled. But this is sheer mockery : the only moral
victory is that achieved, under favourable conditions,
by some living spirit, glad to be expressed or to have been
expressed in some perfect form. The finite only is good :
the infinite tides are worth exactly what they cast up.
There is a bitter idolatry of fate in this system which
might seem splendid to a barbarian ; but how, I asked
myself, can it be anything but horrible to a cultivated
conscience, or to a pupil of the Greeks ?

In the real England the character I dreamt of exists,
but very much mixed, and overbalanced by its contrary.
Many have the minds of true gentlemen, poetically
detached from fortune, and seeing in temporal things only
their eternal beauties. Yet if this type of English character
had been general, England could never have become
Puritan, nor bred so many prosperous merchants and

manufacturers, nor sent such shoals of emigrants to the colonies ; it would hardly have revelled as it does in political debates and elections, and in societies for the prevention and promotion of everything. In the real England there is a strong if not dominant admixture of worldliness. How ponderous these Lord Mayors, these pillars of chapels, these bishops, these politicians, these solemn snobs ! How tight-shut, how moralistic, how overbearing these intellectuals with a mission ! All these important people are eaten up with zeal, and given over to rearranging the world, and yet without the least idea of what they would change it into in the end, or to what purpose. Being so much in earnest, they are convinced that they must be living on the highest principles : what, then, is more intelligible than that they should welcome a philosophy which assures them that such is the case ? They are well pleased to hear, on the highest metaphysical authority, that the first duty of a rich man is to grow richer, and of a settled man to redouble in loyalty to his wife, his community, his party, and his business. The Protestant reformers told them so formerly in biblical language ; the Protestant philosophers tell them so now in the language of Hegel.

Besides, on its technical side, the Hegelian system has a great strength, and was most apposite in the predicament in which, fifty years ago, philosophy found itself in England. It supplied three illusions which idealism sadly needed if it was to become orthodox and popular : the illusions of profundity, of comprehensiveness, and of finality. It was a philosophy of progress—another claim to popularity in the nineteenth century—not only progress in the world at large, but especially in philosophy itself ; and a philosophy of progress cannot ask us to go back, to cry *peccavi*, and reconsider the false assumptions on which we may have been reasoning for two hundred or for two thousand years. It must accept these assumptions and go on building upon them, always a higher and a higher structure. Now the principal assumption of British philosophy, on which German philosophy itself rests, was that nothing can be experienced except experience itself, and nothing known except knowledge. But the Germans

analysed far more accurately than the British had formerly
done what the notions of experience and knowledge contain.
They demonstrated the unity of glance that is essential
to it, and thus refuted (without of course removing) the
successive and episodic character of experience, as the
honest but unwary empiricists had conceived it. Hume
and Mill had remained naturalists in regard to the distribution of those volatile ideas to which they pretended to
reduce the world. John Stuart Mill had a deeper and a
sweeter mind than his critics ; there was something in
him akin to Wordsworth or to Matthew Arnold ; but his
inherited principles were treacherous, and opened the door
to just such a concentration of egotism as the Hegelians
brought about. Moreover, Hume and Mill had seemed
depressing ; they perplexed without filling the mind ;
they made everything that is most familiar and interesting
seem strangely hypothetical ; whereas in Hegel the pageant
of nature and history appeared to be re-formed and to march
round and round the stage of the ego under the strongest
light to the loudest music. There was a sort of deafening
optimism about it ; and not only was a convenient school-
book universe offered you, warranted complete, but all
previous philosophies were succinctly described, refuted,
and linked together, in a manner most convenient for
tutorial purposes. Of course, the true character and eternal
plausibility of each great system were falsified in such a
survey ; each was attached artificially to what happened
to precede and to follow it in time, or in the knowledge of
the historian ; as if history were a single chain of events,
and its march dialectical — a fiction which Hegel did
not blush to maintain. An inner instability was thus
attributed to each view which came only from the slippery
mind of the critic touring amongst them, without the least
intention of finding anywhere a home in which to rest.
Hegel was not looking for the truth—why dream of truth
when you possess learning ?—he was writing an apology
for opinion. He enjoyed understanding and imagining
things plausibly, and had a great intelligence to pour
into his constructions ; but this very heat of thought fused
everything into the mould of his method, and he gave out
that he had understood every system much better than

those who believed in it, and had been carried by its inner contradictions (which its adepts never saw) to the next convenient position in the development of human fancy, and of his own lectures.

Abstraction, such as withdrawal of the mind from worldly affairs, is condemned by this philosophy : you must glut the brain and heart with everything that exists. An even worse abstraction, for a philosopher, is to detach the object from the subject, and believe it to exist independently. But what is abstraction ? Can attention ever render things more discrete than they are in their own nature ? Suppose I abstract a coin from another man's pocket : it is easily proved by Hegel's logic that such an abstraction is a mere appearance. Coins cannot exist as coins except as pocketed and owned ; at the same time they imply an essential tendency to pass into the pockets of other men : for a coin that could not issue from the pocket would be a coin in name only, and not in function. When it actually passes from one man's pocket into another's, this circumstance, far from justifying us in thinking the coin a separable thing, shows that all men's pockets (when not empty and therefore, in function, not pockets at all) are intrinsically related and, in a higher sense, one and the same purse. Therefore, we may conclude, it was not the sly transference of the coin from my neighbour's pocket into mine that was the wrongful abstraction, but only the false supposition that if the coin was his it was not, by right of eminent domain, mine also. A man, in so far as he is the possessor of coins, is simply a pocket, and all pockets, in so far as there is transferable coin in them, are one pocket together. In this way we avoid false abstraction by proving that everything is abstract.

Nor is this all ; for strange as it may seem, Hegel appeals also to one type of religious people, and seems to them to lift religious faith triumphantly above all possible assaults of fact or of science. Are not all facts mere ideas ? And must not all ideas be bred in the mind according to its own free principles of life and effort ? Is not all this semblance of externality in things a blessed foil to spiritual activity ? Does not this universal mutation pay loud

homage to eternal law ?   Things go by threes : that is
the reason why they exist and why they move, and the
sovereign good to be attained by their motion.   If every
truth turns out to be a lie, every lie is a part of some higher
truth ;   if everything becomes unreal, because it passes
into something else, this other thing inherits its reality ;
and if we look at things as a whole instead of *seriatim*, and
spread out our moving film into a panorama, we perceive
that everything has implied everything else from the
beginning, and formed a part of it ; so that only from the
point of view of ignorance is anything earlier, or better,
or truer than anything else.   Here, in the All, we have
rest from our labours.

In this way even the slaves of the world at last learn
to overcome the world ; but it is too late.   This All, even
if it were open to human survey, would have no value : it
defeats each of its constituent lives and is itself responsive
to no living desire.   The indistinction which the vague
idea of it produces in the mind may be soothing to the
weary ; but better than mystical relief at the end would
have been moral freedom in the beginning.   That a different
life will supersede mine is nothing against my happiness ;
that time is swallowing me up is nothing against my
appropriate eternity.   How vain the crabbed hand of the
miser stringing his pearls and never looking at them,
counting the drops that trickle into his cup and never
emptying it, never feeling the intoxication of living now,
of telling the truth frankly, and of being happy here !   If
the devil laughs at me because I am mortal, I laugh at
him for imagining that death can trouble me, or any other
free spirit, so long as I live, or after I am dead.

48

THE PROGRESS OF PHILOSOPHY

THIS war will kill the belief in progress, and it was high
time.   Progress is often a fact : granted a definite end to
be achieved, we may sometimes observe a continuous
approach towards achieving it, as for instance towards

cutting off a leg neatly when it has been smashed ; and such progress is to be desired in all human arts. But *belief* in progress, like belief in fate or in the number three, is a sheer superstition, a mad notion that because some idea —here the idea of continuous change for the better—has been realized somewhere, that idea was a power which realized itself there fatally, and which must be secretly realizing itself everywhere else, even where the facts contradict it. Nor is belief in progress identical with belief in Providence, or even compatible with it. Providence would not have begun wrong in order to correct itself ; and in works which are essentially progressive, like a story, the beginning is not worse than the end, if the artist is competent.

What true progress is, and how it is usually qualified by all sorts of backsliding and by incompatible movements in contrary directions, is well illustrated by the history of philosophy. There has been progress in it ; if we start with the first birth of intelligence and assume that the end pursued is to understand the world, the progress has been immense. We do not understand the world yet ; but we have formed many hypotheses about it corroborated by experience, we are in possession of many arts which involve true knowledge, and we have collated and criticized— especially during the last century—a great number of speculations which, though unverified or unverifiable, reveal the problems and the possibilities in the case ; so that I think a philosopher in our day has no excuse for being so utterly deceived in various important matters as the best philosophers formerly were through no fault of theirs, because they were misled by a local tradition, and inevitably cut off from the traditions of other ages and races. Nevertheless the progress of philosophy has not been of such a sort that the latest philosophers are the best : it is quite the other way. Philosophy in this respect is like poetry. There is progress in that new poets arise with new gifts, and the fund of transmitted poetry is enriched ; but Homer, the first poet amongst the Greeks, was also the best, and so Dante in Italy, and Shakespeare in England. When a civilization and a language take shape they have a wonderful vitality, and their first-fruits are some love-child, some incomparable creature in whom the whole genius of the young race bursts forth uncontaminated and untrammelled. What follows is more valuable in this respect or in that ; it renders fitly the partial feelings and varying fashions of a long decadence ; but nothing, so long as that language and that tradition last, can ever equal their first exuberance. Philosophy is not so tightly bound as poetry is to language and to local inspiration, but it has largely shared the same vicissitudes ; and in each school of philosophy only the inventors and founders are of any consequence ; the rest are hacks. Moreover, if we take each school as a whole, and compare it with the others, I think we may repeat the same observation : the first are the best. Those following have made very real improvements ; they have discovered truths and methods before unknown ; but instead of adding these (as they might have done) to the essential wisdom of their pre-decessors, they have proceeded like poets, each a new-born child in a magic world, abandoned to his fancy and his personal experience. Bent on some specific reform or wrapped up in some favourite notion, they have denied the obvious because other people had pointed it out ; and the later we come down in the history of philosophy the less important philosophy becomes, and the less true in fundamental matters.

Suppose I arrange the works of the essential philosophers —leaving out secondary and transitional systems—in a bookcase of four shelves ; on the top shelf (out of reach, since I can't read the language) I will place the Indians ; on the next the Greek naturalists ; and to remedy the unfortunate paucity of their remains, I will add here those free inquirers of the renaissance, leading to Spinoza, who after two thousand years picked up the thread of scientific speculation ; and besides, all modern science : so that this shelf will run over into a whole library of what is not ordinarily called philosophy. On the third shelf I will put Platonism, including Aristotle, the Fathers, the Scholastics, and all honestly Christian theology ; and on the last, modern or subjective philosophy in its entirety. I will leave lying on the table, as of doubtful destination, the works of my contemporaries. There is much life in some of them. I like their water-colour sketches of self-consciousness, their rebellious egotisms, their fervid reforms of phraseology, their peep-holes through which some very small part of things may be seen very clearly : they have lively wits, but they seem to me like children playing blind-man's-buff ; they are keenly excited at not knowing where they are. They are really here, in the common natural world, where there is nothing in particular to threaten or to allure them ; and they have only to remove their philosophical bandages in order to perceive it.

What sort of a world this is—I will not say in itself, but in respect to us—can be perceived almost at once by any candid spirit, and the Indians readily perceived it. They saw that substance is infinite, out of scale with our sensuous images and (except in the little vortex that makes us up) out of sympathy with our endeavours ; and that spirit in us nevertheless can hold its own, because salvation lies in finding joy in the truth, not in rendering fortune propitious, by some miracle, to our animal interests. The spirit is at home in the infinite, and morally independent of all the accidents of existence : nothing that nature can produce outruns its potential scope, its desire to know the truth ; and its disinterestedness renders it free, free especially from any concern about its own existence. It does not deem it the part of piety to deny the fugitive, impotent, and fantastic nature of human life. It knows that the thoughts of man and his works, however great or delightful when measured by the human scale, are but the faintest shimmer on the surface of being. On the ruin of humanistic illusions (such as make up the religious philosophy of the West) it knows how to establish a tender morality and a sublime religion.

Indian wisdom, intent on the infinity and unity of substance and on the vanity of human life, neglected two inquiries which are nevertheless of the greatest interest to the spirit, so long as this vain life endures. The Indians did not study the movement and mechanism of nature : they had no science. Their poets, in a sort of spectacular physics, were content to paint vividly the images of sense, conscious of their fugitive charm, and of their monstrous and delirious diversity. They also neglected the art of rational conduct in this world ; the refinements of their

moral discipline were all mystical ; they were determined
by watching the movement of inner experience, and allowing
the fancy to distinguish its objects and its stages.   They
thought the spirit could liberate itself by thinking, as by
thinking it seemed to have entangled itself in this mesh of
dreams.   But how could the spirit, if it had been free
originally, ever have attached its fortunes to any lump of
clay ?   Why should it be the sport of time and change and
the vicissitudes of affairs ?   From the point of view of
the spirit (which is that of the Indians) this question is
absolutely insoluble ; a fact which drives them to say that
this entanglement is not " real," but only an illusion of
being entangled.   Certainly substance is not entangled, but
persists and moves according to its nature ; and if what
exists besides substance—its aspects and the spirit in us
that notes them—is not " real " because not substantial,
then the unreal has the privilege, as Democritus pointed out,
of existing as well as the real, and more obviously.   But
this subterfuge, of denying that appearance exists, because
its existence is only the seeming of its objects, was inevitable
in the Indian system, and dramatically right.   The spirit,
left to its own fond logic, remains perfectly ignorant of its
natural ancestry and cannot imagine why it finds itself
caught in the vice of existence, and hanging like Prometheus
on a crag of Caucasus, or like Christ on the cross.   The
myth of reincarnation, whilst it meets certain moral demands,
leaves the problem essentially untouched.   Why should
spirit have fallen in the first instance, or made any beginning
in sin and illusion ?

It would have been better, for the moral and religious
purposes of these sages, to have observed and respected the
prose facts, and admitted that each little spirit falls for the
first time when the body is generated which it is to dwell
in.   It never, in fact, existed before ; it is the spirit of that
body.   Its transcendental prerogatives and its impersonal
aims are by no means inconsistent with that humble fact :
they seem inconsistent only to those who are ignorant of
the life and fertility of nature, which breeds spirit as naturally
as the lark sings.   Aspiration to liberate spirit from absorption in finite existence is in danger of missing its way if it
is not enlightened by a true theory of existence and of

spirit ; for it is utterly impossible to free the spirit materially, since it is the voice of matter, but by a proper hygiene it can be freed ideally, so that it ceases to be troubled by its sluggish instrument, or conscious of it. In these matters the Indians were the sport of the wildest fancy. They mistook their early poetry for a metaphysical revelation, and their philosophy was condemned to turn in the most dreary treadmill of commentaries and homilies, without one ray of criticism, or any revision of first principles. Nevertheless, all their mythology and scholasticism did not invalidate (as they did not in the Catholic church afterwards) the initial spiritual insight on which their system rested. The spirit, viewed from within, is omnipresent and timeless, and must be spoken of as falling, or coming down, or entering (as Aristotle puts it) through the house-door. Spirit calls itself a stranger, because it finds the world strange ; and it finds the world strange because, being the spirit of a very high-strung and perilously organized animal, it is sensitive to many influences not harmonious with its own impulses, and has to beg its daily bread. Yet it is rich in resource ; and it gives itself out for a traveller and tells marvellous lies about its supposed native land, where it was a prince and an omnipotent poet. These boasts serve the spirit as a declaration of independence, and a claim to immense superiority above the world. This independence, however, is really only the independence of ignorance, that must think and act at random ; and the spirit would add sanity to its spirituality if it recognized the natural, precarious, and exquisite life of which it is the spirit.

Sanity, thy name is Greece. The Greek naturalists saw (what it needs only sanity to see) that the infinite substance of things was instinct with a perpetual motion and rhythmic order which were its life, and that the spirit of man was a spark from that universal fire. They made a magnificent beginning in understanding what the order of nature is, and what is the relation of its substance to its spirit. They were much nearer in their outlook and their wisdom to the Indians than we are apt to imagine. The Indians meant to be naturalists too ; all serious philosophers must somehow make a naturalism of their chosen elements ; only the Indians were carried away by an

untutored imagination. The Greeks, for their part, also
meant to be discerners of substance like the Indians, and
sharers in the divine life. The object which they believed
in and studied was precisely the same as that which the
Indians felt to be breathing deeply around and within
them : it was the infinite substance and life of things ;
all things not as they appear but as they truly are. This
is the object which animals envisage in their perceptions
from the beginning. The sciences, and all honest speculation, only substitute more refined ideas for the images of
sense, to be descriptions of the same objects which the
images of sense reveal. The notion that the object of
sense is the very image created in sensation, or is an idea
constructed afterwards by the intellect, is an aberration
of confused psychologists ; the intellectual construction,
like the sensuous image, is and is meant to be only a symbol
for the substance, whatever it may be, which confronts
the living being when he eats or looks or frames a
scientific hypothesis. Natural things, in their undiscovered
inner texture, are the only things-in-themselves, and the
object of every practical perception is the thing-in-itself,
whatever its nature may happen to be.

When we enlarge our thoughts, and take in the world,
as it were, at a glance, the object does not become more
metaphysical than when we take common things singly.
The Greeks, too, looked up into the heavens and cried,
" The All is one." It was just what the Indians had said,
shutting their eyes and drinking in an infinite draught of
nothing ; but the outward glance, the docility to fact,
in the Greeks made a new thought of it, and a true one.
What was now discovered was the system of nature ;
the spirit was naturalized in its source ; it was set like a
young plant in its appropriate flowei-pot, where it might
wax and bloom. It did grow there, but not to its primeval
size. These knowing Greeks were not saints and hermits,
like the venerable Indians ; they were merchants, sniffing
travellers, curiosity-hunters, who turned pebbles over and
culled herbs, breeders of animals, or wandering sooth-
sayers with a monkey on their shoulder ; and in naturalizing
the spirit they stultified it. Why should knowledge of the
world make people worldly ? It ought to do the exact

opposite. The Indians had, in their way, a most profound
and mature knowledge of the world ; they knew perfectly
what it could yield to the spirit, and what it was worth.
But lost in their inner experience they invented for nature
what structure they chose, fantastically attenuating and
inflating it as in a dream. Apparently there is not energy
enough in the human intellect to look both ways at once,
and to study the world scientifically whilst living in it
spiritually.

The Greeks in their sanity discovered not only the
natural world but the art of living well in it. Besides
physics they founded ethics and politics. But here again
progress was prevented by the rejection or perversion of
the greater thing in the interests of the lesser. Specu-
latively at least some just conception of the world we live
in, and of our place and destiny there, is more important
than the choice of a definite way of life ; for animals and
man have, quite legitimately, each his own habits and
pleasures, but they all crawl under the same heaven, and
if they think of it at all, they should not blaspheme against
it. The Greek naturalists had conceived nature rightly ;
and their sentiments and maxims, whilst very properly
diverse, had all of them a certain noble frankness in the
presence of the infinite world, of which they begged no
favours. It was precisely these personal sentiments and
maxims, and policy in the government of cities, that
interested the Greeks most ; and the Sophists and Socrates
affected to care nothing about natural science, unless it
could make their pot boil. This utilitarianism was
humorous in Socrates, and in some of the Sophists unprin-
cipled ; but the habit of treating opinions about nature
as rhetorical themes, or as more or less edifying myths,
had disastrous consequences for philosophy. It created
metaphysics. Metaphysics is not merely speculative
physics, in which natural science is extended imaginatively in congruous ways, anticipating what might some
day be discovered. This is what the naturalists had done,
and their theories were simply physical or cosmological.
But after Socrates a theory constructed by reasoning, in
terms of logic, ethics, and a sort of poetic propriety, was
put in the place of physics ; the economy of the human

mind was projected into the universe ; and nature, in the
works of the metaphysicians, held the mirror up to man.
Human nature and the human mind, which were thus made
to rule the world, are in reality a very small incident in
it ; they are proper to one animal ; they are things of
yesterday and perhaps not of to-morrow. This is nothing
against them in their place, as it is nothing against the
daisy that it is humble, nor against the spray of the sea
that its flight is violent and brief. The Platonic, British,
and German schools of philosophy advance our knowledge
of ourselves ; what a pity that they were not content to
cultivate their own gardens, where so many moral fruits
and psychological flowers might be made to grow, but have
insisted that their domestic vegetables are the signs of the
zodiac, and that the universe was made to illustrate their
horticulture !

Taken for what they really are, these humanistic
philosophies express different sides of human nature.
The best (and earliest) is the Platonic, because the side of
human nature which it expresses and fosters is the spiritual
side. Platonic metaphysics projects into the universe the
moral progress of the soul. It is like a mountain lake,
in which the aspirations and passions of a civilized mind
are reflected upside down ; and a certain tremor and
intensity is added to them in that narrower frame, which
they would hardly have in the upper air. This system
renders the life of the soul more unified and more beautiful
than it would otherwise be. Everything becomes magical,
and a sort of perpetual miracle of grace ; the forms which
things wear to the human mind are deputed to be their
substance ; the uses of life become its protecting gods ;
the categories of logic and of morals become celestial
spheres enclosing the earth. A monstrous dream, if you
take it for a description of nature ; but a suitable allegory
by which to illustrate the progress of the inner life : because
those stages, or something like them, are really the stages
of moral progress for the soul.

The British and German philosophies belong to an
analytic phase of reflection, without spiritual discipline,
and their value is merely psychological. Their subject
matter is human knowledge ; and the titles of many of the

chief works of this school confess that this is their only theme. Not moral life, much less the natural world, but simply the articulation of knowledge occupies them ; and yet, by the hocus-pocus of metaphysics, they substitute this human experience for the whole universe in which it arises. The universe is to be nothing but a flux of perceptions, or a will positing an object, or a tendency to feign that there is a world. It would ill become me, a pupil of this philosophy, to deny its profundity. These are the heart-searchings of " a creature moving about in worlds not realized." It is a wonderful thing to spin out in soliloquy, out of some unfathomed creative instinct, the various phases of one's faith and sensibility, making an inventory of one's intellectual possessions, with some notes on their presumable or reported history. I love the lore of the moral antiquary ; I love rummaging in the psychological curiosity shop. The charm of modern life is ambiguous ; it lies in self-consciousness. Egotism has its tender developments ; there is a sort of engaging purity in its perplexities and faithful labours. The German soul has a great volume, and Hamlet is heroic even in his impotence. When in this little glow-worm which we call man there is so much going on, what must not all nature contain in its immensity ? Yet all these advances in analysis and in psychological self-knowledge, far from enriching the modern philosopher and giving him fresh hints for the interpretation of the great world, have been neutralized, under the guise of scepticism, by a total intellectual cramp or by a colossal folly. This thoughtful dog has dropped the substance he held in his mouth, to snatch at the reflection of it which his own mind gave him. It is wonderful with what a light heart, with what self-satisfaction and even boasts, the youngest children of the philosophical family jettison all their heirlooms. Fichte and Nietzsche, in their fervid arrogance, could hardly outdo the mental impoverishment of Berkeley and Hume in their levity : it had really been a sight for the gods to see one of these undergraduates driving matter out of the universe, whilst the other drove out spirit.

49

THE PSYCHE

ENGLISH poetry and fiction have expressed the inner man far better than British philosophy has defined him. He is a hidden spring, a source of bubbling half-thoughts and characteristic actions, and the philosophers have called him a series of ideas. Ideas are rather his weak point. Idealism, on principle, leaves no room for anything latent ; but in a living being, especially in a nice Englishman, what is latent is the chief thing. The vital organs are under the skin and far more complicated, I suspect, than anatomy would lead us to imagine : the case is somewhat as if some giant in remote space should examine the surface of our earth with a glass, measuring its motion round the sun and perhaps round its own axis, but regarding as perfectly inexplicable and unmeaning the coursing of ships, the march of armies and migrations, the change of forests into cornfields, and of cornfields into deserts. So, perhaps, far beyond the reach of any microscope, the politic congregation of atoms within us is busy in its curiously organic and curiously aimless way : sustaining on the whole, until disease or death supervenes, the inter-national peace and commerce of the animal body. How much wireless telegraphy, how many alliances, and how many diplomatic compromises there must be in our system for the human body to live at all ! But psychological philosophers, like children, think the whole economy of life the simplest thing in the world : experience, they say, just *comes* as it does come ; as the boy, asked where he would get the money necessary for all the fine things he said he would do when he was a man, replied, full of empirical wisdom, " Out of my pocket, like papa ! " Experience is the paternal pocket of these philosophers ; they have not discovered the financial system, the life of the body, which fills that minute and precarious reservoir.

It is not only a stronger glass that the remote giant would need to disclose to him the life of the earth ; he would need imagination akin to the human, which such a giant would probably not possess. For suppose anatomy

had done its best or its worst, and had completely mapped
the machinery of the human automaton ; and suppose
at the same time the modern dream-readers and diviners
had unearthed all a man's infant concupiscences and
secret thoughts : there would still be something essential
undiscovered. I do not mean that behind the whole
physical machinery there would be another material
agency, another force or set of events ; nor that besides
the totality of mental discourse, remembered or un-
remembered, there would be more thinking elsewhere :
the hypothesis is that all that exists in these spheres has
been surveyed, and assigned to its place in the evolving
system. What has been so far ignored is something on
another plane of being altogether, which this automatic
life and this mental discourse involve, but do not
contain. It is the *principle* of both and of their relation ;
the system of repetitions, correspondences, developments,
and ideal unities created by this march of human
life in double column. For instance, men are mortal ;
they are born ; they are begotten by sexual fertilization ;
they have a childhood ; their passions and thoughts flow
in a certain general order ; and there are units in the human
world called persons, nations, interests, purposes. I do
not refer to the *ideas* of these things in the mental discourse
of this or that man ; but to the groups or cycles of facts
designated by these ideas. To perceive these groups or
cycles requires a certain type of intelligence : but intelligence does not invent them without cause ; it *finds* the
order which it designates by some word, some metaphor,
or some image.

That this order of human life is something natural, and
not a fiction of discourse, appears in many ways. The
relation of discourse itself to physical life is one proof of it.
Mental discourse is the inner luminosity or speech that
accompanies dramatic crises in the fortunes of the body ;
it is not self-generated ; it is always the *expression* of
another event, then occurring in the body, as is a cry of
pain ; and it is usually, at the same time, a *report* of still
another event that has already occurred beyond the body,
as is a memory or a perception. Feeling and thought are
perpetually interrupted and perpetually renewed by some-

thing not themselves. Their march, logic, and sanity, no less than their existence, translate into mental language an order proper to material events. A sense of comfort is the symptom of a good digestion ; pain expresses a lively discord in the nervous system, and pleasure a lively harmony. When we can scarcely live, because something is stifling us, we hate that thing ; and when we breathe more freely because something approaches, we love it. Spirit everywhere expresses the life of nature, and echoes its endeavours ; but the animal life which prompts these feelings is itself not arbitrary : it passes through a cycle of changes which are pre-ordained. This predetermined, specific direction of animal life is the key to everything moral ; without it no external circumstance could be favourable or unfavourable to us ; and spirit within us would have no reason to welcome, to deplore, or to notice anything. What an anomaly it would seem to a free spirit (if there could be such a thing) that it should care particularly for what happens in the body of some animal, or that it should see one set of facts rather than another, and this in so partial and violent a perspective ! But spirit does, and must, do this ; and it is an absurd and satanic presumption on its part to profess that it could exist, or be a spirit at all, if it were not the spirit of some body, the voice of some animal heart. To have a station in matter, and to have interests in the material world, are essential to spirit, because spirit is life become articulate, experience focussed in thought and dominated ideally ; but experience and life are inconceivable unless an organism with specific capacities and needs finds itself in an environment that stimulates it variously and offers it a conditioned career.

Science as yet has no answer to this most important of all questions, if we wish to understand human nature : namely, How is the body, and how are its senses and passions, determined to develop as they do ? We may reply : Because God wills it so ; or Because such is the character of the human species ; or Because mechanical causes necessitate it. These answers do not increase our scientific understanding in the least ; nevertheless they are not wholly vain : for the first tells us that we must be satisfied with ignorance ; the second that we must be satisfied with the facts ; and the third, which is the most significant, that these facts are analogous in every province of nature. But how close are these analogies ? Mechanism is one habit of matter, and life is another habit of matter ; the first we can measure mathematically and forecast accurately, the second we can only express in moral terms, and anticipate vaguely ; but that the mechanical habit runs through the vital habit, and conditions it, is made obvious by the dependence of life on food, on time, on temperature, by its routine in health and by its diseases, by its end, and above all by its origin ; for it is a habit of matter continuous with other inorganic habits, and (if evolution is true) arising out of them. In any case, life comes from a seed in which it lies apparently dormant and arrested, and from which it is elicited by purely mechanical agencies. On the other hand, the seed reacts on those agencies in a manner as yet inexplicable by what we know of its structure ; and its development closely repeats (though perhaps with some spontaneous variation) the phases proper to the species.

To this mysterious but evident predetermination of normal life by the seed the ancients gave the name of soul ; but to us the word soul suggests a thinking spirit, or even a disembodied one. It is totally incredible that a thinking spirit should exist in the seed, and should plan and carry out (by what instruments ?) the organization of the body ; and if so wise and powerful and independent a spirit lay in us from the beginning, or rather long before our birth, how superfluous a labour to beget us at all, and how unkind of it to dangle after it, in addition to its own intelligence, these poor blundering and troubled thoughts of which alone we are aware ! Evidently the governing principle in seeds is no soul in this modern sense, no thinking moral being ; it is a mysterious habit in matter. Whether this total habit is reducible to minor habits of matter, prevalent in the world at large, is the question debated between mechanical and vitalist psychologists ; but it is a stupid controversy. The smallest unit of mechanism is an event as vital, as groundless, and as creative as it is possible for an event to be ; it summons fresh essences into existence, which the character of the essences previously embodied in existence by no means implied dialectically. On the other hand, the romantic adventure of life, if it is not a series of miracles and catastrophes observed *ex post facto*, must be a resultant of simpler habits struggling or conspiring together. However minute, therefore, or however comprehensive the units by which natural processes are described, they are equally vital and equally mechanical, equally free and (for an observer with a sufficient range of vision) equally predictable. On the human scale of observation it is the larger habits of living beings that are most easily observed ; and the principle of these habits, transmitted by a seed, I call the Psyche : it is either a complex of more minute habits of matter, or a mastering rhythm imposed upon them by the habit of the species. Many Greek philosophers taught that the Psyche was material ; and even Plato, although of course his Psyche might eventually take to thinking, regarded it as primarily a principle of motion, growth, and unconscious government ; so that the associations of the word Psyche are not repugnant, as are those of the word soul, to the meaning I wish to give to it : that habit in matter which forms the human body and the human mind.[1]

There is, then, in every man a Psyche, or inherited nucleus of life, which from its dormant seminal condition

[1] I beg the learned to notice that the Psyche, as I use the term, is not a material atom but a material system, stretching over both time and space ; it is not a monad ; it has not the unity proper to consciousness ; nor is it a mass of " subconscious," mental discourse. The Psyche may be called a substance in respect to mental and moral phenomena which (I think) are based on modes or processes in matter, not on any material particle taken singly ; but the Psyche is not a substance absolutely, since its own substance is matter in a certain arrangement—in other words, body. Matter may be called mind-stuff or psychic substance inasmuch as it can become on occasion the substance of a Psyche, and through the Psyche the basis of mind ; but of course not in the sense that matter may be an aggregate of thinking spirits. Mental events may be called psychic when we consider their origin rather than their essence, as certain pleasures are called material, although pleasures, in being, are all equally spiritual. " Psychic phenomena " are crudely material, and " psychical research " has for its object, not spirits in another world, but the habits of matter that produce apparitions.

expands and awakes anew in each generation, becoming
the person recognized in history, law, and morals. A
man's body is a sort of husk of which his Psyche (itself
material) is the kernel ; and it is out of the predispositions
of this living seed, played upon by circumstances, that his
character and his mind are formed. The Psyche's first
care is to surround itself with outer organs, like a spider
with its web ; only these organs remain subject to her
central control, and are the medium by which she acts
upon outer things, and receives, in her patient labour, the
solicitations and rebuffs of fortune. The Psyche, being
essentially a way of living, a sort of animated code of
hygiene and morals, is a very selective principle : she is
perpetually distinguishing—in action, if not in words—
between good and bad, right and wrong. Choice is the
breath of her nostrils. All the senses, instincts, and passions
are her scouts. The further she extends her influence the
more she feels how dependent she is on external things,
and the more feverishly she tries to modify them, so as
to render them more harmonious with her own impulses.

At first, when she was only a vegetative Psyche, she
waited in a comparatively peaceful mystical torpor for the
rain or the sunshine to foster her, or for the cruel winter
or barbarous scythe to cut her down ; and she never would
have survived at all if breeding had not been her chief
preoccupation ; but she distributed herself so multitudin-
ously and so fast amongst her children, that she has survived to this day. Later, she found a new means of safety
and profit in locomotion ; and it was then that she began
to perceive distinct objects, to think, and to plan her
actions—accomplishments by no means native to her. Like
the Chinese, she is just as busy by night as by day. Long
before sunrise she is at work in her subterranean kitchen
over her pots of stewing herbs, her looms, and her spindles ;
and with the first dawn, when the first ray of intuition
falls through some aperture into those dusky spaces, what
does it light up ? The secret springs of her life ? The
aims she is so faithfully but blindly pursuing ? Far from
it. Intuition, floods of intuition, have been playing for
ages upon human life : poets, painters, men of prayer,
scrupulous naturalists innumerable, have been intent on

their several visions ; yet of the origin and of the end of life we know as little as ever. And the reason is this : that intuition is not a material organ of the Psyche, like a hand or an antenna ; it is a miraculous child, far more alive than herself, whose only instinct is play, laughter, and brooding meditation. This strange child—who could have been his father ?—is a poet ; absolutely useless and incomprehensible to his poor mother, and only a new burden on her shoulders, because she can't help feeding and loving him. He *sees* ; which to her is a mystery, because although she has always acted as if, in some measure, she felt things at a distance, she has never seen and never can see anything. Nor are his senses, for all their vivacity, of any use to her. For what do they reveal to him ? Always something irrelevant : a shaft of dusty light across the rafters, a blue flame dancing on the coals, a hum, a babbling of waters, a breath of heat or of coolness, a mortal weariness or a groundless joy—all dream-images, visions of a play world, essences painted on air, such as any poet might invent in idleness. Yet the child cares about them immensely : he is full of sudden tears and of jealous little loves. " Hush, my child," says good mother Psyche, " it's all nonsense." It is not for those fantastic visions that she watches : she knits with her eyes shut, and mutters her same old prayers. She has always groped amidst obstacles like a mole pressing on where the earth is softest. She can tell friends from enemies (not always correctly) by a mysterious instinct within her, and the rhythm, as it were, of their approaching step. She is long-suffering and faithful, like Penelope ; but when hard-pressed and at bay she becomes fierce. She is terribly absolute then, blindly bent on vengeance and wild destruction. At other times she can melt and be generous ; in her beehive she is not only the congregation of workers, but also the queen. Her stubborn old-womanish temper makes her ordinarily unjust to her best impulses and hypocritical about her worst ones. She is artful but not intelligent, least of all about herself. For this reason she can never understand how she gave birth to such a thankless child. She hardly remembers the warm ray from the sun or from some other celestial source which one day pierced to her heart, and begat there this strange uneasiness, this truant joy, which we call thought. Seeing how quick and observant the brat is, she sometimes sends him on errands ; but he loiters terribly on the way, or loses it altogether, forgets what he was sent for, and brings home nothing but strange tales about Long-noses and Helmets-of-gold, whom he says he has encountered. He prefers the poppies to the corn, and half the mushrooms he picks are of the poisonous variety ; he sometimes insists on setting apart his food for imaginary beings called the dead or the gods ; and worst of all, he once ravished and married a fairy, whom he called Truth ; and he wished to bring her to live with him at home. At that, good mother Psyche naturally put her foot down. No hussies here ! Yet there are moments when she relents, when her worn old hands rest in her lap, when she remembers and wonders, and two cold tears trickle down from her blind eyes. What is the good of all her labour ? Has it all been, perhaps, for his sake, that he might live and sing and be happy ? Even in her green days, in her cool vegetable economy, there had been waste ; she had unwittingly put forth flowers she could not see and diffused a fragrance that eluded her. Now her warmer heart has bred this wilder, this diviner folly : a wanton sweetness shed by her longer travail and a flower of her old age. But he forgets her in his selfishness, and she can never, never understand him.

50

REVERSION TO PLATONISM

I HEAR that Oxford is reading Plotinus—a blessed change from Hegel. The pious mind is still in the age of mythology ; science has confused its own lessons, for want of a philosopher who should understand them ; and what matters, so long as the age of mythology lasts, is that the myths that occupy the fancy should be wise and beautiful, and should teach men to lay up their treasures in heaven. The philosophy of Plotinus does this, and does it magnificently. Like that of Plato and of Aristotle it is little more

than a rhetorical inversion or perpetual metaphor, expressing the aim of life under the figure of a cosmos which is
animate and which has already attained its perfection.
Considering the hurried life which we are condemned to
lead, and the shifting, symbolic ideas to which we are
confined, it seems hardly worth while to quarrel with such
inspired fabulists, or to carp at the cosmic dress in which
they present their moralities.   Gentle, secluded, scholastic
England does well to platonize.   It had never ceased to do
so.   In spite of the restiveness, sometimes, of barbarian
blood, in spite of Hebraic religion and Germanic philosophy, the great classical tradition has always been seated
here ; and England has shared, even if with a little reserve
and mistrust, in the ecclesiastical, courtly, military, and
artistic heritage of Europe.   A genuine child of the past,
who is bred to knowledge of the world, and does not plunge
into it greedily like a stranger, cannot worship the world ;
he cannot really be a snob.   Those who have profited by
a long life cannot possibly identify the divine life with
the human.   They will not be satisfied with a philosophy
that is fundamentally worldly, that cannot lift up its heart
except pragmatically, because the good things are hanging
from above, or because the long way round by righteousness
and the ten commandments may be the shortest cut to
the promised land.   Their love of wisdom will not be merely
provisional, nor their piety a sort of idyllic interlude,
penitent but hopeful, comforting itself with the thought
that the sour grapes will soon be ripe, and oh, so delicious !
They will not remember the flesh-pots of Egypt with an
eternal regret, and the flesh-pots of Berlin and New York
will not revive their appetite.

Spirit is not an instrument but a realization, a fruition.
At every stage, and wherever it peeps out through the
interstices of existence, it is a contemplation of eternal
things.   Eternal things are not other material things by
miracle existing for ever in another world ; eternal things
are the essences of all things here, when we consider what
they are in themselves and not what, in the world of fortune,
they may bring or take away from us personally.   That is
why piety and prayer are spiritual, when they cease to be
magic operations or efforts of a celestial diplomacy : they

lead us into the eternal world. Platonism is a great window in the same direction. It is well to open it afresh. I should not say of the typical Englishman, any more than of the typical Greek, that he was spiritual ; both are healthy, and the spirit in them is not so developed as to sickly o'er their native hue with the pale cast of thought, nor to surround their heads with any visible aureole of consuming fire. Yet I think that their very health saves them both from worldliness : for life would not be healthy and free, but diseased and slavish, if it were ultimately turned only towards its instruments and to the pressing need of keeping itself going ; a life so employed would not be worth living, and a healthy spirit would abandon it. The normal Englishman, like the normal Greek, is addressed to spiritual things, even if distantly ; so that when for any reason his spiritual life is intensified, he will create or adopt a spiritual philosophy, like that of Plotinus. His inner man is selective ; he is accustomed not to accept unquestioningly the suasion of custom and not to tremble before material grandeur. He is an explorer ; he has some notion of the extent and variety of nature, with enough appreciative contempt for its tropical splendours, moral and geographical ; it is with a clear inward satisfaction, even if with some grumbling of the flesh, that he turns his back upon them for the sake of his sweet, separate, cool, country life at home. He loves the earth, not the world. His ideal is that people everywhere should be steady and happy, in their way, as he is in his ; and if he feels some glow at the power and influence of his country, or the spread of his religion, it is not because he covets domination or a Roman grandiloquent greatness, but because he feels that when others take to his ways he will be safer in them himself, and the world more decent. He wishes to be free, free to choose his walks, his friends, his thoughts, his employments ; and this freedom, although it may be employed only on commonplace and earthly things, is the very principle of spirituality, and a beginning in it.

What spirituality is when developed fully may be seen clearly in the system of Plotinus. It is a system of morals inverted and turned into a cosmology ; everything in his magic universe is supposed to be created and moved by

the next higher being, to which by nature it aspires : so
that life everywhere is a continual prayer, and if it cannot
actually shake off its fetters and take wing into a higher
sphere, at least it imitates and worships the forms which
beckon to it from there. All this is a true allegory ; if
any one takes it for natural science he must think it a
very poor speculation ; because if the higher thing in each
instance were really the *source* of the lower, it never could
have determined the time, place, number, distribution, or
imperfection of its copies ; and the whole drama of creation,
in everything except its tendency and meaning, must be
due to specific and various predispositions in matter, for
which this system, in its scientific impotence, has forgotten
to make room. It would be easy, however, to supply
this defect. We might start, as nature actually did, at
the bottom, and pass at once to the level at which the
Psyche, having organized the vital functions of the human
animal, begins to ask itself what it is living for. The
answer is not, as an unspiritual philosophy would have it :
In order to live on. The true answer is : In order to
understand, in order to see the Ideas. Those Ideas which
the Psyche is able and predestined to discern are such as
are illustrated or suggested by its own life, or by the
aspects which nature presents to it. Each Idea will be
the ideal of something with which the Psyche is naturally
conversant ; but the good of all these psychic labours
will lie precisely in clarifying and realizing that ideal.
To envisage and clearly to discern the Idea of what we are
about is the whole of art, spiritually considered ; it is all
the mind can or need do ; and the more singly the spirit
is rapt in the meaning and vision of the work, the more
skilfully the hand and the tongue will perform it. And
the standard and criterion of their skill is in turn precisely
the same vision of the Idea : for, I ask, what makes an
action or a feeling right, except that it clears away obstruc-
tions and brings us face to face with the thing we love ?
The whole of natural life, then, is an aspiration after the
realization and vision of Ideas, and all action is for the sake
of contemplation.

Plato and Aristotle had been satisfied to stop at this
stage ; but Plotinus carries us one step further. What is

the good of seeing the Ideas ? I do not ask, of course, what is its utility, because we have left that behind, but what is the nature of the excellence which various Ideas seem to have in common, like beauty, or affinity with the harmonious and perfected life of the Psyche. Plotinus says that what lends excellence to the Ideas is the One ; and I cannot connect—perhaps we ought not to connect—any idea with those words. But by looking at the matter naturalistically perhaps we may discover whence the excellence of Ideas and of the vision of them actually flows. It flows from health, which is a unity of function, and it flows from love, which is an emotional unity pervading that function, and suffusing its object, when it comes before the mind, with beauty and inexpressible worth. Here, if I am not mistaken, we have the key to the whole mystery, both in Plotinus and in Plato. The One or the Good is the mythical counterpart of moral harmony in the spirit ; it is the principle by which the Ideas were disentangled from the detail of experience and the flux of objects, and it is again the principle by which the Ideas themselves are consecrated, illumined, and turned into forms of Joy.

Spirituality, then, lies in regarding existence merely as a vehicle for contemplation, and contemplation merely as a vehicle for joy. Epicurus was far more spiritual than Moses. But Epicurus could free the spirit only in the presence of the simplest things ; the universe terrified him, quite without reason, so that his spirituality was fumbling, timid, and sad. For Plotinus the universe had no terrors ; he liked to feel himself consumed and burning in the very heart of the sun, and poured thence in a flood of light from sphere to sphere. We, in this remote shore of time, may catch that ray and retrace it ; it will lead us into good company.

51

IDEAS

How comes it that the word Idea, so redolent of Platonism, has been the fulcrum on which British philosophy has turned in its effort to dislodge Platonism from its foundations, and to lay bare the positive facts ? The vicissitudes of words are instructive ; they show us what each age understood or forgot in the wisdom of its predecessors, and what new things it discovered to which it gave the old names. The beauty which Plato and the English saw in Ideas was the same beauty ; they both found in Ideas the immediate, indubitable object of knowledge. And nevertheless, hugging the same certitude, they became sure of entirely different things.

The word Idea ought to mean any theme which attention has lighted up, any aesthetic or logical essence, so long as it is observed in itself or used to describe some ulterior existence. Amid a thousand metaphysical and psychological abuses of the term this purely ideal signification sometimes reappears in polite speech ; for instance when Athalie says, in Racine :

> J'ai deux fois, en dormant, revu la même idée.

Here, perhaps by chance, the word is used with absolute propriety and its chief implications are indicated. An Idea is something seen, an *immediate* presence ; it is something seen in a dream, or *imaginary* ; and it is the same Idea when seen a second time, or a *universal*. That universals are present to intuition was the secret of Plato ; yet it is the homeliest of truths. It comes to seem a paradox, or even inconceivable, because people suppose they see what they believe they are looking at, which is some particular thing, the object of investigation, of desire, and of action ; they overlook the terms of their thought, as they overlook the perspective of the landscape. These terms, which are alone immediate, are all universals. Belief—the expectation, fear, or sense of events hidden or imminent—precedes clear perception ; but it is supposed to be derived from it. Perception without belief would be mere intuition of Ideas, and no belief in things or ulterior events could ever be based on it. A seraph who should know only Ideas would be incapable of conceiving any fact, or noting any change, or discovering his own spiritual existence ; he would be mathematics actualized, a landscape self-composed, and love spread like butter. The human mind, on the contrary, is the expression of an animal life, swimming hard in the sea of matter. It begins by being the darkest belief and the most helpless discomfort, and it proceeds gradually to relieve this uneasiness and to tincture this blind faith with more and more luminous Ideas. Ideas, in the discovery of facts, are only graphic symbols, the existence and locus of the facts thus described being posited in the first place by animal instinct and watchfulness. If we suspend these eager explorations for a moment, and check our practical haste in understanding the material structure of things and in acting upon them, it becomes perfectly obvious that the data of actual intuition are sounds, figures, movements, landscapes, stories—all universal essences appearing, and perhaps reappearing, as in a trance.

I think that Plato in his youth must have seen his Ideas with this mystical directness, and must have felt the irritation common to mystics at being called back out of that poetic ecstasy into the society of material things. Those essences were like the gods, clear and immortal, however fugitive our vision of them might be ; whereas things were in their inmost substance intricate and obscure and treacherously changeable ; you could never really know what any of them was, nor what it might become. The Ideas were our true friends, our natural companions, and all our safe knowledge was of them ; things were only vehicles by which Ideas were conveyed to us, as the copies of a book are vehicles for its sense.

Nevertheless, the happy intuition of pure essences of all sorts, as life vouchsafes it to the free poet or to the logician, could not satisfy the heart of Plato. He felt the burden, the incessant sweet torment, of the flesh ; and when age —as I think we may detect in the changed tone of his thoughts—relieved him of this obsession, which had been also his first inspiration, it only reinforced an obsession of a different kind, the indignation of an aristocrat and the sorrow of a patriot at the doom which hung visibly over his country. The fact that love intervened from the be-ginning in Plato's vision of the Ideas explains why his Ideas were not the essences actually manifested in ex-perience, as it comes to the cold eye or the mathematical brain. When love looks, the image is idealized ; it does

not show the obvious, but the dreamt-of and the desired.
Platonism is not pure intuition, but intuition charged with
enthusiasm. Then, to reinforce this mystification of the
Ideas by love, there was the passionate political impulse
to contrast the form things actually wore with that which
they ought to have worn. This double moral bias, of love
and of hate, with its dismissal of almost all given essences
as not the right essences, produced the curious hierarchy of
Platonic Ideas ; themes belonging to the realm of essence
by their ontological texture or mode of being, yet clinging,
like a faithful shadow or simplified echo, to the morphology
of earthly things. The poet in Plato had been entrapped
by the moralist, and the logician enslaved by the legislator.
He turned away from the disinterested vision of the Ideas
in their endless variety ; he lost, he almost blushed to have
possessed, the genial faculty of his anonymous ancestors,
the creators of mythology, who could see gods in all things.
He cultivated instead the art of a nearer progenitor of his,
Solon, and attempted to make laws for Athens, for mankind, and even for the universe. He did it admirably ;
the *Timaeus,* his book on nature, is a beautiful myth, and
his book on the *Laws* is a monument of wisdom. But Plato
had grown forgetful of the Ideas, and of the life of intuition ; his gaze had become sad, troubled, and hopeless ;
he was preoccupied with making existence safe. But
how should existence be safe ? How should those tiny
nut-shells—his walled city and his walled cosmos—keep
afloat for ever in this rolling sea of vagueness and
infinity ?

When breeding or conscience suppresses a man's genius,
his genius often takes its revenge and reasserts itself, by
some indirection, in the very system that crushed it. This
happened to paganism when, being stamped out by Christianity, it turned Christianity into something half pagan.
It happened also to Plato when, the world having distracted
him from his Ideas, he made a supernatural world out of
them, to govern and correct this nether world, in which he
was forced to live. To say that Ideas govern the world is
safe and easy, if these Ideas are merely names for the forms
which the world happens to wear. Nature is bound to
present some Idea or other to the mind ; but the Ideas it

presents actually will be only a few, and not the most welcome, since this world is a most paradoxical, odd, and picturesque object, and not at all the sort of world which the human mind (being a highly specialized part of it) would have made or can easily believe to be real. The Ideas which a philosopher says govern the world are not likely to be its true laws ; and, if he has really drawn them from observation, they cannot possibly be all, nor the best, Ideas on which his free mind would have chosen to dwell. The truth, which is a standard for the naturalist, for the poet is only a stimulus ; and in many an idealist the poet debauches the naturalist, and the naturalist paralyses the poet. The earth might well upbraid Plato for trying to build his seven - walled cloud - castle on her back, and to circumscribe her in his magic circles. Why should she be forbidden to exhibit any other essences than those authorized by this metaphysical Solon ? Why should his impoverished Olympian theology be imposed upon her, and all her pretty dryads and silly fauns, all her harpies and chimeras, be frowned upon and turned into black devils ? How these people who would moralize nature hate nature ; and if they loved nature, how sweetly and firmly would morality take its human place there without all this delusion and bluster ! But I am not concerned so much with the violence done by Plato to nature ; nature can take care of herself, and being really the mother even of the most waspish philosopher, with his sting and his wings and his buzzing, she can comfortably find room for him and his system amongst her swarming children. I wish I knew if the real wasps, too, have a philosophy, and what it is ; probably as vital and idealistic as that of the Germans. But I am grieved rather at the servitude and at the stark aspect imposed on the Platonic Ideas by their ambition to rule the world. They are like the shorn Samson in the treadmill ; they have lost the radiance and the music of Phoebus Apollo. Socrates taught that to do wrong is to suffer harm ; and his Ideas, in establishing their absurd theocracy over nature, were compelled to bend their backs to that earth - labour, and to become merely a celestial zoology, a celestial grammar, and a celestial ethics. Heaven had stooped to rule the earth, and the crooked features of the earth had cast their grotesque shadow on heaven.

This is the first chapter in the sad history of Ideas. Now for the second.

The honest Englishman does not care much for Ideas, because in his labour he is occupied with things and in his leisure with play, or with rest in a haze of emotional indolence : but finding himself, for the most part, deep in the mess of business, he is heartily desirous of knowing the facts ; and when, in his scrupulous inquiry into the facts, he finds at bottom only Ideas, and is constrained to become a philosopher against his will, he contrives, out of those very Ideas, to elicit some knowledge of fact. Ideas are not intrinsically facts, but suppositions ; they are descriptions offering themselves officiously as testimonials for facts whose character remains problematical, since, if there were no such facts, the Ideas would still be the same ; yet, says the melancholy Jaques to himself, " Is it not a fact that I have made this dubious supposition ? Am I not entertaining this Idea ? This sad but undeniable experience of mine, not the fact which I sought nor the Idea which I found, is the actual fact, and the undeniable existence." Thus the occurrence of any experience, or the existence of any illusion, assumes the names both of fact and of idea in his vocabulary, and the existence of ideas becomes the corner-stone of his philosophy.

The most candid and delightful of English philosophers (who was an Irishman) was Berkeley. In his ardent youth, like Plato, he awoke to pure intuition : he saw Ideas, or at least he saw that he did not see material things ; but instead of studying these Ideas for their own sake with a steadier gaze, he took up the disputatious notion of denying that material things existed at all, because he could not *see* them. It was a great simplification ; and if he had not had conventional and apologetic axes to grind, he might have reached the radical conclusion, familiar to Indian sages, that nothing could exist at all, least of all himself. Language, however, and the Cartesian philosophy, made it easy for him to assume that of course he existed, since he saw these Ideas ; and he was led by a malicious demon to add, that the Ideas existed too, since he saw them, so long as they were visible to him. But if he existed only in that he saw the Ideas, and the Ideas existed in that he saw them, was there any difference at all between himself seeing and the Ideas seen ? None, I am afraid : so that he himself, whom he had proudly called a spirit, would be in truth only a series of ideas (I spell them now with a small *i*), and the ideas—in which he had not stopped to recognize eternal essences—would be only the pulses of his fugitive existence.

Here is substance for an excellent ironical system of the universe, such as some philosopher in Greece might have espoused ; a flux of absolute intensive existences, variously coloured and more or less warm, like the sparks of a rocket. Some scientific philosopher in our day or in the future may be tempted to work out this system, and it might have been the true one. But I see an objection to it from the point of view of British philosophy, which covets knowledge of fact. The philosopher conceiving this system, if the system was true, would be only one of those sparks ; he could have no idea except the idea which he was ; the whole landscape before him would be but the fleeting nature of himself. Although, therefore, by an infinitely improbable accident, his philosophy might be true, he could have no reason to think it true, and no possibility of not thinking it so. A genuine sceptic might be satisfied with this result, enjoying each moment of his being, and laughing at his own perpetual pretension of knowing anything further. And since extremes meet, such a mocking sceptic might easily become, like Plato, a lover of pure Ideas. If he really abandons all claims, all hopes, all memory which is more than fantasy, and simply enjoys the illusion of the moment, he dwells on an Idea, which is all that an illusion can supply. The immediate has a mystical charm ; it un-veils some eternal essence, and the extreme of renunciation, like a sacrificial death, brings a supreme security in another sphere. Berkeley and Hume were little more than boys when they fell in love with Ideas ; perhaps, if we knew their personal history, we should find that they were little children when they first did so, and that pure Essence was the Beatrice that had secretly inspired all their lives. But though they were youths of genius, there was a touch in

them of the prig ; the immediate, dear as it is to fresh and
honest hearts, was too unconventional for them legally to
wed and to take home, as it were, to their worldly relations.
In England to love Ideas is to sow one's intellectual wild
oats. There may be something healthy and impetuous in
that impulse which is engaging ; but it must not go too
far, and above all it must not be permanent. The British
philosopher dips into idealism in order to reform belief, to
get rid of dangerous shams or uncongenial dogmas, not for
the sake of pure intuition or instant assurance. He wishes
to remove impediments to action ; he hates great remote
objects as he hates popery and policy ; imposing things
are impositions. Better get rid, if possible, of substance
and cause and necessity and abstractions and self and
consciousness. The purpose is to reduce everything to
plain experience of fact, and to rest neither in pure intuition
nor in external existences. For instance, he has two arguments against the existence of matter which he finds
equally satisfactory : one that matter cannot exist because
he can form no idea of it, and the other that matter cannot
exist because it is merely an idea which he forms. He
descends to the immediate only for the sake of the ulterior,
for the immediate in some other place. If he found himself
reduced to essences actually given now, he would be terribly
unhappy, and I am sure would renounce philosophy as a
bad business, as he did in the person of Hume, his most
profound representative.

Thus European speculation, like the Athalie of Racine,
has twice in its dreams beheld the same Ideas ; but like
that uneasy heroine it has been troubled by the sight, and
has stretched out its arms to grasp the painted shadow.
The first time, instead of Ideas, it found a celestial hierarchy
of dominations and powers, a bevy of magic influences,
angels, and demons. The second time, instead of Ideas,
it found an irrevocable flux of existing feelings, without
cause, purpose, connection, or knowledge. Perhaps if on
a third occasion the Ideas visited a less burdened and preoccupied soul, that could look on them without apprehension, they might be welcomed for their fair aspect and for
the messages they convey from things, without being, in
their own persons, either deified or materialized.

52

THE MANSIONS OF HELEN

CONCERNING the visions which men have of the gods there is much uncertainty. It is written that no man can see God and live ; but I think some evil god or evil man must be spoken of, and that they come nearer to the truth who say that the vision of God brings perfect happiness. I suspect this is true in a humbler and more familiar sense than is intended in discourses about the state of the soul in heaven ; for there is a heaven above every place, and the soul mounts to it in all its thoughts and actions, when these are perfect. I incline also to another opinion, which would surprise those religious friends of mine who call me an atheist ; namely, that whenever we see anything, we have, or might have if we chose, a partial vision of God, and a moment of happiness. For all experience comes to us fatally, from an alien source which in physics is called matter, in morals power or will, and in religion God ; so that by his power (as I learned when a child in my Spanish catechism) God is present in everything. The same authority added (and how full of meaning that word is to me now !) that he was also present in everything by his essence ; since what is brought unimpeachably before us in any vision is some essence which, being absolutely indestructible, is in that respect divine. It is indestructible because, if all trace and memory of it were destroyed, it would in that very obscuration vindicate its essential identity, since not *it*, but only things different from *it*, would now exist. Every essence, therefore, lies eternally at the very foundations of being, and is a part of the divine immutability and necessity ; an intrinsic feature in that Nous or Logos which theologians tell us is the second hypostasis of the divine nature. Yet to say that we see God when we see him only in part is perhaps hazardous and open to objection, because a part of anything, separated from the rest, becomes a different being, qualitatively and numerically ; and it will be better to speak of our visions as visions of angels or messengers or demigods, having one divine parent and one human. In everything, if we regard it as it is in itself, and not selfishly, we may find an incarnation or manifestation of deity.

How the divinity of our daily visitants shines out at certain moments and then again is obscured by our practical haste and inattention, is admirably expressed in the history of Helen. Her birth was miraculous, and yet quaintly natural, for her father Zeus, having taken the form of a swan when he wooed her mother Leda, she was hatched from a great white egg ; and there was always something swanlike in the movements of her neck, in the composure of her carriage, as if borne on still waters, in the scarcely flushed marble of her skin, and in the lightness and amplitude of her floating garments. She was hardly of this world, and it seemed almost a desecration to have wedded her to any mortal. Yet she offered no resistance to love ; it was indifferent to her whom she might enamour, or into what nest of robbers she might be carried by force. Was it not violence, she said to herself, to exist on earth at all ? What mattered a shade more or less of violence ? If she remained in a manner chaste and inviolate, it was only because she was too beautiful to tempt the lusts of men. Neither of her two husbands loved or understood her. Menelaus because he was a dullard, and Paris because he was a rake, approached her as they would have approached any other woman, and they found no great pleasure in her society. Yet wherever she appeared, every one stopped talking and was motionless ; and she was worshipped by all who saw her pass at a distance. Supreme beauty is foreign everywhere, yet everywhere has a right of domicile ; it opens a window to heaven, and is a cause of suspended animation and, as it were, ecstatic suicide in the heart of mortals.

Helen passed her childhood dazed, but with a pleasing wonder, because she loved her brothers, and they, absorbed though they were habitually in their violent sports, were tender to her. When they died, how gladly would she have followed them and become the third star with them in heaven ! But she found herself married to Menelaus the king ; and this her first mansion at Sparta, the narrowest of citadels, was far from happy. The palace was a great

farm-house, and the talk in it was all of harvests and
cattle and horses and wars. The men were boors, and their
scruples about sacrifices and auguries annoyed her; being
half divine, she felt no need for religion. " What advantage
is it," she said in her thoughts, " to be a queen when I
am a prisoner, or to be called beautiful where nobody
looks at me."

Accordingly it was with a vague hope and a secret
desire for vengeance that she heard of the approach of a
brilliant stranger, from a far more populous and flourishing
city than Sparta, who came with gifts and a glib tongue
to view the wonders of the island world. When his eyes
fell on her, his unfeigned surprise filled her with exultation.
To be so discerned, for her, was to be won. Those eyes
could recognize divinity. No doubt he was preparing new
fetters for her and new sorrows, but for a moment she
would be free, and in following him she would feel herself
once more the goddess.

In fact, so long as they sailed the dark-purple sea, or
rested in caves or in island bowers, all was pleasantness
between them. Their very galley, with its white sails
spread, took on something of Helen's beauty, and seemed
a cloud wafted across the Aegean, or the swan, her father,
riding on the rippled reaches of the Meander. Paris
proved a candid and light-hearted lover; never vexed,
he was all grace and mastery in small matters: one of those
lordly travellers who can feel the charm of nature and of
woman in every clime, however exotic, however pure, or
however impure; and the incomparable Helen seemed
indeed incomparable to his practised mind. He adored
her, but he preferred other women. Moreover, she found
that at Troy he counted for nothing. He moved amid
battles and councils, quite at home in the scene, but never
consulted; a prince turned shepherd, a familiar but superfluous ornament, like a fop or a ballet-dancer that everybody smiled upon and nobody respected. It was given
him in the end to slay the redoubtable Achilles with a
chance arrow, Apollo secretly directing the shaft, but he
was no warrior. It was a useless triumph, as his abduction
of Helen had been an innocent crime: both were the work
of gods laughing at human arrogance. There were doubt-

less street rhetoricians in Ilium who upbraided Paris and
Helen, as there are reasoning philosophers and politicians
to-day who attribute the ascendancy or decay of nations
to the ideas that prevail there, forgetting to ask why
those particular ideas have been embraced by those
peoples, when all ideas, in the universal market, are to
be had gratis. The wise old Priam and his counsellors
knew better. They did not disown Paris for his escapade,
as they might so easily have done, nor did they return Helen
to her wronged husband, useless as she was at Troy. They
knew that the confused battles of earth must be fought
over some nominal prize ; men and animals will always
be fighting for something, not because the thing is
necessarily of any value to them, but *because* they wish
to snatch it from one another. Helen had lent her name
and image to colour an ancient feud, and make articulate
the dull eternal contention between Asia and Europe.
It was for existence that each party was fighting ; but it
added to their courage and self-esteem to say they were
fighting for beauty, and that the victory of their side would
be a victory for the gods. But the gods were in both camps,
and in neither, as in her heart was Helen herself. In her
isolation, her conscience sometimes reproached her, and
she wondered that she never heard these reproaches from
the lips of others. Hector and Priam and the other old
men, even the queen and the gossiping women, treated
her with deference ; but they cared only for Troy and for
their own affairs. If less beset than in her strict old home,
she was more neglected in these spacious palaces, and no
less melancholy. Was it a miracle of generosity that
nobody blamed her, or was it a supreme proof of indifference,
that standing in the centre of the stage she remained unheeded ? Was she so much a goddess that they thought
her a statue ? Would she be borne away by the victors
like an inert Palladium, to be set up elsewhere on a new
pedestal ? She did not understand that it is not the
vision that men have of the gods that works their safety
or ruin, but that fatal maladjustments, or natural vigour
in them, in shaping their destiny, call that vision down.
Nor is it an idle vision ; for the sight turns the dreary
length of their misery into a tragedy flashing with light

and tears ; and the presence of Helen on those beleaguered walls, which might have irritated the foolish, consoled the wise. She was not the cause of their danger nor of their coming disaster, as she had not been the cause of the harsh virtues of her Spartan clan ; but as those harsh virtues had created her beauty, so the wealth and exuberant civilization of Ilium had recognized it, and made it their own ; and she was a glory to both nations, for not every city, of all the cities that perish, has had a queen like her.

When Troy fell at last, when Hector and Paris and Priam were dead, and Aeneas had escaped just in time, she waited, impassible, at the gate of the smoking acropolis, neither glad nor sorry, not ashamed to see her first husband again and his shouting friends—for she despised them— nor unwilling to be removed, as it were, into the evening shadow of her old queenliness. Something told her that in her second life at Sparta she would be more feared and more respected ; in her advancing age and intangible isolation she would be as a priestess whom no one—not even Menelaus—would dare to approach. Her crime would be her protection ; her rebellion, proudly acknowledged and never retracted in spirit, would lift her above all mankind. Even while still in this world, she would belong to the other.

There is an obscure rumour that after the fall of Troy Helen never returned to Sparta but was spirited away to Egypt, whilst a mere phantasm resembling her accompanied her dull husband back to his dull fastness by the pebbly Eurotas. This turn given to the fable hints darkly at the unearthly truth. Helen was a phantom always and everywhere ; so long as men fought for her, taking her image, as it were, for their banner, she presided over a most veritable and bloody battle ; but when the battle ceased of itself, and all those heroes that had seen and idolized her were dead, the cerulean colours of that banner faded from it ; the shreds of it rotted indistinguish- ably in the mire, and the hues that had lent it for a moment its terrible magic fled back into the ether, where wind and mist, meteors and sunbeams, never cease to weave them. The passing of Helen was the death of Greece, but Helen herself is its immortality. Yet why seek to interpret the

parable ? There is more depth of suggestion in these
ancient myths than in any abstract doctrine which we
may substitute for them. Homer and his companions
certainly were not writing intentional allegories ; but
they had a sense for beauty and a sense for the flux of
things, and in those two perceptions the whole philosophy
of Ideas is latent. Sight, thought, love arrest essences ;
and time, perpetually undermining the existence that
brings those essences before us, drives them, as fast as we
can arrest them, like a sort of upward flaw, back into
heaven.

53

THE JUDGEMENT OF PARIS

I DO not conceive the Judgement of Paris as Rubens has
painted it : an agricultural labourer leering at three fat
women of the town who have gone into the country for a
lark. This disrobing of goddesses, though there may be
some ancient authority for it, does not conform to my
principles of exegesis, and I pronounce it heretical.
Goddesses cannot disrobe, because their attributes are
their substance. They are like the images of the Virgin
in Spanish churches ; if you are so ill-advised, you may
take off their crown, their veils, and their stiffly embroidered
conical mantle ; but what will remain will not be our
Lady either of Mercies or of Sorrows, but a pole, with a
doll's head and two hands attached. The spell lies in the
ornaments, because they alone are symbolical and richly
mysterious. Similarly the virtue of those pagan goddesses
did not lie in what each might be in herself, either as a
conscious spirit or as a beautiful titanic body endowed
with free and immortal life ; their relevant virtue was
tutelary, and lay in their patronage of particular crafts
or passions in man. For this reason it was not absurd
that they should be rivals in beauty. Of course in itself
every nature, celestial or even earthly, is incomparable
and perfect in its own way. But goddesses may well
compete for the prize of beauty in the eyes of a mortal ;
it is not their persons that he sees or can see, but their

gifts ; and it is inevitable and right that these should not attract him equally. The Judgement of Paris is essentially like the Choice of Hercules, a moral choice and an expression of character. Only Paris was not asked to choose between good and evil, but between different goods ; his three goddesses were rivals like competing nations or religions : they proposed to him contrasted pursuits and forms of experience, such as each was wont to secure for her votaries. Their offers were not bribes, but tests ; and yet the suspicion is quite justified that they were tempting him ; because in fact none of them had true happiness to give. They represented interests, not reason ; each secretly felt the weakness of her own cause, and wished to have her claims to superiority (which she knew to be false) confirmed before the world, even by the suffrage of fools. A bad conscience loves to be flattered and reassured ; company consoles it for loss of honour. That is why these assiduous goddesses run to every youth and whisper their soft eloquence in his ear.

Methinks I see Juno appearing in a sunlit cloud, with a diadem of stars, and clothed in a floating garment which Minerva had so cunningly woven that when seen in a certain light (in which Juno saw it) it represented the labours of Hercules, but from any other angle all the colours (which were those of the peacock) shifted their places and represented the treacheries of Jupiter. She bore the model of a city girt with seven walls, every gate, bastion, and battlement complete, and in the midst of the towering acropolis a great temple, doubtless that of Juno, surrounded by smaller temples for the other gods. Raising a white and queenly hand, as if in warning or in blessing, she spoke as follows :

" I will give thee dominion over the world and over thyself, if thou wilt first deliver up thyself and the world into my keeping. I am skilled in the governance of men, and my ancient laws, though they seem hard, bring discipline into their lives, and fortify them in seemly habits of labour and holiness."

" Perhaps," Paris replied, " if the other gods cannot offer me freedom, I might accept from thee a noble servitude."

Minerva took heart at these words, thinking herself nothing if not emancipated, and interposed her form, shining in its golden armour, yet obscured by the azure light of her eyes. " I will give thee," she cried, " philosophy natural, moral, logical, and rhetorical. I will endue thy mind with a perfect image of the spheres musically enclosing the earth. Thou shalt possess knowledge of all genera and species of animals, herbs, seeds, gestations, and diseases. All measures and proportions, both of numbers and of forms, shall be clear to thee as the light of day. The arts of tillage and planting and mining and weaving and building—all save trade and voyages, forbidden to a good man—shall have no secrets for thee : to the advantage of thy fellow-citizens, if ever they should choose thee for their legislator."

" Perhaps," Paris again answered, " when I grow weary of being a shepherd, I may not disdain to become a philosopher. It is a better pastime for old age. But as I am no shepherd in reality, but a prince, dwelling on Mount Ida in this vernal season for pleasure and for the sake of these rural sights and savours of solitude, so later I should be no sophist with illusions ; I should merely entertain my wintry leisure with the fictions of the learned, as a prince may : for they are other pictures."

Venus, whose marble nakedness was not remarked, so divine was it and so constitutional, smiled to hear the youth say this, because it was what she secretly approved, and she added disdainfully : " Thou art wise enough already in the use of words ; but what hast thou tasted of experience ? Consider the gift I can give thee : Possession of the Immediate. Is not this the best ? "

" Yes," he replied, smiling in return, " but I have that in any case."

It might seem that this version of the Judgement of Paris errs in not giving a clear victory to Venus and in saying nothing of Helen ; but such a reproach would be hasty. Possession of the Immediate had always seemed to Paris the highest, if not the only, good, as his bucolic life and pastoral amusements could prove : and when the heart has chosen, it is not necessary to express in words the preference for a deity so clearly favoured. To real shep-

herds, born and bred on the mountain-side, Arcadia is full
of dirt, hardship, and poverty ; sunrise and sunset are
heavy to them ; they fatten their sheep in order to shear
and to slaughter them, and they love a green pasture
because it fattens the sheep. So too the eclogues of town
poets, and the toy Arcadias of Versailles or of the carnival,
in their satin slippers and gilded crooks, are a forced
labour, and tedious ; at best a new masquerade in which
the jaded may continue to make love. But there is a
poetic Arcadia none the less, the real Arcadia mirrored in
a contemplative mind. Idle vision neither is what it looks
at, nor apes it : it is infinitely other, yet in looking forgets
itself, and lends its heart gladly to the spectacle. Paris
shirked none of the labours or bestialities of the country
swain ; with a semi-divine tolerance he relished those
rough sports and those monotonous pipings : anything a
creature can love, some god finds lovable. He tussled
with those wenches, and the crude scent of those smoking
kettles did not turn his stomach. Had it been less mal-
odorous at court ? Was there not more freedom, more
laughter, and greater plenty here ? If Paris was not a
hero, at least he was not a snob. He was a truant prince,
a fop become a shepherd, with a body and a mind capable
of great things, but doing easy things from choice. In his
very softness, since it was voluntary, there was a kind of
strength, the strength of indifference, and freedom, and
universal derision. And his cynicism was voluptuous. Idle
vision in him gilded alike everything it saw. He had
chosen, and would never lose, possession of the Immediate.

As to Helen, I have not ignored her. The gods called
Paris Alexander, and a private oracle has revealed to me
that they also had another name for Helen, which was
Doxa or Epiphaneia, that is to say, Glory or Evidence or
(being otherwise interpreted) Seeming or Phantom. She
was not substantial, but a manifestation of something else.
Her beauty was her all, and what was her beauty to herself ? A myriad potential appearances wait in the intricate
recesses of substance, or in the ethereal web of lights and
motions that vibrates through the infinite, ready for the
quick eye that can discern them. This discernment is at
once a birth and a marriage. No sooner is the fair phantom

called into existence than she has already leapt, as if carried by destiny, into her lover's arms ; for nothing can be more longed for, or more rapturously beautiful when it appears, than perfect evidence is to the mind. And the womb of nature, too, in its dark fertility, must be relieved to bring something to light at last. Yet this rare concourse of desires, and this blissful marriage, proves in the end most unhappy, for there is sin in it.

As all desperate lovers, in the absence of their true love, embrace what best they can find, though a false object, so spirit which, if not entangled in circumstance and heavy with dreams, would embrace the truth, must embrace appearance instead. There is a momentary lyrical joy even in that, because appearance has a being of its own ; it has form, like Helen, and magic comings and goings, like visions of the gods : and if spirit were not incarnate and had nothing to fear or pursue, appearance would be the only reality it would care to dwell on. It was princely of Paris to love only the Immediate, but it was inhuman and unwise ; and Venus had seduced him not only to his ruin (we must all die sooner or later) but to his disgrace and perpetual misery. A spirit lodged in time, place, and an animal body needs to be mindful of existence ; it needs to respect the past, the hidden, the ulterior. It should be satisfied with what beauties are visible from its station, and with such truths as are pertinent to its fate. It should study appearance for the sake of substance. But as the joy of a free spirit is in perfect evidence, in Doxa or Epiphaneia, it inevitably flouts substance and embraces appearance instead. The Rape of Helen is this adulterous substitution, dazzling but criminal.

54

ON MY FRIENDLY CRITICS

Now that for some years my body has not been visible in the places it used to haunt (my mind, even then, being often elsewhere), my friends in America have fallen into the habit of thinking me dead, and with characteristic haste and kindness, they are writing obituary notices, as it were, on my life and works. Some of these reach me in this other world—the friendly ones, which their authors send me—and without the aid of any such stratagem as Swift's, I have the strange pleasure of laughing at my own epitaphs. It is not merely the play of vanity that enters into this experience, nor the occasional excuse for being unfair in return ; there comes with it a genuine discovery of the general balance of one's character. A man has unrivalled knowledge of the details of his life and feelings, but it is hard for him to compose his personage as it appears in the comedy of the world, or in the eyes of other people. It is not true that contemporaries misjudge a man. Competent contemporaries judge him perfectly, much better than posterity, which is composed of critics no less egotistical and obliged to rely exclusively on documents easily misinterpreted. The contemporary can read more safely between the lines ; and if the general public often misjudges the men of its own time, the general public hears little of them. It is guided by some party tag or casual association, by the malignity or delusion of some small coterie that has caught its ear : how otherwise should it judge ideas it has not grasped and people it has not seen ? But public opinion is hardly better informed about the past than about the present, and histories are only newspapers published long after the fact.

As to my person, my critics are very gentle, and I am sensible of the kindness, or the diffidence, with which they treat me. I do not mind being occasionally denounced for atheism, conceit, or detachment. One has to be oneself ; and so long as the facts are not misrepresented—and I have little to complain of on that score—any judgement based upon them is a two-edged sword : people simply condemn what condemns them. I can always say to myself that my atheism, like that of Spinoza, is true piety towards the universe and denies only gods fashioned by men in their own image, to be servants of their human interests ; and that even in this denial I am no rude iconoclast, but full of secret sympathy with the impulses of idolaters. My detachment from things and persons is also affectionate, and simply what the ancients called philosophy : I consent that a flowing river should flow ; I renounce that which betrays, and cling to that which satisfies, and I relish the irony of truth ; but my security in my own happiness is not indifference to that of others : I rejoice that every one should have his tastes and his pleasures. That I am conceited, it would be folly to deny : what artist, what thinker, what parent does not over-estimate his own offspring ? Can I suppress an irresistible sense of seeing things clearly, and a keen delight in so seeing them ? Frankly, I think these attitudes of mine are justified by the facts ; but I entirely understand how offensive they must be to any one who thinks they are not justified, or who fears that they may be. Let the irritant work. The arrows of anger miss their mark. Aimed at some imaginary evil bird in the heavens, they scarcely startle the poet wandering in his dell. He hears them pass over his head and bury their venom far away in the young grass. Far away too his friends are designing his vain cenotaph, and inscribing it with seemly words in large capitals.

On the other hand, in respect to my impersonal opinions, I notice a little bewilderment, and some obtuseness. Of course, if people are repelled by the subject or by the manner (which is an integral part of the thought) and find it all unintelligible, that is no fault of theirs, nor of mine ; but I speak of the initiated and of such as are willing to lend their minds to my sort of lucubration. For instance, when more than twenty years ago, I wrote some *Interpretations of Poetry and Religion*, this is what William James said of them : " What a perfection of rottenness . . . how fantastic a philosophy !—as if the ' world of values ' *were* independent of existence. It is only as *being* that one thing is better than another. The idea of darkness is as good as that of light, as ideas. There is more value in light's *being*." William James was a " radical empiricist," so that for him the being of light could not have meant anything except its being in idea, in experience. The fantastic view must therefore be some other ; apparently that in the realm of unrealized essences, apart from any observer, one essence can be better than another. But how could any one attribute such a view to me ? The whole conten-

tion of my book was that the glow of human emotion
lent a value to good poetry which it denied to bad, and to
one idea of God which it denied to another. My position
in this matter was that of empirical philosophy, and of
William James himself. In his book on Pragmatism he
says that the being of atoms is just as good as the being
of God, if both produce the same effects in human experience ; and I remember once mildly protesting to him
on that point, and asking him if, apart from these effects
on us, the existence of God, assuming God to be conscious,
would not have a considerable value in itself ; and he
replied, " Of course ; but I was thinking of our *idea*."
This was exactly the attitude of my book ; I was thinking
of our religious and poetic ideas, and reducing their value
to what they stood for in the elements of our experience,
or in our destiny.

I think I see, however, where the trouble lies. The
practical intellect conceives everything as a source of
influence. Whether it be matter or other people, or
tutelary spirits, that which we envisage in action and
passion is not our idea of these objects, but their operation
on us, or our operation on them. Now a source of influence
cannot be non - existent. Accordingly, what concerns
earnest people in their religion is something, they know
not what, which is real. They are not interested in forming
poetic or dramatic pictures of the gods, as the Greeks did
in their mythology, but rather in finding a living God to
help them, as even the Greeks did in their home cultus and
their oracles. This living God, since he is to operate and
to be worked upon, must exist ; otherwise the whole
practice of religion becomes a farce. So also in love or
in science, it would be egotistical and affected to gloat
on our own ideal, turning our backs on the adorable person
or the natural process before us. It is the danger of
empirical and critical philosophy, that it turns our attention stubbornly to the subjective : legitimately, I think,
if the purpose is merely to study the growth and logic of
our beliefs, but illegitimately, if the purpose is malicious,
and if it is assumed that once we have understood how our
beliefs are formed we shall abandon them and believe
nothing. Empiricism and idealism are, as Kant called

them, excellent cathartics, but they are nasty food ; and
if we try to build them up into a system of the universe
the effort is not only self-contradictory (because we ought
then to possess only ideas without beliefs) but the result
is, in the words of William James, fantastic and rotten.

Now, however much I may have studied the human
imagination, I have never doubted that even highly
imaginative things, like poetry and religion, express real
events, if not in the outer world, at least in the inner
growth or discipline of life. Like the daily experience
of the senses and like the ideas of science, they form *a
human language*, all the terms of which are poetical and its
images dream-images, but which symbolizes things and
events beyond it and is controlled from outside. This
would be perfectly evident to any other animal who should
discover how men see the world or what they think of it :
why should we be less intelligent than any other animal
would be about ourselves ? Enlightenment consists in
coming nearer and nearer to the natural objects that lend
a practical meaning to our mental discourse ; and when
the material significance of our dreams is thus discovered,
we are lost in admiration at the originality, humour, and
pictorial grandeur of the imagery in which our experience
comes to us, as we might be at the decorative marvels of
tapestry or of stained glass : but now without illusion.
For we can now discriminate the rhythms and colour
proper to our mental atmosphere from the extrinsic value
of discourse as a sign for things and events beyond it.
These external things and events make up what we call
nature. It is nature, or some part of nature, or some
movement of nature occurring within us or affecting us,
that is the true existent object of religion, of science, and
of love. The rest is a mere image.

My naturalism is sometimes taxed with being dogmatic,
and if I were anxious to avoid that reproach, I might easily
reduce my naturalism to a definition and say that if experience has any sources whatever, the sum and system of
these sources shall be called nature. I know what speculative difficulties cluster about the notion of cause, which in
one sense is quite unnecessary to science ; but so long as
time, process, and derivation are admitted at all, events

may be traced back to earlier events which were their sources ; and this universal flux of events will be called nature. Any existing persons, and any gods exercising power, will evidently be parts of nature. But I am not concerned to avoid dogmatism on such a point. Every assertion about existence is hazarded, it rests on animal faith, not on logical proof ; and every argument to support naturalism, or to rebut it, implies naturalism. To deny that there are any facts (if scepticism can be carried so far) is still to dogmatize, no less than it would be to point to some fact in particular ; in either case we descend into the arena of existence, which may betray our confidence. Any fact is an existence which discourse plays about and regards, but does not create. It is the essence of the practical intellect to prophesy about nature, and we must all do it. As to the truth of our prophecy, that is always problematical, because nature is whatever nature happens to be ; and as to our knowledge, starting as it does from a single point, the present position of the thinker, and falling away rapidly in clearness and certainty as the perspective recedes, it cannot pretend to draw the outlines of nature *a priori* : yet our knowledge of nature, in our neighbour-hood and moral climate, is very considerable, since every known fact is a part of nature. It is quite idle to deny, for instance, that human life depends on cosmic and hygienic influences ; or that in the end all human operations must run back somehow to the rotation of the earth, to the rays of the sun, to the moisture and fructifica-tion of the soil, to the ferment there of vegetative and dreaming spirits, quickened in animals endowed with loco-motion into knowledge of surrounding things : whence the passionate imaginations which we find in ourselves. I know that things might have been arranged otherwise ; and some of those alternative worlds may be minutely thought out in myth or in philosophy, in obedience to some dialectical or moral impulse of the human mind ; but that all those other worlds are figments of fancy, interesting as poetry is interesting, and that only the natural world, the world of medicine and commerce, is actual, is obvious ; so obvious to every man in his sane moments, that I have always thought it idle to argue the

point. Argument is not persuasive to madmen ; but
they can be won over by gentler courses to a gradual
docility to the truth.   One of these gentler courses is this :
to remember that madness is human, that dreams have
their springs in the depths of human nature and of human
experience ;   and that the illusion they cause may be
kindly and even gloriously dispelled by showing what
the solid truth was which they expressed allegorically.
Why should one be angry with dreams, with myth, with
allegory, with madness ?   We must not kill the mind,
as some rationalists do, in trying to cure it.   The life of
reason, as I conceive it, is simply the dreaming mind
becoming coherent, devising symbols and methods, such
as languages, by which it may fitly survey its own career,
and the forces of nature on which that career depends.
Reason thereby raises our vegetative dream into a poetic
revelation and transcript of the truth.   That all this life
of expression grows up in animals living in the material
world is the deliverance of reason itself, in our lucid
moments ; but my books, being descriptive of the imagination and having perhaps some touches of imagination in
them, may not seem to have expressed my lucid moments
alone.   They were, however, intended to do so ; and I
ought to have warned my readers more often that such was
the case.

I have no metaphysics, and in that sense I am no
philosopher, but a poor ignoramus trusting what he hears
from the men of science.   I rely on them to discover gradually exactly which elements in their description of nature
may be literally true, and which merely symbolical : even
if they were all symbolical, they would be true enough for
me.   My naturalism is not at all afraid of the latest theories
of space, time, or matter : what I understand of them, I
like, and am ready to believe, for I am a follower of
Plato in his doctrine that only knowledge of ideas (if we
call it knowledge) can be literal and exact, whilst practical
knowledge is necessarily mythical in form, precisely because
its object exists and is external to us.   An arbitrary sign,
indication, or name can point to something unambiguously,
without at all fathoming its nature, and *therefore* can be
knowledge of fact : which an aesthetic or logical elucida-

tion of ideas can never be. Every idea of sense or science is a summary sign, on a different plane and scale altogether from the diffuse material facts which it covers : one unexampled colour for many rays, one indescribable note for many vibrations, one picture for many particles of paint, one word for a series of noises or letters. A word is a very Platonic thing : you cannot say when it begins, when it ends, how long it lasts, nor where it ever is ; and yet it is the only unit you mean to utter, or normally hear. Platonism is the intuition of essences in the presence of things, in order to describe them : it is mind itself.

I am quite happy in this human ignorance mitigated by pictures, for it yields practical security and poetic beauty : what more can a sane man want ? In this respect I think sometimes I am the only philosopher living : I am resigned to being a mind. I have put my hand into the hand of nature, and a thrill of sympathy has passed from her into my very heart, so that I can instinctively see all things, and see myself, from her point of view : a sympathy which emboldens me often to say to her, " Mother, tell me a story." Not the fair Sheherazad herself knew half the marvellous tales that nature spins in the brains of her children. But I must not let go her hand in my wonder, or I might be bewitched and lost in the maze of her inventions.

A workman must not quarrel with his tools, nor the mind with ideas ; and I have little patience with those philanthropists who hate everything human, and would reform away everything that men love or can love. Yet if we dwell too lovingly on the human quality and poetic play of ideas, we may forget that they are primarily signs. The practical intellect is always on the watch for ambient existences, in order to fight or to swallow them : and if by chance its attention is arrested at an idea, it will instinctively raise that idea to the throne of power which should be occupied only by the thing which it stands for and poetically describes. Ideas lend themselves to idolatry. There is a continual incidental deception into which we are betrayed by the fictitious and symbolical terms of our knowledge, in that we suppose these terms to form the whole essence of their objects. I think I have never failed to point out this danger of illusion, and to protest against idolatry in thought, so much more frequent and dangerous than the worship of stocks and stones ; but at the same time, as such idolatry is almost inevitable, and as the fictions so deified often cover some true force or harmony in nature, I have sometimes been tempted in my heart to condone this illusion. In my youth it seemed as if a scientific philosophy was unattainable ; human life, I thought, was at best a dream, and if we were not the dupes of one error, we should be the dupes of another ; and whilst of course the critic must make this mental reservation in all his assents, it was perhaps too much to ask mankind to do so ; so that in practice we were condemned to overlook the deceptiveness of fable, because there would be less beauty and no more truth in whatever theory might take its place. I think now that this despair of finding a scientific philosophy was premature, and that the near future may actually produce one : not that its terms will be less human and symbolical than those to which we are accustomed, but that they may hug more closely the true movement and the calculable order of nature. The truth, though it must be expressed in language, is not for that reason a form of error. No doubt the popularizers of science will turn its language into a revelation, and its images into idols ; but the abstract character of these symbols will render it easier for the judicious to preserve the distinction between the things to be described and the science which describes them.

Was it, I wonder, this touch of sympathy with splendid error, bred in me by long familiarity with religion and philosophy, that offended my honest critics ? Now that I show less sympathy with it, will they be better satisfied ? I fear the opposite is the case. What they resented was rather that in spite of all my sympathy, and of all my despair about science, it never occurred to me to think those errors true, because they were splendid, except true to the soul. Did they expect that I should seriously debate whether the Ghost in *Hamlet* really came out of Purgatorial fires, and whether Athena really descended in her chariot from Olympus and pulled Achilles by his yellow hair when he was in danger of doing something rash ? Frankly, I have assumed—perhaps prematurely—that such questions are settled. I am not able nor willing to write a system of magic cosmology, nor to propose a new religion. I merely endeavour to interpret, as sympathetically and imaginatively as I can, the religion and poetry already familiar to us ; and I interpret them, of course, on their better side, not as childish science, but as subtle creations of hope, tenderness, and ignorance.

So anxious was I, when younger, to find some rational justification for poetry and religion, and to show that their magic was significant of true facts, that I insisted too much, as I now think, on the need of relevance to fact even in poetry. Not only did I distinguish good religion from bad by its expression of practical wisdom, and of the moral discipline that makes for happiness in this world, but I maintained that the noblest poetry also must express the moral burden of life and must be rich in wisdom. Age has made me less exacting, and I can now find quite sufficient perfection in poetry, like that of the Chinese and Arabians, without much philosophic scope, in mere grace and feeling and music and cloud-castles and frolic. I assumed formerly that an idea could have depth and richness only if somehow redolent of former experiences of an overt kind. I had been taught to assign no substance to the mind, but to conceive it as a system of successive ideas, the later ones mingling with a survival of the earlier, and forming a cumulative experience, like a swelling musical movement. Now, without ceasing to conceive mental discourse in that way, I have learned, with the younger generation, to rely more on the substructure, on the material and psychical machinery that puts this conscious show on the stage, and pulls the wires. Not that I ever denied or really doubted that this substructure existed, but that I thought it a more prudent and critical method in philosophy not to assume it. Certainly it is a vast assumption ; but I see now an irony in scepticism which I did not see when I was more fervid a sceptic ; namely, that in addressing anybody, or even myself, I have already made that assumption ; and that if I tried to rescind it, I should only be making another, no less gratuitous, and far more extravagant ; I should be assuming that the need of making this assumption was a fatal illusion, rather than a natural revelation of the existence of an environment to a living animal. This environment has been called the unknowable, the unconscious and the subconscious—egotistical and absurd names for it, as if its essence was the difficulty we have in approaching it. Its proper names are matter, substance, nature, or soul ; and I hope people will learn again to call it by those old names. When living substance is thus restored beneath the surface of experience, there is no longer any reason for assuming that the first song of a bird may not be infinitely rich and as deep as heaven, if it utters the vital impulses of that moment with enough completeness. The analogies of this utterance with other events, or its outlying suggestions, whilst they may render it more intelligible to a third person, would not add much to its inward force and intrinsic beauty. Its lyric adequacy, though of course not independent of nature, would be independent of wisdom. If besides being an adequate expression of the soul, the song expressed the lessons of a broad experience, which that soul had gathered and digested, this fact certainly would lend a great tragic sublimity to that song ; but to be poetical or religious intrinsically, the mystic cry is enough.

I notice that men of the world, when they dip into my books, find them consistent, almost oppressively consistent, and to the ladies everything is crystal - clear ; yet the philosophers say that it is lazy and self-indulgent of me not to tell them plainly what I think, if I know myself what it is. Because I describe madness sympathetically, because I lose myself in the dreaming mind, and see the world from that transcendental point of vantage, while at the same time interpreting that dream by its presumable motives and by its moral tendencies, these quick and intense reasoners suppose that I am vacillating in my own opinions. My own opinions are a minor matter, and there was usually no need, for the task in hand, that I should put them forward ; yet as a matter of fact, since I reached the age of manhood, they have not changed. In my adolescence I thought this earthly life (not unintelligibly, considering what I had then seen and heard of it) a most hideous thing, and I was not disinclined to dismiss it as an illusion, for which perhaps the Catholic epic might be substituted to advantage, as conforming better to the impulses of the soul ; and later I liked to regard all systems as alternative illusions for the solipsist ; but neither solipsism nor Catholicism were ever anything to me but theoretic poses or possibilities ; vistas for the imagination, never convictions. I was well aware, as I am still, that any such vista *may* be taken for true, because all dreams are persuasive while they last ; and I have not lost, nor do I wish to lose, a certain facility and pleasure in taking those points of view at will, and speaking those philosophical languages. But though as a child I regretted the fact and now I hugely enjoy it, I have never been able to elude the recurring, invincible, and ironic conviction that whenever I or any other person feign to be living in any of those non-natural worlds, we are simply dreaming awake.

In general, I think my critics attribute to me more illusions than I have. My dogmatism may be a fault of temper or manner, because I dislike to stop to qualify or to explain everything ; but in principle it is raised more diffidently and on a deeper scepticism than most of the systems which are called critical. My " essences," for instance, are blamed for being gratuitous inventions or needless abstractions. But essences appear precisely when all inventions are rescinded and the irreducible manifest datum is disclosed. I do not ask any one to *believe* in essences. I ask them to reject every belief, and what they will have on their hands, if they do so, will be some essence. And if, believing nothing, they could infinitely enlarge their imagination, the whole realm of essence would loom before them. This realm is no discovery of mine ; it has been described, for instance, by Leibniz in two different ways ; once as the collection of all possible worlds, and again as the abyss of non-existence, *le néant*, of which he says : " The non-existent . . . is infinite, it is eternal, it has a great many of the attributes of God ; it contains an infinity of things, since all those things which do not exist at all are included in the non-existent, and those which no longer exist have returned to the non-existent." It suffices, therefore, that we deny a thing for us to recog-

nize an essence, if we know at all what we are denying.
And the essence before us, whether we assert or deny its
existence, is certainly no abstraction ; for there is no other
datum, more individual or more obvious, from which the
abstraction could be drawn. The difficulty in discern-
ing essences is simply the very real difficulty which the
practical intellect has in abstaining from belief, and from
everywhere thinking it finds much more than is actually
given.

Profound scepticism is favourable to conventions,
because it doubts that the criticism of conventions is any
truer than they are. Fervent believers look for some
system of philosophy or religion that shall be *literally*
true and worthy of superseding the current assumptions
of daily life. I look for no such thing. Never for a
moment can I bring myself to regard a human system—a
piece of mental discourse—as more than a system of
notation, sometimes picturesque, sometimes abstract and
mathematical. Scientific symbols, terms in which calcula-
tion is possible, may replace poetic symbols, which merely
catch echoes of the senses or make up dramatic units out
of appearances in the gross. But the most accurate
scientific system would still be only a method of description,
and the actual facts would continue to rejoice in their own
ways of being. The relevance and truth of science, like
the relevance and truth of sense, are pragmatic, in that
they mark the actual relations, march, and distribution
of events, in the terms in which they enter our experience.

In moral philosophy (which is my chosen subject) I
find my unsophisticated readers, as I found my pupils
formerly, delightfully appreciative, warmly sympathetic,
and altogether friends of mine in the spirit. It is a joy,
like that of true conversation, to look and laugh and cry
at the world so unfeignedly together. But the other
philosophers, and those whose religion is of the anxious
and intolerant sort, are not at all pleased. They think
my morality very loose : I am a friend of publicans and
sinners, not (as they are) in zeal to reform them, but because
I like them as they are ; and indeed I am a pagan and a
moral sceptic in my naturalism. On the other hand (and
this seems a contradiction to them), my moral philosophy

looks strangely negative and narrow; a philosophy of abstention and distaste for life. What a horrible combination, they say to themselves, of moral licence with moral poverty! They do not see that it is because I love life that I wish to keep it sweet, so as to be able to love it altogether: and that all I wish for others, or dare to recommend to them, is that they should keep their lives sweet also, not after my fashion, but each man in his own way. I talk a great deal about the good and the ideal, having learned from Plato and Aristotle (since the living have never shown me how to live) that, granting a human nature to which to appeal, the good and the ideal may be defined with some accuracy. Of course, they cannot be defined immutably, because human nature is not immutable; and they cannot be defined in such a way as to be transferred without change from one race or person to another, because human nature is various. Yet any reflective and honest man, in expressing his hopes and preferences, may expect to find many of his neighbours agreeing with him, and when they agree, they may work politically together. Now I am sometimes blamed for not labouring more earnestly to bring down the good of which I prate into the lives of other men. My critics suppose, apparently, that I mean by the good some particular way of life or some type of character which is alone virtuous, and which ought to be propagated. Alas, their propagandas! How they have filled this world with hatred, darkness, and blood! How they are still the eternal obstacle, in every home and in every heart, to a simple happiness! I have no wish to propagate any particular character, least of all my own; my conceit does not take that form. I wish individuals, and races, and nations to be themselves, and to multiply the forms of perfection and happiness, as nature prompts them. The only thing which I think might be propagated without injustice to the types thereby suppressed is harmony; enough harmony to prevent the interference of one type with another, and to allow the perfect development of each type. The good, as I conceive it, is happiness, happiness for each man after his own heart, and for each hour according to its inspiration. I should dread to transplant my happiness

into other people ; it might die in that soil ; and my
critics are the first to tell me that my sort of happiness
is a poor thing in their estimation. Well and good. I
congratulate them on their true loves : but how should I
be able to speed them on their course ? They do not
place their happiness in the things I have, or can give.
No man can set up an ideal for another, nor labour to realize
it for him, save by his leave or as his spokesman, perhaps
more ready with the right word. To find the comparatively right word, my critics seem to agree, is my art.
Do I not practise it for their benefit as best I can ? Is it
I who am indifferent to the being of light ? Who loves
it more, or basks in it more joyfully ? And do I do
nothing that the light may come ? Is it I who tremble
lest at its coming it should dissolve the creatures begotten
in darkness ? Ah, I know why my critics murmur and
are dissatisfied. I do not endeavour to deceive myself,
nor to deceive them, nor to aid them in deceiving themselves. They will never prevail on me to do that. I am
a disciple of Socrates.

55

HERMES THE INTERPRETER

A TRAVELLER should be devout to Hermes, and I have
always loved him above the other gods for that charming union which is found in him of youth with experience,
alacrity with prudence, modesty with laughter, and a ready
tongue with a sound heart. In him the first bubblings of
mockery subside at once into courtesy and helpfulness.
He is the winged Figaro of Olympus, willing to yield to
others in station and to pretend to serve them, but really
wiser and happier than any of them. There is a certain
roguery in him, and the habit of winking at mischief. He
has a great gift for dissertation, and his abundant eloquence,
always unimpeachable in form and in point, does not hug
the truth so closely as pious people might expect in a god
who, as they say sagaciously, can have no motive for lying.
But gods do not need motives. The lies of Hermes are
jests ; they represent things as they might have been, and

serve to show what a strange accident the truth is. The
reproach which Virgil addresses to his Juno, " Such malignity in minds celestial ? " could never apply to this amiable
divinity, who, if he is a rascal at all (which I do not admit),
is a disinterested rascal. He has given no pawns to fortune,
he is not a householder, he is not pledged against his will to
any cause. Homer tells us that Hermes was a thief ; but
the beauty of mythology is that every poet can recast it
according to his own insight and sense of propriety ; as, in
fact, our solemn theologians do also, although they pretend
that their theology is a science, and are not wide awake
enough to notice the dreamful, dramatic impulse which
leads them to construct it. Now, in my vision, the thievery
of Hermes, and the fact that he was the patron of robbers,
merchants, rhetoricians, and liars, far from being unworthy
of his divine nature, are a superb and humorous expression
of it. He did not steal the cattle of Apollo for profit.
Apollo himself—a most exquisite young god—did not give
a fig for his cattle nor for his rustic employment ; in
adopting it he was doing a kind turn to a friend, or had
a love-lorn scheme or a wager afoot, or merely wished for
the moment to be idyllic. It was a pleasant *scherzo* (after
the *andante* which he played in the heavens, in his capacity
of sun-god and inspirer of all prophets) to lean gracefully
here on his herdsman's staff, or to lie under a tuft of trees
on some mossy hillock, in the midst of his pasturing kine,
and to hold the poor peeping dryads spellbound by the
operatic marvels of his singing. In purloining those oxen,
Hermes, who was a very little boy at the time, simply
wanted to mock these affectations of his long-haired elder
brother ; and Apollo, truly an enraptured artist and not
a prig, and invulnerable like Hermes in his godlike freedom,
did not in the least mind the practical joke, nor the ridicule,
but was the first to join in the laugh.

When Hermes consents to be the patron of thieves and
money-lenders it is in the same spirit. Standing, purse in
hand, in his little shrine above their dens, he smiles as if
to remind them that everything is trash which mortals can
snatch from one another by thieving or bargaining, and
that the purpose of all their voyages, and fairs, and high-
way robberies is a bauble, such as the dirty children playing

in the street set up as a counter in their game. But
Hermes is not impatient even of the gutter-snipes, with
their cries and their shrill quarrels. He laughs at their
grimaces ; their jests do not seem emptier to him than
those of their elders ; he is not offended at their rags, but
sends sleep to them as they lie huddled under some arch-
way or stretched in the sun upon the temple steps. He
presides no less benignly over thieves' kitchens and over
the shipyards and counting-houses of traders ; not that he
cares at all who makes the profit or who hoards the
treasure, but that sagacity and the hum of business are
delightful to him in themselves. He likes to cull the
passion and sparkle out of the most sordid life, and the
confused rumble of civilization is pleasant to his senses,
like a sweet vapour rising from the evening sacrifice.

His admirable temper and mastery of soul appear in
nothing more clearly than in his love-affair with the
beautiful Maia. She is ill-spoken of, but he is very, very
fond of her, and deeply happy in her love. It is a secret
relation, although everybody has heard of it ; but the
nymph is a mystery ; in fact, although everybody has
seen her at one time or another, no one has ever known
then that it was she. Hermes alone recognizes and loves
her in her own person, and calls her by her name ; but
privately. Sometimes, with that indiscretion and over-
familiarity which the young allow themselves in their cups,
his brothers ask him where he meets her ; and he only
smiles a little and is silent. She is said to be a wild un-
manageable being, half maenad and half shrew; a waif
always appearing and disappearing without any reason,
and in her fitful temper at once exacting and tedious.
Her eyes are sometimes blue and sometimes black, like
heaven. Empty-headed and too gay, some people think
her ; but others understand that she is constitutionally
melancholy and quite mad. They say she often sits alone,
hardly distinguishable in the speckled sunshine of the
forest, or else by the sea, spreading her hair to the wind
and moaning : and then Hermes flies to her and comforts
her, for she is an exile everywhere and he is everywhere
at home. It is rumoured that in the East she has had a
great position, and has been Queen of the Universe ; but

in Europe she has no settled metaphysical status, and it is not known whether she is really a goddess, mistress over herself, or only a fay or a phantom at other people's beck and call ; and she has nowhere any temple or rustic sanctuary or respectable oracle. Moreover, she has inexpressibly shocked the virtuous, who think so much of genealogy, by saying, as is reported, that she has no idea who is the father of her children. Hermes laughs merrily at this, calling it one of her harmless sallies, which she indulges in simply because they occur to her, and because she likes to show her independence and to flout the sober censors of this world. He is perfectly confident she has never had any wooer but himself, nor would dream of accepting any other. Even with him she is always reverting to stubborn refusals and denials and calling him names ; but when the spitfire is raging most angrily, he has only to gaze at her steadily and throw his arm gaily about her, as much as to say, " Don't be a fool," for her to be instantly mollified and confess that it was all make-believe, but that she couldn't help it. Then it is wonderful how reasonable she becomes, how perfectly trustful and frank, so that no companion could be more deeply delightful. She is as light as a feather, then, in his arms. The truth is, she lives only for him ; she really has no children, only young sisters who are also more or less in love with him and he with them ; and she sleeps her whole life long in his absence. In all those strange doings and wanderings reported of her she is only walking in her sleep. The approach of Hermes awakes her and lends her life—the only life she has. Her true name is Illusion ; and it is very characteristic of him, so rich in pity, merriment, and shrewdness, to have chosen this poor child, Illusion, for his love.

Hermes is the great interpreter, the master of riddles. I should not honour him for his skill in riddles if I thought he invented them wantonly, because he liked to puzzle himself with them, or to reduce other people to a foolish perplexity without cause. I hate enigmas ; and if I believed that Hermes was the inspirer of those odious persons who are always asking conundrums and making puns I should renounce him altogether, break his statue, turn his

picture to the wall, and devote myself exclusively to the
cult of some sylvan deity, all silence and simple light.   But
I am sure Hermes loves riddles only because they are no
riddles to him ; he is never caught in the tangle, and he
laughs to see how unnecessarily poor opinionated mortals
befool themselves, wilfully following any devious scent
once they are on it by chance, and missing the obvious for
ever.   He gives them what sly hints he can to break the
spell of their blindness ; but they are so wedded to their
false preconceptions that they do not understand him, and
are only the more perplexed.   Sometimes, however, they
take the hint, their wit grows nimble, their thoughts catch
fire, and insight, solving every idle riddle, harmonizes the
jarring cords of the mind.

The wand of Hermes has serpents wound about it,
but is capped with wings, so that at its touch the sting
and the coil of care may vanish, and that we may be
freed from torpor and dull enchantment, and may see,
as the god does, how foolish we are.   All these mysteries
that befog us are not mysteries really ; they are the
mother-tongue of nature.   Rustics, and also philosophers,
think that any language but theirs is gibberish ; they are
sorry for the stranger who can speak only an unintelligible
language, and are sure he will be damned unless the truth is
preached to him speedily by some impertinent missionary
from their own country.   They even argue with nature,
trying to convince her that she cannot move, or cannot think,
or cannot have more dimensions than those of their understanding.   Oh for a touch of the healing wand of Hermes
the Interpreter, that we might understand the language of
the birds and the stars, and, laughing first at what they
say of us, might then see our image in the mirror of
infinity, and laugh at ourselves ! Here is a kindly god
indeed, humane though superhuman, friendly though inviolate, who does not preach, who does not threaten, who
does not lay new, absurd, or morose commands on our
befuddled souls, but who unravels, who relieves, who shows
us the innocence of the things we hated and the clearness
of the things we frowned on or denied.   He interprets us
to the gods, and they accept us ; he interprets us to one
another, and we perceive that the foreigner, too, spoke a

plain language : happy he if he was wise in his own tongue. It is for the divine herald alone to catch the meaning of all, without subduing his merry voice to any dialect of mortals. He mocks our stammerings and forgives them ; and when we say anything to the purpose, and reach any goal which, however wantonly, we had proposed to ourselves, he applauds and immensely enjoys our little achievement ; for it is inspired by him and like his own. May he be my guide : and not in this world only, in which the way before me seems to descend gently, quite straight and clear, towards an unruffled sea ; but at the frontiers of eternity let him receive my spirit, reconciling it, by his gracious greeting, to what had been its destiny. For he is the friend of the shades also, and makes the greatest interpretation of all, that of life into truth, translating the swift words of time into the painted language of eternity. That is for the dead ; but for living men, whose feet must move forward whilst their eyes see only backward, he interprets the past to the future, for its guidance and ornament. Often, too, he bears news to his father and brothers in Olympus, concerning any joyful or beautiful thing that is done on earth, lest they should despise or forget it. In that fair inventory and chronicle of happiness let my love of him be remembered.